Finding
the Killers

Finding the Killers

Control the Power

Of Your Mind

A W Anderson

McMurdo Press

For bulk sales, promotions, seminars and educational use
Contact: info@mcmurdopress.com

ISBN 978-1-9991969-0-5

Cover Image by Freepik
Cover design by Tanja Prokop
Logo design by Tanja Prokop

McMurdo **Press**

www.mcmurdopress.com
info@mcmurdopress.com

To Lorraine,

*No words can express the happiness
I feel when I'm with you.*

The day science begins to study non-physical phenomena; it will make more progress in one decade than in all the previous centuries of its existence.

Nikola Tesla–Inventor (1856–1943)

Contents

Contents ix

Introduction xi

Chapter 1   The Secret—The Enemy—The Answers 15

Chapter 2   Stop the *MADNESS* 23

Chapter 3   Prepare To Win.. 31

Chapter 4   Clarifying Your Desires................................... 35

Chapter 5   Removing the Agony of Effort 45

Chapter 6   Behavior and Conditioning 61

Chapter 7   Limitations of The Conscious Mind 75

Chapter 8   The Cycle of Change 89

Chapter 9   The Power of Suggestion................................ 97

Chapter 10 Overriding the Subconscious Mind.............. 109

Chapter 11 The Programmable Brain 119

Chapter 12 Training Your Imagination 133

Chapter 13 Hackers, Hijackers and Renegade Thoughts. 147

Chapter 14 Your Power—Use It or Lose It 157

Chapter 15 Intuition—Your Sixth Sense 171

Chapter 16 W Y S I W Y G... 189

Chapter 17 Your Master Program 195

Chapter 18 The Transformation Point............................ 203

Chapter 19 Active Programs & Killers 209

Chapter 20 What's Important—To You 219

Chapter 21 The Power Booster 231

Chapter 22 The Snipers.. 237

Chapter 23 External Killers 247

Chapter 24 Why Is This Happening Again?..................... 259

Chapter 25 The Main Cause of Failure 267

Chapter 26 Assassins, Killers & Zombies 283

Chapter 27 Sleepers and The Law of Attraction..............291

Chapter 28 The Communication Saboteurs 307

Chapter 29 Where it goes *WRONG*.................................317

Chapter 30 It's Time to Win..325

Epilogue 331

Bibliography 332

Appendix "A" Controlling My Self-talk............................336

Appendix "B" Listening to My Solar Plexus 338

Appendix "C" Simulation and Visualization 339

Appendix "D" My Master Program..................................341

Appendix "E" The Power of Believing..............................343

Appendix "F" My Beliefs and Programs 344

Appendix "G" Clarifying My Values................................346

Appendix "H" Assessing My Attitude 349

Appendix "I" Emotions and Snipers................................350

Appendix "J" Identifying External Killers........................351

Appendix "K" Repeating Behaviors 354

Appendix "L" Planning and Goal Setting 356

Appendix "M" Locating Hidden Programs.......................363

Appendix "N" Communication Saboteurs........................366

Appendix "O" Suggestions for Self-Coaching..................367

Acknowledgements 375

About the Author...376

Introduction

This book is written for you and is all about you. It is designed for you to develop and increase your personal discipline and mind power to combat the challenges of today's fast-paced society. You will learn how to stand up to dominating and frustrating personalities. You will discover why exercise programs, diets and New Year's resolutions fail within three to six weeks and how your best intentions and willpower are destroyed by hidden killers. These carefully explained processes will enable you to develop your mind and willpower to attract success and have more time for the activities that you enjoy.

Finding the Killers will lead you through an amazing path of discovery that will not only identify the killers but provide you with exceptional insight into how your mental powers are undermined, and how you are controlled by others. You will learn how to control an energy within you that for over three thousand years was labeled a mystery or a secret. It was deemed a right only to be used by royalty, clerics and religious leaders.

For over three decades, I have personally coached and helped individuals from all walks of life develop the powerful skills and techniques that are presented in this book. The techniques are simple but unique. When implemented, they will become as natural as breathing. They have been referred to as the laws of the universe and are essential to master anything you want to achieve. In this book are all the skills you will ever need to reach your desired weight, stay on an exercise program, attract more money, choose a compatible partner and become a confident and dynamic person.

The secret or skill to start a new venture or activity and stay with it until it becomes a natural part of life, is one of the common challenges or barriers people face. There are self-defeating programs within your subconscious mind that operate on a subliminal level and constantly defeat you. They are killers that target your willpower and cause you to quit, fail or miss opportunities that are right in front of you. *Finding the Killers* is written for you to become a great detective and find these elusive killers. Only by understanding how your desire, resolve, determination or drive is killed can you develop your mind power.

Your first realization will be that you operate like a computer that requires specific programming. If you can program a smartphone, TV recorder or any electronic device, you can master these skills. This book will become the operating manual that you were never given when you were growing up. You will be provided with specific instructions on how to master the power of your mind. The skills and techniques to gain self-mastery will be linked to self-help and personal development, mind control, the laws of attraction, intuition, the sixth sense, meditation, and autosuggestion. You will develop techniques to avoid 10 common traps that have been killing your efforts to succeed.

Finding the Killers will show you how your brain tricks you into doing what you do not want to do, rather than what you really want to do. You will identify how you have been letting others control your life and how to stop those unwanted demands. You will come to appreciate that you are an entity that has been programmed, conditioned or brainwashed by others. By completing a few exercises, you will prove to yourself that you have the power to control your mind and influence or control others. You will become a free thinker and an independent decision maker.

As you read this book, you will realize that the skills for self-mastery are no longer a secret. They have been debated and written about for over three hundred years. You will find how this energy and inner force work against you and how you are no different than a digital computer or electronic device that requires programming and specific instructions. You will learn how to program your inner computer.

When you comprehend that your conscious mind is severely limited in what it can do, it will be easy to see how people are often fooled or duped. Your conscious actions and reactions are performed by an inner computer, your subconscious mind. However, there is a third component, the command center, that can be controlled by the conscious mind, the subconscious mind and external entities. You will be shown how this construct can work for or against you. Through easy to follow exercises you will realize that change is possible but requires mental effort. To be successful, it is imperative that your instructions proceed in a specific and orderly process, just like programming your smartphone or personalizing any computer application.

Just when you think that you have everything under control, you will find that your inner computer and control center can be hacked by others. You will be shown how to maintain control. Your path, unbeknownst to you at the start, will lead you through a mine field where killers lurk at every turn.

There are 20 powerful constructs of your mind that when combined with 12 other aspects make up and control your internal computer. These are the core principles of self-help books and personal development programs. Your discoveries will convince you that you have the resources and weapons to overpower these killers. The explanation for each of these aspects and skills is like learning to read and write. Once learned, the techniques can be applied silently and instantly to defend yourself from any attack at any time.

Success is not limited to money or status and requires a balance in life. Without this balance, you will remain wanting and disappointed. You will be shown the importance of applying mind power to all aspects of your life. As you introduce these techniques into your daily activities, you will experience a particular inner sensation and know that you are winning.

Finding the Killers will expand your awareness and become a significant turning point for you. No one will fight your battles for you, only you can do that. Once you find and subdue the killers of your time, happiness and best intentions, you will enjoy more of what life has to offer. It is one thing to find those killers but quite another to outsmart and subdue them. This book is designed to show you exactly how to do that.

Identifying and dealing with the enemies within will free you to achieve more than you ever thought possible. You will immediately be able to apply the techniques to all your real-life challenges. By becoming aware and applying the powers of your mind, you will enjoy many new successes and achievements. This book is for those who want more out of life.

Finding the Killers

Chapter 1

The Secret — The Enemy — The Answers

Many believe that there are hidden secrets for applying mind power. For centuries, mind power created intrigue and mystique that perpetuated this belief. The definition of the word secret is simply—not known or seen or not meant to be known or seen by others. Often, those who learned mind power techniques exploited others who were less educated. Religious leaders intentionally suppressed independent thinking to maintain control and branded anyone who dared to question their authority as evil or demonic. It is not surprising that the power of the mind remained hidden from the general population for centuries.

Scientific and philosophical debates have been ongoing for over 3,000 years. But only in the last 150 years has education become available to the masses. As people became more educated and independent thinkers, they began to challenge religious controls. Free thinkers began to reveal the secrets—but at a cost. Teachers of the new concepts lived in fear of losing their lives. Yet politicians, religious organizations and profiteers continued to apply these same techniques to manipulate the masses for personal, political, religious and financial gains.

Without an awareness of the techniques required to use mind power, you are severely disadvantaged. Your successes and achievements are undermined by internal enemies. These ruthless, conniving killers reside within your mind and instantly destroy your best intentions. Their dominance over you can be suppressed when you apply the power of your mind. The killers that initiate your behaviors and thinking processes are not smart or savvy because they are programs, like computer apps. Collectively, they become the autopilot or guidance system for your behaviors and actions. By design, these programs protect themselves and block all attempts to add anything contrary to their constructs. They are automatons, and like zombies, they attack as effectively as computer viruses and undermine your efforts when you least expect them.

We tend to ignore how easily the mind can be influenced and programmed by others. A child born in one country may be adopted by a different family or raised in another country. The child learns the culture, language or religion of the new family without knowing the traditions of his or her family of origin. The learned concepts, beliefs and values that they are exposed to become program settings or their guidance system.

Like that child, we too have been programmed. Our mind is programmed to attract good and bad circumstances throughout life. You may be surprised to discover that several negative situations you experienced were the result of how you were conditioned or programmed. These are your enemies. Your guidance system settings prompted you to attract, notice and engage in activities that manifested your experiences.

Change can only occur by assessing how you view, manage and respond in all aspects of your life. This includes career and finances, family and relationships, physical activities, health, education, friends, social activities and your spiritual well-being or peace of mind. As you progress, you will begin to identify the effects that the power of your mind has on your life. You will develop techniques to disarm and outmaneuver those who discourage or interfere with your goals, plans or lifestyle.

Regardless of the external influences, breaking free and becoming "you" is an internal battle. Killers are relentless, hold you captive and continually undermine your plans. Staying focused requires simple but specific actions.

Becoming aware of the controls and influences others have had on you may first appear as a shock and then as a resentment, especially when you realize how subtly they occurred or that you were conned by a best friend. As your exploration continues, you will realize that you have been unknowingly tricked, and then trapped on a treadmill of manipulation that has become your way of life. Unless the cycle is interrupted and new directions are set on your guidance system, nothing will change.

The killers and enemies that hide in your subconscious mind disguise themselves in peculiar forms. Without identifying and neutralizing them, they prevent you from attracting or achieving what you desire. They will relentlessly undermine your intentions until you decide to take proactive and firm action. This decision will cause your killers to fight back with greater force.

Enemies hide in plain sight and prompt you to become a follower rather than a free thinker. Unaware that you can defend yourself, internal and external forces influence and control your mind. External forces such as corporations, political parties, organized causes, religion, celebrities, athletes or fashion, subliminally intercept your command center and set guidance system settings to control or influence you. Their survival depends on controlling the masses, and that includes you. Their presentations sway you to believe in their causes, change your behaviors to portray yourself in a particular physical manner, display the newest or coolest gadgets, wear the latest fashions or join a specific club or event.

Even though you know you are not that type of individual or can't afford the bling, not feeling a part of their group creates a sense of loss that attacks your self-worth. To dispel this feeling, you participate in their offerings. The decision to follow may not be your genuine desire, but it soon feels comfortable and enjoyable. That decision resulted from external entities that successfully programmed your guidance system to influence your actions.

As you become aware of the disappointments created by being an unconscious follower, you recognize the need to make changes. However, stress and anxiety increase when you dare to be different. You may suffer rejection by your friends or your family. Peer pressure or a need to be seen and accepted in roles set by others feels like a magnetic force pulling at you. The constant exposure to these compelling forces develops subliminal killers that attack and destroy all efforts to be your true or authentic self. Only by exercising the power of your mind can you combat these forces.

For those of you who have already explored the topics of mind and personal development, new perspectives can revitalize ideas that have fallen by the wayside. Concepts that you felt did not work previously can be approached with new insights and be revived from the point where a killer silently and successfully caused you to quit or fail. If the secret or the answer mysteriously eluded you in your quest to understand mind power, then your situation is no different than the thousands of others with whom I have shared my approach. The secrets and answers are merely an understanding of processes that program the mind to attract or respond to various situations.

My realizations occurred during a time when I learned to overcome migraine headaches. For years, I suffered through debilitating pain without obtaining lasting relief from the medical profession. Finally, at the age of twenty-four I asked my physician whether hypnosis would be beneficial. His advice was to be careful as hypnosis was not for everyone. He suggested that it was a viable option for me because I was cautious and open minded.

Locating an experienced and qualified hypnotist was a challenge. It was not a simple task considering the number of disreputable practitioners that existed. The law of attraction seemed to unfold exceptionally well when I located Dr. Hans Nütt. He first shared with me his daring escape from a German concentration camp during World War II. He described how he joined the French Resistance and eventually the British Intelligence. He trained spies to speak a new language, including the accent and dialect of the specific region where they would be deployed. I quickly became his student—but not for long. Following his advice, I implemented preventative techniques and my migraines were no longer an issue.

The cure for my migraines might seem incredible but that was not what I found most enlightening. I was fascinated by the mind and the effect it had on behaviors, including my health. Although the sessions were enormously valuable, Dr. Nütt's guidance to further explore and develop my mind was the catalyst that altered my life. He advised me to begin by reading a specific book that unfortunately was out of print. He said, "If you are serious, locate that book. After reading it, you will know what to do." Finding that book was an experience in itself that I will share later.

One is not required to be a hypnotist or have a degree in psychology to understand the concepts of mind power. Locating your answers requires time to reflect and explore how you were influenced or programmed. All thoughts, interactions and events that you have experienced are recorded in your subconscious mind.

A lack of understanding of how your mind power works creates the perfect conditions for killers to hide, thrive and undermine your achievements.

My hypnotist did not provide me with specific instructions. What he did provide were directions about where to begin my search to find answers and the encouragement to follow my instincts. Lastly, he emphasized, "You will know what to do, and you will not need to see me again."

Initially, I felt abandoned and unprepared to embark on this daunting journey. I began reading books on topics about the mind and how it is influenced and controlled. Within a short time, I was launched onto a fascinating road of self-exploration. Information on mind power, meditation, self-hypnosis, behavior, religions, cultures, advertising and personal motivation was abundant.

The results of my research were three-fold. The first and foremost realization was that we are entities with computer-like capabilities that are as programmable as digital computers. Next, I discovered that self-help books generally focus on a single topic whereas multiple factors influence each facet of our behavior. Finally, I concluded that self-help books are of little value if they do not provide a practical or meaningful format for implementing the information. Positive stories are enjoyable to read but if you do not know what to do when you set a book down, it is just an enjoyable read. For change to occur, the subconscious mind requires specific instructions. Those instructions are presented throughout this book.

One of the challenges I encountered in my search was that the descriptions provided by early mind explorers were confusing. It took over 200 years for inspirational writers, physicists and psychologists to agree on the name *cybernetics* for this field of study. Renowned explorers included—Émile Coué (1857-1926), Maxwell Maltz (1889-1975), Norbert Wiener (1894-1964) and William Ross Ashby (1903-1969).

Various sources and dictionaries credit Norbert Wiener for devising the word cybernetics in the 1940s from the Greek word *kubernētēs*, meaning a steersman or *kubernan*, to steer or control. From the late 1800s to 1975, experts attempted to explain mental programming or conditioning to a world devoid of computer terminology. Cybernetics and Psycho-Cybernetics became descriptors but were not mainstream vocabulary until the 1970s and 1980s.

Imagine the difficulties early explorers faced in describing causes, effects, programming and processes without today's computer terminology and lingo. The modern language of computers enables us to describe the constructs of mind power and the power of suggestion. Computers are central to our offices, vehicles, phones, appliances, equipment and home media centers. They are programmable and function as programmed. You are the same.

The mystery of the mind has been a controversial topic since the time of Socrates. Regrettably, Socrates was sentenced to death in 399 BCE for teaching youth to be free thinkers. His concepts threatened the religious beliefs of the region, and his teachings were quickly suppressed. The fear of execution caused Plato (429 BCE – 347 BCE) and Aristotle (384 – 322 BCE) to distance themselves from Socrates, yet they continued promoting the same concepts. When one considers that the information has not changed for centuries, one must question why it is not commonly taught in our schools.

It was centuries before philosophers like René Descartes (1596-1650), and Baruch Spinoza (1632-1677) braved the wrath of church and government to explore and promote independent thinking and the development of our mental powers. The information did not become mainstream until inspirational writers from the mid to late 1800s dared to challenge the authorities. They included, among others, Helen Blavatsky (1831-1891), William James (1842-1910), Nikola Tesla (1856-1943), James Allen (1864-1912), Florence Scovel Shinn (1871-1940), Alice Bailey (1880-1949), Napoleon Hill (1883-1970), Emmet Fox (1886-1951), Joseph Murphy (1898-1991), U.S. Andersen (1871-1940), Earl Nightingale (1920-1989) and Og Mandino (1923-1996).

These explorers of mind and behavior made valuable contributions during the last 400 years. During the time of Plato (400 BCE), the term teleology was conceived to express the phenomena of processes that work but are unexplainable. In the field of modern science, explanations for multiple processes of the brain remain undefined and unknown. Science is behind in confirming what many already know and have experienced. Einstein's theories continue to be validated one hundred years after they were formulated. Sadly, the masses are discouraged from exploring concepts that are not scientifically explained; yet for millennia religious doctrines have promoted superstitions and unfounded dogmas. For over 2400 years, Socrates' wisdom has been available for us to follow:

> *Employ your time in improving yourself*
> *[by the writings of others], so that you*
> *shall gain easily what others have labored*
> *[for long and] hard.*
> *Socrates – Philosopher – (469–399 BCE)*

Many regularly process, experience and understand the cause and effect relationships created by thought processes. Unfortunately, the connection and significance of their findings are publicly dismissed if science cannot agree or provide an explanation. This restrictive mindset is not new, as Nikola Tesla stated a century ago:

> *The day science begins to study non-physical*
> *phenomena; it will make more progress in one*
> *decade than in all the previous centuries of its*
> *existence.*
> *Nikola Tesla–Inventor (1856–1943)*

We continuously search for solutions to improve our lives and achieve more. The answers we seek are obvious when we take the time to reflect on how we function. A generic response cannot be provided as each of us has different life experiences, cultures and educational backgrounds. This book is designed for you. It provides numerous processes and explanations for you to discover your mental powers and resolve challenges and situations that are specific to you.

Your defense against internal and external influences (killers) requires applying a silent energy that we all possess. When not controlled, this energy can be hijacked and turned against you. No one can protect you. The battle is in your mind. You alone have to take control. The techniques required to manage this power are the answers you seek. Through a process of exercises and self-exploration you will understand how these killers formed and what is required to suppress them.

The answers we seek are not hidden but society's excessive stimuli often overpower our minds and prevent us from recognizing and applying simple solutions. Many describe their lives as a world of manic madness that does not allow them a moment to relax or think. Others recognize this madness but have not discovered ways to function more effectively amid the busyness of life. Managing this madness is your first challenge and the topic of the next chapter.

Chapter 2

Stop the MADNESS

Without exception, the demands of family, career and social expectations create stress and anxiety. We regularly hear people say that they have no time for themselves or can't slow down and just "be" for a while. The hype for individuality, living the dream and displaying success by owning the next trendy item increases consumerism and financial stress. The exploding culture of social media develops an addiction to stay connected and simulate what others do. Stress increases as each new posting raises the bar to outdo the previous one, whether it be a birthday party, destination event, gender reveal or attending an opening of the newest club. And if that isn't enough, we have agitating and inciteful reports of false or fake news on political, racial, religious, environmental and health issues.

The driving force behind these influences is powerful and did not evolve by accident. Cleverly designed constructs to control the masses subtly engage the power of our minds to work against us. Rather than become our authentic selves, we succumb to temptations and distractions and become followers of trends and causes. Peer pressure, social expectations and a plethora of distractions prevent us from evaluating how our time, energy and resources are consumed. The control that reigns over us goes unnoticed.

Societal control isn't new. What is new is that we can detect and manage this enemy. Unfortunately, the busyness of our lives causes us to lose focus. You cannot develop mind power amidst distractions. Noisy environments interfere with our mental abilities and subtly influence our actions. The noise and busyness will only increase. It is you who has to adapt. Learning to manage mind power enables you to calmly navigate noisy environments and reclaim a sense of peace and tranquility.

The technological advancements of devices are intriguing and add to our distractions. Features are continually added that entice us to engage more with others or purchase new products. A natural curiosity to explore new features robs us of valuable time that diminishes the unique human experience of sensing and expressing who we are. We have devices to track our time, sleep, steps, breathing, food consumption and weight, as well as social media to follow what others do and say, regardless of its triviality. With each new gadget, app or device that we acquire, a dependency is created that forms into an addiction. Addictions begin by our voluntary participation and grow until the addiction controls us.

For many, social media has become an addiction. Detoxing from it is a challenge. Governments, special interest groups, advertisers and promoters of fake news use the technology to control us. Within seconds, messages are propagated around the world with a single posting. Promoters focus on the human weaknesses of fear, hate and curiosity to compel anyone to rapidly click and connect to their messages. They lure the unsuspecting with the ease of a click to follow enticing or agitating headlines.

Social media platforms entrap friends and acquaintances by developing a habit of needing to know who said what, who rated that or how many hits, tags or likes their blogs or sites received. The hype and madness escalate. The all-consuming desire to stay current consumes our precious time, individuality and finances. You can verify this by monitoring the number of times you are distracted by your device to follow a post or observe the activities of others. Without a doubt, we are easily influenced by external forces.

Don't get me wrong. I am not a fanatic who wants to return to "olde worlde" ways. I love my computer and the internet which provide incredible access to a world of information and services. Electronic devices are valuable and save massive amounts of time and effort. The danger lies in the subtle traps that create addictions. Apps are intentionally designed to capture your attention and keep you connected as long as possible. Freeing yourself from the control of your device or the prompt to respond immediately enables you to take control of the madness in your world.

Statistics support that anxiety attacks, sleep disorders and depression are increasing and that accidents and injuries caused by electronic distractions are now everyday occurrences. Physicians attribute the cause to an intense compulsion to partake in the activities on electronic devices. Many experience an anxiety when requested to turn off their cell phone during specific activities.

Surrendering to the power of others isn't limited to electronic devices. Our mind power can be strategically controlled by those who understand thought processes and the power and vulnerabilities of the mind. We are influenced by multiple entities, from large corporations and agenda-driven organizations to our local community's petty politics. Subtle influences dictate our actions and we comply without question, either blindly or with a silent reluctance. We submit to these forces and become automatons. Without understanding and developing mind power, you become a pawn for others to manipulate.

Ignoring the power of mind develops passivity, a human weakness that is easily exploited. Frequently, this exploitation is not by force. Your passivity makes you unaware that you are being controlled and you freely give up your power. Governments, corporations and policymakers introduce change as you accept and gradually *get used to it*. You remain passive. Marketers count on your need to accept or buy into fads, fashions and activities. They sell you the glamour of the fun you can have and how popular you will be if you own the coolest glitter, gadgets and gear.

Humans are part of the animal kingdom. We have an inherent character trait that compels us to want to control others. Through the evolution of psychology, some have perfected their predatory skills to identify weaknesses in others under the guise of being helpful or providing a service. This approach is common in politics, business, religion, special causes, phone scammers and status seeking activities where having an advantage over others is beneficial. Whether it is at a local community level or in our employment, acceptance and achievement is a hierarchical process where advancement is frequently attained at the expense of others.

In the absence of war, financial conquests are achieved through dominance, control of the financial system or the marketing of items and services. Corporations, in their pursuit of profit, know that financial success requires a repetitive cycle. Repeat customers are necessary for growth and profit. The process requires the public to be conditioned with purchasing habits that favor their product or service. Slick promoters achieve this by instilling emotional connections through advertising or a dependency on essential services like banking, utilities and insurance. Software companies are switching from selling one-time computer programs to subscription-based programs, no different from utility companies with monthly recurring fees. Hence, repetition and conditioning create cash flow.

We are targets that are regularly and strategically under attack. Increasing profit isn't the only reason for controlling the masses. Less tangible forces like status, social expectations and the desire for consumer products are just as controlling as physical force. Eventually you will recognize that you are a small cog in the gears of big business or play insignificant roles in smaller groups. Unfortunately, it is at your expense. You remain a paying passenger if your behaviors continue to be that of a follower. Control is taken from you slowly and subliminally as you are conditioned without your conscious awareness. The entrapments of societal expectations strangle people just as effectively and efficiently as serial killers.

The lure of a quick fix or easy money is enticing bait aimed at our human weaknesses and captures our attention to buy into a concept, activity or product. With an abundance of get-rich-quick schemes, instant diets and labor-saving apps, you are not told upfront that for the app to work, you still have to do all the physical work.

Smart homes, smartphones and a plethora of new smart devices are introduced daily. They are useful, but as complex as they are, electronic devices have their limitations. They cannot romantically invite that attractive person to dinner, negotiate a deal or perform your exercises. Devices can't calm an upset client or your employer when there is a risk of losing your job or instill confidence to excel in a new venture. Devices can only remind you of a task or sense your inaction by alerting you that you are not mobile. Unfortunately, too much dependency is created on external devices rather than developing your independence and personal power.

When it comes to earning more money, losing weight, exercising, attracting a harmonious relationship or improving an existing one, no device can replace human dynamics. People become disappointed and despite their best intentions, they continue to fail. They fail to stick to their diets, exercise programs and New Year's resolutions or to do what is required to earn more money. They feel that they cannot improve their situations. They don't realize that the enemy that prevents their success lurks deep within themselves and is further concealed by the madness of our society.

The enemy is a force of seasoned killers that effectively destroys your efforts. These enemies are programmed and respond like zombies. They reside in your subconscious mind and strike without warning, much like a computer virus. You remain unaware of their existence or purpose. For killers to be present, they were either created by you or they formed due to your lack of awareness. There were times when your approval was implied by not responding or you were too afraid to say "no." Fortunately, killers can be identified and suppressed. The challenge is in recognizing who or what they are and how they efficiently kill your efforts and plans.

With each passing day, month and year, the difficulty of identifying killers increases for two reasons. First, killers are subtle habits, actions and thoughts that easily escape our awareness. Second, the time invested in social commitments, activities or on our devices to connect or observe others during our hectic routines leaves little or no time to reflect on ourselves. When the distractions of a fast-paced society, social media and implied messages of success are combined, our minds become overwhelmed.

Our independence diminishes as we follow others, reinforcing our role as pawns. Our passivity fools us into believing that we are choosing through free will when the reality is, we are actually following a conditioned lifestyle of repetitive daily behaviors. We are evolving into a society of automatons where the freedom and power of our minds are being controlled. The madness of our lives becomes a prison. Fortunately, you can escape.

Easy targets are the got-to-have-it-now crowd or those who are driven to be the first to look cool and trendy. What is presented as state-of-the-art technology in bright shiny packages with gimmicky new catchwords or easy downloads, quickly becomes outdated technology. Within months, outdated electronics are tossed into drawers or recycle bins or replaced with new apps. It is natural for these devices to follow the same fate as old exercise equipment or electronic devices usurped by new technologies. Discovering how temptation routinely targets you is the first step to awareness.

The danger of following trendy fads is that we find ourselves back at the starting line each time a new trend is introduced. In the fashion industry, the lure of the latest and greatest garments for others to admire perpetuates an exhausting cycle—no different than drug addicts looking for their next fix. A Scientific American article paralleled this pattern to the Hawthorne Effect (Tufekci, 2019). Introducing a new process or gadget may create a short-term spike in performance or satisfaction, but we inevitably return to how we were as the novelty wears off.

When gadgets and fashion fail to entice you to act, personal attacks on your self-worth and self-discipline are sure to follow. Advertisers target those who have a pattern of failing at diets, fitness programs or achieving their personal goals.

Somewhere in this madness, each of us has been under attack at one time or another. The madness prevails by exploiting the weaknesses of our inner being – our self-image and self-respect. The attacks are effective because the individuals who are targeted have not achieved the personal success they crave. Each new temptation places us at that eternal starting line to run and fail again. As passengers, we board another train of false hope and expectation and blindly follow—not knowing our destination or the outcome.

The madness is fueled by our insecurities, a need for acceptance and peer pressure. Advertisers spend billions of dollars targeting your vulnerabilities to capture your time and money. They have perfected the process to generate revenue, even when you do not make a purchase. Each click on a product link or online article creates revenue for the advertiser or media platform. The temptations create a conflicting mental battle, much like an angel on one shoulder urging us to "Do this" and the devil on the other insisting "No, no— do this." The recurring internal conflict results in stress, anxiety, inaction or inappropriate and costly behaviors.

Sooner or later, you become dissatisfied or frustrated with what you have and yearn for something more meaningful. These feelings are your true and authentic "Self" begging to emerge so that you can be You. Killers are programmed to suppress your true Self and keep you hostage. You cannot escape until you develop an awareness that you are trapped.

Without assessing how your life is controlled, you remain vulnerable to chasing the next quick fix. Invariably, the winners are the marketers and advertisers. They are acutely aware of the killers within us and skillfully apply effective and subtle techniques that activate our internal killers to work for them.

Contrary to social and media hype, success isn't about being famous, having millions of dollars or being the best in a particular field, sport, or activity. Successful people become successful when they realize what creates happiness for them and choose activities that increase those positive experiences. Occasionally, they develop products or services that make them wealthy but often that was not their original goal. Successful people are not born into money nor are they given special advantages. Often, they do not have supporting families that encourage them. They achieve self-mastery by identifying obstacles or interferences and developing techniques to overcome them. Their obstacles are the same obstacles that you and I encounter. When you do not control or manage your challenges, your inner power becomes an enemy.

Lack of time is one of your killers. Maintaining a hectic schedule prevents you from allocating time to learn and adopt the techniques of successful people. The techniques are quick and simple to implement, but you have to take the time to understand them.

Our lives are complicated compared to people living a century ago. Yet, according to the observations of Nikola Tesla (Tesla, 1919), we have not evolved sufficiently to recognize or control the distractions in our lives.

> ***Most [people] are so absorbed in the contemplation of the outside world that they are wholly oblivious to what is passing on within themselves.***
>
> ***Nikola Tesla (1856-1943)***

Finding the Killers

Those who would benefit from you becoming a pawn or a cog in a large gear will never disclose the fact that they are exploiting you. The techniques to free yourself from entrapment are revealed in a specific order. Explaining a construct or process is often more time consuming than the action itself. Be patient. Your perseverance will be rewarded.

Only by stopping the madness long enough to explore these processes can you detect the killers that prevent you from noticing opportunities and achieving new goals. If this sounds exciting – it is! But first, you must be prepared to win. That is the topic of the next chapter.

Chapter 3

Prepare To Win

Breaking free of the opposing forces that control you is a frustrating process. Whether it is staying on a diet or exercise program, attracting money or developing new skills, initiating the first step is easy. Failing to remain on task by taking the next step and then the next is when killers attack.

If you are under the guidance of a health care practitioner, the information presented in this book is not intended to replace any therapy or therapeutic advice you are receiving. However, if you are ready to explore and challenge ideas that you thought were true, reflect on how you respond to situations or examine how people influence or intimidate you, this will be an enlightening experience.

Significant benefits are attained by completing the exercises in the order they are presented. Occasionally, you will be required to set the book aside to internalize a process or look away to contemplate a response. The exercises are designed to identify barriers and for you to experience the sensations and thought processes required to control mind power.

It is common knowledge that when learning new concepts, we remember 10% of what we hear or read, 30% of what we see and 80% when we participate in a process. Completing the exercises increases your retention from 10% to around 80%. If you do not experiment with the exercises and continue reading, critical steps necessary for mind power development will be missed. If you feel a reluctance to complete these exercises, the reluctance you sense is a game-changing clue to identifying killers that prevent you from achieving your goals.

At no time is the information intended to imply a right or wrong response, even when your answers and feelings reveal unpleasant scenarios. The exception is that if the choices are illegal or immoral, then those choices are not supported or recommended. The intent is for you to identify and convert undermining thoughts and desires into positive mind power.

Unlike social media, your notes are private and you are under no obligation to share them with others. When you explore a personal issue, it is to your benefit not to share your thoughts or feelings until you specifically identify what you want to achieve.

The situations and constructs are easy to relate to, and you will notice yourself saying, Yeah, that is what happens; or Wow, that's cool. It is the act of questioning and challenging your thinking that provides the most significant insights.

> *If you would be a real seeker after truth, it is*
> *necessary that at least once in your life you*
> *doubt, as far as possible, all things.*
> *René Descartes – 1641*

You are about to discover that a distinct cause and effect relationship exists between your thoughts and what transpires in life. The cause and effect is not readily apparent to you, as the dynamics of each situation have become your norm. Soon, you will be looking at this very differently.

Given the impressive number of self-help books and online training courses, it is normal to be overwhelmed by the options available. Outrageous claims are often made that mimic tabloid headlines on display at supermarket checkouts. A quick search on the internet for myths about pop-psychology reveals the absurdity of the titles and claims. *Finding the Killers* differs from pop-psychology or pseudo-science by guiding you step by step through a process to experience the power of your mind. What you will sense, feel or experience does not require a trendy label or an endorsement from science or an acclaimed authority.

If you are concerned about reading the right books, my recommendation is simple. To prevent mind entrapment by a single philosophy, never hold one book as the ultimate authority. Read as many books as possible. Ensure they offer you the freedom to choose and do not convey what you should do based on a format of laws or principles established by a group, organization or one who claims to be a supreme authority holding unique secrets. If a book does not offer the opportunity to challenge its concepts, be concerned. This book encourages you to think differently than you have in the past and does not promote enrollment in additional seminars to advance to a higher level. The information presented is all-inclusive.

By drawing on your experiences, you will undeniably acknowledge the presence of an energy or force that opposes your efforts. You have the power to control this energy and suppress killer habits that block you from achieving what you desire.

What appear as secrets are cause and effect relationships created by thought processes that you may never have contemplated. Your understanding of mind power will expand dramatically when you recognize how your thoughts and feelings sabotaged goals that you had previously set out to achieve. As you learn to identify and control the power of your mind, an indescribable feeling of peace, contentment and confidence will ensue.

During this journey, you will have several "Aha" moments when you relate to coincidences or become aware that what you experienced was not a coincidence, but a unique form of magnetism. There may be times while you are going about your daily routine and suddenly experience a sensation that compels you to enter a shop that you did not plan to visit. To your astonishment, you notice an item you have been seeking for days, weeks or months. As you reflect on what transpired, then or months later, you have an epiphany. The notion of entering that store on that day could not have been a coincidence, considering the length of time that you have been thinking about that specific object.

During your exploration, the examples and questions may feel like an attack on you, your lifestyle or your choices. You may have an urge to trash this book. If you find yourself thinking this way, be encouraged. It is this feeling of discomfort that will lead you to understand how your conditioning sabotages your efforts. Your feelings expose the defense systems that enemies and killers engage to keep you the way you are. Killers are habits that do not want you to introduce new ideas or behaviors as it would destroy them. Their survival desperately depends on you ditching this book. Should you not proceed, you instantly fail and remain as you are.

Overpowering this urge is foundational for developing mind power. It is normal to feel uncomfortable when addressing personal issues. However, sensitive feedback that is viewed constructively identifies where modifications would improve your life and personal interactions. The advantage of identifying sensitive issues in private eliminates the embarrassment of others informing you or relying on feedback from those who are reluctant to be truthful.

Self-transformation is not to be entered into lightly, nor should you delude yourself by thinking that your friends, family and associates will enjoy the new you. When your confidence and independence increase, others may not appreciate that they cannot continue to manipulate you.

Exploring the concepts in this book will lead you through a series of defining moments. You will have to decide if you want to continue to fail because of your conditioning or develop powerful skills to overcome habits that control you. If the latter, you are on the road to becoming your true Self. Whether we credit Lao Tzu, sixth century BCE Chinese philosopher, or an old biblical proverb, the message is as meaningful today as it was 2,600 years ago—if you are given a fish, you are fed for today—but if you are taught how to fish, you can feed yourself for life. Likewise, the techniques you develop are yours for life. As you apply these techniques, the enemies that have prevented you from achieving what you have long desired are subdued. Clarifying those desires is the topic of the next chapter.

Chapter 4

Clarifying Your Desires

Life is a constant balancing act between the activities we enjoy and the challenges and situations that consume our time, energy and resources. Happiness is attained by doing more of the things we enjoy and understanding how to effectively resolve unpleasant issues. Before you can focus on what you enjoy, you must clarify what makes you happy.

During your goal clarifying process, multiple questions will arise. The first question is: Am I motivated to achieve this for me? And secondly: Am I following the lives of others so much that every day I lose more of myself and become less of the person I long to be?

Mind power is a source of motivation and energy. As you will soon discover, the mind is programmable and easily influenced. Your mind requires diligent guidance and control. The word *influenced* does not imply that you consciously agreed to or willingly accepted the ideas and activities that make up your life. To your surprise, you will learn that since you were born you have been subliminally conditioned to accept undesirable values as habits. Your upbringing, education, casual encounters and even people that you dislike all contributed to how you were conditioned and programmed.

Feeling motivated and working toward a goal is energizing, uplifting and rewarding. Unfortunately, if the activity is not what you desire, it is difficult to remain motivated.

Motivation requires a personal desire to do, be or achieve something. When I consulted to organizations and corporations, I encouraged clients to refrain from referring to me as a motivational speaker. A client once invited me to give a motivational speech to his employees. When I inquired what he wanted to achieve, he merely replied, "Oh, I just want to motivate them." My reply was, "Would it not be better if we focused on improving performance, communication, morale or sales? What if you have a few troublemakers, complainers and idiots? If I motivate them, then your workforce will consist of motivated troublemakers, complainers and idiots. Is that your goal?" When his laughter subsided, we discussed the importance of specific goals to enhance his company's performance. Your life is the same.

Various techniques are presented to apply mind power, but they are not meaningful if you do not understand them or apply them to your life. A simple format on pages 39-40 provides you with an outline to identify what success, happiness and peace of mind mean to you. The aspects of life that impact you the most are your health, relationships, social life, career, finances, leisure, physical activities and spirituality or your overall peace of mind. The aspects are not ranked in any specific order, yet each aspect is impacted by the level of success or happiness you experience in each of the other aspects.

It is difficult to be productive or enjoy life when your mind is focused on troublesome issues. If that isn't enough, you may be required to work and deal with people you simply don't like.

> *We are affected by every aspect of our life.*
> *We cannot do well in one area of our life,*
> *While doing poorly in another.*
> (*Author Unknown*)

Enjoying more of life requires conquering the daily challenges and mental interruptions that waste energy. By learning to direct your energies to attract what you desire, a new lifestyle will unfold.

Mind power has the connotation of a mysterious process of wizards or robed priests or priestesses waving magical wands to make problems disappear. Your successes will increase when you understand how the power of your mind attracts new opportunities and overcomes everyday challenges.

Mind power is futile when it is misdirected. Your power can be turned against you and defeat you with devastating results. Completing the exercise will identify aspects of your life that create stress and prevent you from enjoying other activities.

Stress results from not developing skills to deal with issues that arise at work, home or social situations. Stress increases when the days and weeks are restricted to work and family obligations and do not include time for friends, partner, exercise, hobbies or yourself. As you apply new techniques to channel your energies into workable solutions, stress automatically dissipates and your circumstances improve.

The first exercise provides an opportunity for you to contemplate meaningful changes. At Socrates' trial, history documents his defense as—*an unexamined life is not worth living.* Although this is not a blanket statement for everyone or a declaration of what life should be, his teachings encourage us to improve and enjoy more of what we desire rather than blindly follow others. Sadly, for encouraging others to be free thinkers, he was sentenced to death.

Examining your life may conjure up conflicting feelings. If you experience a reluctance, don't want to or don't feel like completing these exercises, that reluctance is the negative energy or the killer described on page 31. Those feelings and an unwillingness to act are forces that prevent you from achieving your goals or exploring new opportunities.

As you contemplate each aspect, evaluate your feelings from your perspective. If your thoughts echo what others say or think you should do, continue exploring until you identify what it is that "you" desire.

Rate the degree of happiness or pleasure you receive from each aspect by circling a number between 6 and 9. Circle a number between 1 and 4 if this aspect is problematic, disappointing or requires improvement. A rating of "5" is not offered as it is misleading and does not indicate whether a situation is improving or requires additional attention.

To maximize your benefits, here are a few guidelines. For the aspect of Family and Relationships, ensure that you encompass everyone in your personal life. If an individual requires dedicated attention, assess them separately.

Under the aspect of Social, include the people you desire to interact with and anyone in your social circle who does not add value to your life. Rarely do we assess the negative influences created by our social lives. Some friends cause many problems and are difficult to address or manage. It may be beneficial to reduce the number of friends you have or eliminate those who cost you money, inconvenience or are unpleasant to be around. This may be an opportunity to develop new friendships, explore new interest groups or pursue activities that you have been considering.

The aspect of education is not limited to formal learning. Education has no boundaries and includes all forms of reading, coaching and online tutorials. Topics can include self-improvement, career, hobbies, personal interests, relationships, health, nutrition, managing money and anything that is of interest to you.

To clarify a goal or desire, ensure that it is specific and not a general comment. For example, in the aspect of career, do not state that you *want a better job*. Specifically identify what aspects you want to be different. You could clarify your goal as, I want to attract a job where I can do, be or achieve [*identify your desire*]; or where the salary is a specific range or [*describe the location or activity of a company or organization*].

To effectively engage mind power and the law of attraction, a goal must be free of limiting parameters. Opportunities are missed when you limit your focus on acquiring employment with a specific organization like Apple, Microsoft, Tesla, NASA, Green Peace or Google. The law of attraction produces better results when the focus is on the parameters of a position in a desired industry. The same applies for relationships. Instead of focusing on a specific individual by name, focus on attracting a person who is compatible with your personality, lifestyle and values.

For assessing your finances, do not enter *Win a Lottery*. An excessive amount of money is not a practical solution if your current situation is the result of your inability to manage your current finances. Identify options that would enhance this aspect of your life—a new job, second job, promotion, become certified, develop money management skills or curb a habit of overspending, gambling or lending money.

Physical and Health includes physical activities, sports, exercise, walking and active volunteering. Health includes diet and nutrition, attaining a desired weight or managing specific conditions. Occasionally, situations involving health cannot be altered. A focus may require a shift from the limitations created to exploring options that enhance one's life within those parameters.

Spirituality and Peace of Mind are the essence of who you are and your overall enjoyment of life. Feeling uneasy in this aspect often identifies conflicts in other aspects.

Most people seek a personal relationship or a compatible companion. Some prefer to remain on their own. Without attaining harmony and compatibility in this aspect, every aspect of life will be affected. Your desire may be to improve an existing relationship, attract one or terminate one that has become destructive to your well-being. The choice is yours. Begin by assessing your personal relationships.

Assessing My Life

Family and Relationships:
Partner/Spouse
I would rate my relationship as: 1 2 3 4 − 6 7 8 9
In my relationship, I would like to: *(fill in)*

_____

_____

Kids
I would rate my happiness as: 1 2 3 4 − 6 7 8 9
With my kids, I would like to: *(fill in)*

_____

_____

Others _____
In relation to dependent children and family members:
I would rate my happiness as: 1 2 3 4 − 6 7 8 9
Concerning others, I would like to: *(fill in)*

_____

_____

Education:
I would rate my education as: 1 2 3 4 − 6 7 8 9
As for my education, I would like to: *(fill in)*

_____

_____

Physical and Health

I would rate this aspect as: (1) 2 3 4 – 6 7 8 9
Regarding physical activities and health, I would like to: *(fill in)*

_____

_____

_____

Career and Finances

I would rate this aspect as: (1) 2 3 4 – 6 7 8 9
As for my career and finances, I would like to: *(fill in)*

_____

_____

_____

Social

Person or activity #1 _____
I would rate this aspect as: 1 2 3 4 – 6 7 8 9
Regarding this aspect, I would like to: *(fill in)*

_____

_____

Person or activity #2 _____
I would rate my happiness as: 1 2 3 4 – 6 7 8 9
Regarding this aspect, I would like to: *(fill in)*

_____

_____

Spirituality and Peace of Mind

I would rate my happiness as: 1 2 3 4 – 6 7 8 9
Regarding this aspect, I would like to: *(fill in)*

_____

_____

_____

Other Situations or Issues

Identify other scenarios that could improve or enhance your life. I would like to:

_____

_____

_____

On completion, it is common to observe that a rating of 9 was not achievable for every aspect. A rating of 8 or less indicates that there is always potential for improvement.

Applying mind power requires a clear focus. For each aspect that you did not rate as 9, in the space provided, ensure that you filled in what it is that you desire to do, be or achieve. It is critical to focus on what you desire and not on the barrier that prevents you from achieving it. Blocks and barriers will be identified in the next exercise.

To immediately implement a practical application of mind power, identify at least two personal situations that you can refer to as you proceed through this book. Several techniques and explanations will require you to refer to personal situations to discover how the power of your mind controls you. When you recognize how your mind assessed and recorded your perspective of a situation, you may realize that the situation is significantly different from what you first perceived. After reading this book, you may want to redefine your goals.

Unexpected complications occur when the repercussions of a new desire have a negative impact on your life or on those around you. The subconscious mind retains all goals and desires. This makes it critical that you relinquish the desire for goals that are no longer practical. Clarifying your desires is a foundational requirement to channel the power of your mind to work in your favor. The subconscious mind energizes a magnetic force, called the law of attraction, that continues to fulfill unachieved goals that you once desired.

The next step is to identify where your energies are consumed and what you perceive is blocking your success. This step is critical for determining why you did not rate various aspects as a 9. The blocks, barriers or interferences that you will identify in the next exercise are not your killers. You may insist that they are but you will learn otherwise. The killers are habits or conditioned responses that cause you to repeat ineffective behaviors that prevent you from overcoming what you perceive as a block.

The responses must be from your perspective. Avoid generalities and seriously consider what it is that you desire or what is preventing your success. To save time and prevent killers from throwing you off track, the following guidelines are provided.

Avoid the excuse of *a lack of time*. Not one person of the billions in the world has one minute more or less than you do. If time is the issue, determine whether it is poor time management, an organizational matter or whether you take on too many tasks and projects. It may be that you can't say "No" when you don't have time or the interest to comply with a request. Only you can identify what prevents you from having the time to enjoy more activities in life.

If a situation involves another person, don't name the person solely as the cause, issue or obstacle but identify precisely what they do or do not do that impedes the situation. If you feel uncomfortable asking others for help or dealing with sensitive issues, developing skills to address the situation would be a better investment of your energies.

Regarding finances, avoid the term *lack of money*. Improving your finances includes locating financially rewarding employment and learning to budget, shop, negotiate and manage your finances. A negative financial situation may be the result of behaviors and habits that undermined you. Spending and money management habits need not be permanent. As you learn how to apply mind power, your habits will automatically change, and so will your life.

Refine your answer until you can comfortably describe the block or barrier in one phrase or sentence. As mentioned above, there may be someone who hinders your progress, but the real reason is that you don't have the confidence or the communication skills to confront them for fear of making the situation worse. Should that be the case, then the block is better defined as a lack of communication skills or confidence to address negative situations. It is better to develop techniques that can be applied to multiple situations rather than address one person or situation at a time.

A lack of education and skill sets prevent you from taking advantage of new job opportunities. If an opportunity exists and you are not prepared, you cannot succeed. If you are prepared but do not notice opportunities, again, you cannot succeed. The formula for success is simple: **Preparation + Opportunity = Success**

This exercise will identify various killers. The same issue may affect other aspects. In a few instances, your blocks and barriers will mysteriously disappear, merely by assessing the issue objectively.

Blocks and Barriers

Family and Relationships:
Partner/Spouse

What restricts or creates conflict with my partner?

_____

Child 1 _____

What do I have to overcome in this situation?

_____

Other _____

The situation that requires attention is:

_____

Education:

What prevents me from furthering my education?

_____

Physical and Health (weight, exercise, sports and activities.)

What prevents me from enjoying health and physical activities?

_____

Career and Finances

What is the primary issue?

_____

Social

What creates conflict or frustration in my social life?

_____

Spiritual and Peace of Mind

My happiness and peace of mind are inhibited by:

_____

Other situations or noted issues on page 40:

The situation that prevents me from improving this aspect is:

_____

_____

Review what you have identified as blocks and barriers that you believe prevent you from being successful. If you could develop new skills to overcome blocks and barriers, what would they be?

1. *I would like to be able to* _____

_____

2. *I would like to* _____

_____

New worlds and possibilities appear when you discover and apply techniques that are powerful and effective. When a new concept is introduced, apply the explanation to your personal situation. This book won't tell you how to live your life, but it does reveal the power of the mind that will enable you to overcome blocks and enjoy more activities. The techniques are universal.

By applying the techniques, you will develop skills to keep you on task and advance with confidence. Be encouraged as the quest for a goal, whether it targets diet, exercise, increased finances, a partner or developing the law of attraction, does not have to create drudgery or agony. This is the topic of the next chapter.

Chapter 5

Removing the Agony Of Effort

Rarely do people enjoy change or a new routine required for exercises, diets or their jobs. They prefer to maintain the status quo. When asked why it is challenging to implement change, a common response is that the effort required to change is often agonizing. This belief is a classic trap yet simple to overcome when mind power is applied. The trick is not to focus on breaking the old habit as old habits are programs that cannot be broken or erased. Believing that you can break an old habit is an illusion and a killer that wastes valuable mind power. Success is attained when new habits are created that become stronger than existing habits that undermine your efforts.

When a music selection on the radio is no longer enjoyable, one simply selects another station or soundtrack. The music changes when one consciously selects another program. The same applies to your behaviors.

Your mind performs exactly like a computer. All habits, behaviors and body functions are controlled by an autonomic process in the subconscious mind that dispatches instructions through a hub or command center. Your habits are programs that are comparable to your music library that you select from and play. By comparison, the program library of your mind is a guidance system that is comprised of programmed settings that regulate your behaviors. The following is an example of your mind redirecting your behaviors on short notice without any conscious thought or effort. You may find that you have experienced this exact situation or one similar to it.

Recall a time when you returned home and were exhausted. You assessed that you were too tired and it would take too long to tidy up, so it could wait. Instead, you decided to make a lazy dinner, a.k.a. junk food, and crash in front of the TV for the evening. As you proceeded to settle into your nesting spot, the phone rang, informing you that friends were in the vicinity and wanted to stop by for a visit.

An explanation of what transpired next describes the power of the brain, mind and body and how a simple idea activates your biocomputer and creates motivation. When the phone rang, you answered, "Hello. What? You're where? That's great! I'll see you in twenty minutes!" As you ended the phone call, you gasped, "OMG, look at this place!" For the next fifteen minutes, you rushed around like a crazed person on steroids cleaning, dusting, tidying and changing your clothes, with only seconds to spare before the doorbell rang. You enthusiastically opened the door and jubilantly greeted your friends and then sat back to enjoy an exciting evening that extended late into the night.

You were exhausted before the phone call and it would have been agony to tidy up. You just wanted to kick back and veg out. After the phone call, instead of objecting to the chores that you had dreaded earlier, you exploded with energy and immediately completed them. Without summoning any assistance, a mysterious energy consumed your mind and physical body and elevated you to a new level of enthusiasm. Where that energy came from is not a mystery and can be called upon at any time.

Generating and controlling this energy is achieved through mind power. If you don't channel the energy, internal enemies seize control and undermine your efforts to achieve your goals. This energy is the epicenter of the law of attraction or the magnetism that prompts you to recognize new opportunities, financially or otherwise, and develop the discipline required to maintain a diet or exercise program and manage difficult people or challenging situations.

Your most outstanding achievement may not be the goals you achieve, but how your overall life improves with your ability to direct this energy on command. In the example above, your conscious being, the tired self, was jolted into action. Without being consciously aware, a subliminal guidance system commanded your body to move quickly and with conviction to prepare for your visitors.

You did not deliberately choose to act. It was your subconscious mind that detonated you into action. A combination of programs based on your feelings, values and desires created a perfect subliminal storm that dispatched clear instructions to your command center, enabling you to tidy your place and present yourself respectably to your visitors. It was the subconscious mind that supplied your physical body with an extra boost of energy and enthusiasm as you became supercharged for the evening. Yet moments before, you were exhausted. Imagine having the ability to turn that same energy on to accomplish tasks and achieve goals you never thought possible. Each of us has this energy, but few are shown how to nurture and apply it. The killers within suppress this energy by instilling an aura of agony associated with effort.

It is impossible to remain constantly supercharged. Our physical bodies have limitations, and when pushed too far, we burn out. Operating at maximum physical and mental output day after day, whether for work, studies, sports or family obligations is an impossibility. To effectively apply mind power, the physical body needs to be relaxed and rested. Stress, anxiety and fatigue erode your physical and mental abilities, leaving you at that exhausted level you felt just before your friends called.

Without being consciously aware, you occasionally manage mind power. For example, others may be experiencing a heart-breaking or disastrous loss that requires compassion rather than a display of enthusiasm. You may feel excited about a personal event and want to offer cheerful assistance. You choose not to because of sensitivity and an awareness of their situation. Suppressing your enthusiasm is achieved by applying the same mind power techniques that are required to remove the agony of the effort when developing new skills and habits or achieving a goal.

Learning to manage mind power is often explained in the medical fields of cognitive science, psychology and neuroscience. Few are comfortable with medical terminology as it can be complex and difficult to comprehend. In this book, the terms and concepts are stated in clear everyday language to enable everyone to personally experience the processes, regardless of their level of education. For those who enjoy the technical language of science, neuroscience and medicine, further reading and exploration of the command center or hub can be researched under the terms of the *reticular activating system, amygdala, corpus callosum* and the *hippocampus*.

The objective here is to have you experience what has long been referred to as a mysterious energy and how your brain, mind and thinking processes determine your successes and failures. After thousands of years of debate, there continues to be a lack of consensus within the philosophical and scientific communities as to whether the brain and mind are one or two separate entities. Undoubtedly, there is the physical organ called the brain. As you explore this book, the intangible realm of mental energy, memory and thoughts, which I refer to as the mind, may at times be viewed as part of the brain and at other times as a separate entity.

Applying mind power requires an understanding of how we can consciously alter or override our biomechanical motions and behaviors. Mind power requires an understanding that we are as programmable as digital computers and programmable devices. Digital computers require executable programs comprised of lines of code or steps that direct an internal processor to perform specific functions.

Your biocomputer is the same. We tend to think in terms of habits. To refer to our habits as programs requires a paradigm shift. Regardless of how you wish to label them, habits are programs. A program for your biocomputer begins as a thought or idea and through repetition, manifests itself into a construct that becomes a guidance system setting.

Although the mind is complex, there are basic mind power commands that can be applied to override some autonomic responses of your biocomputer. This is the essence of mind power and the processes required to notice and attract opportunities, increase your finances, attract a compatible partner, overcome challenges, attain a desired weight or achieve the things that continue to elude you. The instructions you will be shown are equivalent to a programmer hacking into and controlling another computer system.

There are a few basic similarities and differences between a digital computer and your biocomputer. First, your behaviors and actions are the result of executable programs or commands that are stored in the subconscious mind. The programs that we call habits have become your guidance system settings. A command center receives instructions from the subconscious mind via your autonomic nervous system and simultaneously completes behaviors based on your past conditioning or programming.

Second, you or external entities can physically intercept the command center the same way you interrupt or stop a computer program or suppress your behaviors when they are inappropriate.

The Components of Your Mind

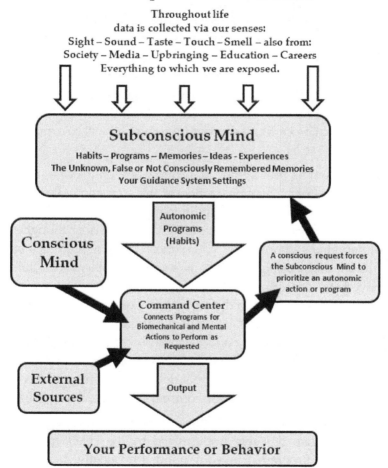

Third, when a digital computer is executing a program that is incorrectly programmed or corrupted, it stops, crashes or processes errors. When a biocomputer program is interrupted, it cannot stop processing or remain idle. If it does not instantaneously receive a replacement command from you consciously, it will default to a previous guidance system setting. The instructions may be random thoughts, an unrelated monologue or the autonomic execution of previously established programs, whether they are productive or counterproductive.

For example, you can consciously override your subconscious mind temporarily to hold your breath. Within a minute, your subconscious mind resumes control through its autonomic survival system and forces the lungs to exhale and begin breathing. The same applies when developing new habits or programs to achieve a goal. If your new command is ambiguous, disrupted or you lose conscious focus of the process, the subconscious mind instantaneously reverts to repeating its past conditioning or existing habits or programs. These processes determine your success or failure. Each process and supporting command will be explained in detail.

Overcoming the agony of change can only occur through conscious effort. Conscious action is the supreme authority and overrides all habits and past conditioning. This cannot be refuted. As you progress, you will understand that your conscious thoughts are the supreme authority over your subconscious mind. It is a small window of consciousness that is sought by others to influence, convert or control you to become a follower, consumer or subservient participant in their activities. Control of your conscious thoughts is a continuous battle between you and your programs (habits) and conditioning and external forces or entities. Whether your choices and actions are solely yours or influenced by others, it is the repetition of the process that develops programs that control your behaviors. But staying the course need not place you in agony.

Any past effort that was not successful is explainable. Your best intentions were probably undermined by the killers (previously conditioned programs) in your mind. Impatiently racing ahead without supporting plans or processes is like taking off in an airplane without learning the procedures to navigate, communicate with control towers, decipher critical instrument readings and safely land the aircraft. Training and practice are necessary. Learning to apply mind power is the same.

Success and the achievement of goals require specific programs or guidance settings. If your efforts have not been successful, your programming and the settings on your guidance system are not compatible with what you desire. Frustration, agony and an internal conflict ensue. It is at this point of frustration that many choose to attempt a quick fix.

If you are ill, you would not go to a pharmacy and ask for just any medication. You would have the pharmacist or physician diagnose your ailment and prescribe medication that addresses your condition. The same is true for applying easy solutions or quick fixes without analyzing or identifying the real issue.

When you analyze a situation first and then focus on solutions to address the barriers that restrict you, superior results are achieved. Failing to apply an organized approach punts you back to the starting line. You go through the motions, emotions and agony, yet success continues to elude you.

Identifying a goal is easy but staying focused requires mind power. Focus is an action that individuals fail to maintain when beginning new processes designed to improve their health, finances or relationships. After considering a process, many silently say, Oh, I know what to do. Unfortunately, they are right, and they are wrong. They have identified what to do externally but not what is required to develop internal or subliminal programs for the change to become permanent.

Learning to play a musical instrument, racquet sport, golf or perform a surgical procedure requires practicing the movements until a level of competency is achieved. With practice, the new process starts to feel natural and comfortable. You may want to call it a new habit. Regardless of its label, that natural feeling is the result of having successfully developed an effective program or setting for your subconscious mind to process or execute autonomically. The agony you endured while forcing your will to get it right mysteriously fades away.

Staying focused requires the combined skills of a bridge builder and a stage manager directing a performance. You are building a bridge from where you are to where you want to be. Your actions are your performance. Without maintaining a focus, your old habits or killers sneak in and destroy your best intentions in a fraction of a second. The killers in your subconscious mind are relentless and possess zombie-like traits that enable them to randomly materialize.

A conscious decision or new program setting is required before your subconscious mind can guide you to your goal or perform an action. Consciously releasing the energy that caused you to explode into action when your friends called requires an awareness of the five elements of motivation and how they combine and intensify your focus.

Motivation is an energy that is fueled by **Desire**. Desire is the first and most powerful element but is commonly misunderstood. People use the word desire in conversation to express that they would enjoy an activity. They casually say that it would be nice to do, be or have something when their desire is nothing more than an idle wish. The desire that creates motivation is activated by an intense wanting from within.

Before setting out on a venture, you need to confront your killers by asking, How strong is my desire to achieve this goal, and am I prepared to do everything that is required to achieve it? A confrontation will ensue in your mind that determines whether you or the killer will secure control of your energy.

It is at this juncture that a lack of focus or a weak desire becomes an open invitation for killers to attack. When you are pondering whether to engage in a project or activity and feel lethargic, or it seems like too much work, the discouraging thoughts and feelings are the weapons killers use to prevent you from progressing. If you do not learn how to suppress them, they are guaranteed to kill your plans and efforts instantly.

When your desire is strong, an invisible force pushes you and generates self-motivation. You wake up earlier and begin tasks without procrastinating. It is common to set out to work on a project for just a few minutes, and before long, an hour or two has passed. Your desire and the sheer enjoyment of the activity keep you energized and focused. Time and effort become irrelevant. The active thoughts in your conscious mind can either summon the subconscious mind to generate the energy required to continue or cause you to sense tiredness, discouragement or loss of interest.

When your passion for a goal is weak, or at best lackadaisical, be assured that a killer will cause you to fail. Killers attack passive efforts and drag you back to a state of inaction. Conversely, desire mysteriously energizes you to put your heart and soul into an activity that you enjoy. If you select a goal that you have dreamed about and craved for some time, you have the desire to achieve it.

Motivation causes your desire to evolve into a passion that may appear as an obsession to others. Discipline and balance prevent passion from becoming an obsession. The urge to stay up late to watch TV, play video games, surf the net or engage in activities that are detrimental to your health, well-being, career or relationship is not a constructive desire but an addiction.

Many achieved mega-success because their desire became an obsession no different than an addiction, causing other aspects of their lives to suffer. Numerous biographies describe financially successful people whose lives were void of time with partners, children and friends. Their focus and desire to achieve were all-consuming and became the only focus that mattered. This book does not advocate that intense obsession to achieve at any cost but instead advocates a healthy and balanced lifestyle. The previous chapter provided a format to identify your specific desires for increasing enjoyment and achieving a balanced lifestyle. As you progress, you will recognize that the strength of your desire influences your actions or inactions and determines your success.

The second element that energizes and reinforces subliminal programs is when your desire has a *Purpose*. The purpose cannot be determined by your friends, parents, partner or employer. Purpose is derived from a personal perspective. It requires a personal and emotional connection for your sole enjoyment or for sharing with others. Part of the process is to understand the purpose of the goal(s) you desire. A purpose energizes desire. Clarifying your purpose begins by evaluating—am I doing this because I want to do it, or did someone imply that I should do it? If the identified purpose is not a personal desire, your enthusiasm gradually evaporates and the goal is rarely achieved. Your heart just isn't in it.

Many of us have embarked on ventures, tasks or projects that we did not care about and completed them only to please an employer, relative, friend or social expectation. When such an activity becomes a long-term expectation, our enthusiasm fades and we invest the least amount of effort. Our purpose fades and we transition to just getting through the activity.

The third element is *Planning*. A specific plan assists the subconscious mind to rapidly process and identify the goal or end result and transmit unambiguous instructions to the command center. Planning channels your mind power to neutralize distractions created by thoughts, objects and external entities.

A visual document or a mental picture provides a focus and target for the subconscious mind. Any distraction that enters your conscious mind is a killer that mysteriously destroys your motivation. The distraction could be the urge to overthink what you should do. When you overthink a situation, you are in a conscious mode. Deliberate and excessive conscious thoughts or internal debates clog the command center and suppress autonomic instructions that the subconscious mind can provide. It is in this intense conscious mode that mind power becomes our trusted friend or worst enemy. A plan is a simple resource and powerful tool for harnessing mind power.

The fourth element is *Action*. Action requires you to act and continue acting. It is natural to be excited at the beginning of a new job or a diet, exercise or study program. Retaining that excitement requires continuous action. When the forces of desire, purpose and planning are combined, motivation increases and the required actions become effortless. Motivation flows from the subconscious mind and stimulates you to act immediately – not tomorrow or next week. When motivation is low, you can instantly generate enthusiasm through mind power. You can consciously instruct your command center to increase your energy from tired and sluggish to enthusiastic and energetic.

The fifth element that generates motivation and reinforces focus is the act of *Evaluating*. There are two types of evaluations. The first is creating a conscious awareness of your advancement toward your goal. The second is interpreting the internal feedback from your subconscious mind. Analyzing internal feedback creates an awareness of the changes that were successful and those that require alternate action. When your goals and desires are compatible, the subconscious mind begins to prompt your conscious mind to recognize opportunities or identify barriers that require corrective action. The feedback is an autonomic aspect of mind power communicating with your consciousness. You will be provided with techniques and processes to analyze the feedback.

Occasionally, your efforts become agony as you trudge and push yourself forward. You feel that the task is a drag and you want to quit. This sensation is valuable feedback indicating that you are losing focus. Although it feels discouraging, it should be celebrated as a welcome warning. The discomfort of performing a task or project is positive feedback that you are overcoming old programs that are fighting to retain control. As you consciously instruct your command center to perform the tasks, killers activate the sensation of agony to prevent the change that is about to occur. If you submit to the agony, the subconscious mind has no option but to conform to your old conditioning and the change you desire fades away. When you do not maintain control, your subconscious mind responds like a traitor and works against you and your best intentions.

The agony that you feel is a weapon the killer employs to tempt you to quit. When a new action is introduced consciously, the subconscious mind autonomically protects the existing default program that has become a setting on your guidance system. Your conscious desire to do something differently is in direct conflict with the program the subconscious mind is protecting. This conflict is the source of your agony and discomfort. When asking others to assist with a new task, recognize that their reluctance or resistance is the result of their internal conflict.

You have multiple killer programs that prevent you from achieving your goals and desires. They continue to function until they are replaced by new programs or you consciously and consistently override them. Multiple programs reside in memory, but it is the strongest or most dominant program that the biocomputer executes by default.

Suppressing a killer is similar to changing an application running on your electronic device. As you progress and complete the exercises, you will recognize that you are as programmable as a smartphone, tablet, TV, DVR or other electronic devices. The difference is that you and your subconscious mind do not have Ctrl, Esc, Enter or Delete keys.

In the diagram below, *Today* is your starting point or a new beginning. By continuing with your existing routines, the habits and programs in your subconscious mind remain strong. Without any interceptions or disruptions, you will arrive at the box marked *Your Future*.

Habit and Program Protection

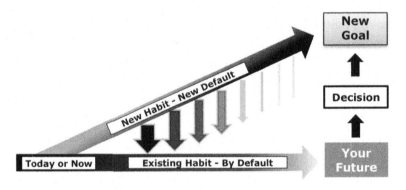

By assessing the probable outcomes of what the future may be, you can ascertain if it is where you want to be or what you desire. A decision is required to remain as you are or select a new Goal or Destination. Merely choosing a new goal does not automatically create the internal programs or habits required to instruct your command center to guide you to success. When you choose a new goal, a relentless force continually tempts you to abandon the new goal or avoid a critical step required to achieve that goal. This is the force that causes you to reach for that candy, skip your exercises or ignore calling a client. To successfully achieve your new goal requires the action of consciously overpowering this relentless force. It does not require physical effort. It requires mental effort. It is at this precise moment that mind power is required to maintain control. Failure to do this ensures change does not occur, and you return to your old routine or that discouraging starting line.

Until a new routine becomes a habit or the new dominant program, your new choice must be consciously and consistently repeated. It is the conscious action that intercepts the command center and wrestles control away from the existing programs in the subconscious mind. Unfortunately, the subconscious mind remains loyal to the existing programs and has a built-in protection system to reject your new choices. At first, it appears that the harder you work to break away from an old habit, the stronger the old habit becomes. A technique to influence your subconscious mind to switch its loyalties to your desire is required.

Change occurs only when a new program becomes more compelling than the old habit. The internal force that pulls at you, the down arrows, is a killer that is powerful and relentless. You may have experienced this earlier when you were encouraged to complete the personal assessment (Pages 39-40) but felt you did not want to do it. That not wanting to do the new action is an existing habit or killer preventing change. For an old habit to maintain its existence, it must kill your good intentions and discourage you from performing a new action. The moment you relax or consciously stop instructing your command center, a killer, or the enemy within, attacks and regains control. You can feel the draw or compulsion to perform the action you specifically want to avoid. The force is a combination of programs in your subconscious mind that kills your efforts as it instructs your command center to stop the diet or exercise regime, sneak that candy, quit reading this book, don't call that client and *BANG!* The Killer wins. Your new goal, plan or idea is as good as *DEAD!*

The power of program protection and the force it has on you are easily demonstrated. To find out if you are addicted to or follow social media excessively, set a plan to not post or check your social media for four to six hours. Set your phone aside and continue with your day. Within minutes, the sensation of an irresistible force pulls at you to check your phone. Just one little peek. The force you sense is a conditioned habit that started innocently through one or two usages. With repetition it has become a killer that protects itself so that a new choice or action does not replace it. This powerful force is a weapon that killers use to control you. Each time you recognize this energy pulling, prompting, urging or causing you to falter, you have identified a killer program protecting itself.

As shown by the top arrow in the diagram on page 56, creating a new habit requires a conscious focus as you diligently repeat a new action. With repetition, the new action grows stronger and becomes a new default program or habit. Control by the old default program is suppressed, but it is not erased. It becomes a sleeper program and attacks when you have a lapse in focus or let your guard down. The old program remains in your subconscious mind and can be activated by you or another person, event or any stimulus that can access your command center.

The inability to remove killer programs ensures they remain programmed to ruin diets and exercise programs or to conceal obvious opportunities by subtle distractions that undermine your best intentions. New goals are simple to choose but are effortlessly usurped by the killer force. It is crucial to develop an awareness when opposing forces begin to challenge your efforts. Awareness is a point of power. The battle is won by applying specific actions that will be systematically revealed in the following chapters.

When striving for a new goal, not only is it necessary to battle your thoughts, but you must deflect the enormous pressure of external influences and temptations. When offered a dessert or invited to participate in an activity that you specifically want to avoid, the temptation to surrender is overwhelming. Temptations of chocolate, cigarettes, ice-cream and alcoholic beverages can be challenging to resist. When you are about to exercise, study or complete a proposal, your discipline is under attack. You receive invitations from friends, social media posts and distractions that surface as avoidance behaviors. These distractions are killers. Combating temptation requires knowing how your command center can be hijacked. The moment you fall for the bait, you lose control.

A new habit creates a new lifestyle but that new lifestyle remains vulnerable. Constant monitoring and protection are required. It was the same when you learned to drive a car or ride a bicycle. You cannot remove your hands from the handlebars or steering wheel for longer than a few seconds, yet the effort to keep the vehicle on course is minimal. As you persist in mastering a new habit, old programs become zombies and attack when you least expect them.

The force that tempts you to quit a new activity creates the agony that you must battle. Habits, like driving or cycling, are developed through practice and repetition. They require minimum effort to continue or maintain except when an issue arises. A storm or bad road conditions can instantly challenge your physical skills. A conscious effort is required to control your vehicle and ensure your mind stays focused on your driving. Your response is to consciously grasp the steering wheel or handlebars firmly and focus on what is coming at you. Situations often occur when resurging old habits become mental storms that rage for only a few seconds. But in the end, who won—you or the old habit?

Remaining in control ensures the old habit is suppressed, but a new habit requires the same attention as a plant, pet or relationship. It requires regular maintenance. Should you neglect the new habit and become passive or lazy, the old habit silently returns. As your subconscious mind calmly and efficiently processes the old habit as a default program, your old lifestyle returns to what it was. Overpowering the internal resistance does not require physical effort. It does require a constant focus on the benefits or the purpose of your actions, rather than on the agony you experience.

The agony of effort fades away,
When you focus on the benefits you gain.

This is a crucial tipping point to identify whether you move forward and succeed or crash and burn. It is the introduction of a new process or technique that causes you to feel uncomfortable or self-conscious. The sensation of discomfort or self-consciousness is an internal conflict activated by an existing killer. The conflict creates a standoff, but it is a confirmation that your actions are appropriate and change will occur. Only you or the killer can be victorious. The newly created awareness of this internal conflict is often an epiphany or an "Aha" moment. The power of your mind wins the battle, not physical effort.

Think of a puzzle that you struggled to solve. As soon as you saw the solution, your consciousness instantaneously shifted into a state of awareness where you could not comprehend the concept of not knowing the solution. You will discover that these techniques are similar. Once you recognize a few cause and effect relationships in your life, it will no longer be a puzzle.

As you develop your mind power and conquer these negative forces, the agony of your effort fades away. It is the ability to channel this mysterious energy that makes your efforts worthwhile. Killers continually stalk and disrupt our daily activities. Being aware of when they are attacking and applying mind power to take control of the situation are paramount. Taking control to intercept a behavior (habit or conditioning) will be expanded on in the next chapter.

Chapter 6

Behavior and Conditioning

A cliché that has endured the test of time is that we are creatures of habit. As stated earlier, prior to modern computer terminology, the construct of a habit was a challenge to comprehend. In modernity, our habits and conditioning can be defined as stored programs or guidance system settings. Hence, habits are programs that are executed by our biocomputer or subconscious mind.

When we introduce a new idea or make a request of others, we have an expectation as to how they will respond. Should they not respond as expected, tensions or conflicts can arise. Their behaviors are based on their conditioning and life experiences.

We experience similar internal conflicts when we introduce alternate behaviors to achieve a new goal or outcome as demonstrated in the previous chapter. If we desire a different outcome, different actions and program settings are required. The programs or guidance system settings in our subconscious mind are in conflict with our new choices and activate a program protection to ensure our response is the same as in the past. We can predict future outcomes with reasonable accuracy by observing our past behaviors and whether our current plans and actions incorporate different settings.

It's important to note that massive or radical changes are not required. At times, it is a single action that produces the most significant or immediate results. We encounter multiple mini-crises in our lives. We may have slept in, received an urgent phone call, missed a transit connection, didn't complete a report, forgot to pick up an item, were interrupted by txt after txt or forgot to charge our phone. Mini-crises are never-ending events in life.

The disruptions we experience are simple to model. On the following page is a computer program with five lines of program numbered: 10, 20, 40, 50 and 60 to randomly print out an event in life. Each disruption is displayed as an **"EVENT IN LIFE."** The pattern printed indicates how we waste energy bouncing back and forth each time a new interruption occurs. It is the bouncing back and forth that causes life to become chaotic.

A Random Program:

The Program:
```
10 FOR A=0 TO 6.3 STEP.2
20 Y = RND(1)
40 LPRINT TAB(20 * Y + 20); "EVENT IN LIFE"
50 NEXT A
60 END
```

The Result:

```
                    EVENT IN LIFE
                              EVENT IN LIFE
        EVENT IN LIFE
                 VENT IN LIFE
                                    EVENT IN LIFE
            EVENT IN LIFE
                    EVENT IN LIFE
                         EVENT IN LIFE
                                 EVENT IN LIFE
               EVENT IN LIFE
                         EVENT IN LIFE
           EVENT IN LIFE
                    EVENT IN LIFE
       EVENT IN LIFE
            EVENT IN LIFE
                    EVENT IN LIFE
       EVENT IN LIFE
                            EVENT IN LIFE
              EVENT IN LIFE
                                EVENT IN LIFE
          EVENT IN LIFE
              EVENT IN LIFE
                    EVENT IN LIFE
       EVENT IN LIFE
              EVENT IN LIFE
                               EVENT IN LIFE
        EVENT IN LIFE
                         EVENT IN LIFE
            EVENT IN LIFE
                               EVENT IN LIFE
         EVENT IN LIFE
```

Suppose we were to classify the events on the right as activities that are exciting and enjoyable and those on the left as negative or disruptive. It is easy to see when one is scattered, life becomes the epitome of the madness described earlier. A lack of focus causes one to be jerked in any direction. Interruptions break our concentration, disrupt our focus and consume excessive energy. We invite interruptions and chaos when we are at the mercy of social media, texting or any situation where we feel we are expected to respond immediately. When we observe people who are continuously stressed out, they often say that their lives are out of control.

Random, unscheduled and unexpected situations are natural occurrences in life. Stress occurs when we are not prepared to take the disruption in stride. Some feel helpless and conclude that the craziness is normal and continue as best they can.

We do not initiate change because we believe that our issues are too numerous or that change is hopeless. A fatal choice ensues. We choose not to act, which is in itself, a choice. We unconsciously decide to exert excessive amounts of energy to slog through the chaos rather than divert that same energy to create a less stressful life. The continued acceptance of the existing chaotic situation is another killer.

Stress and anxiety are not only caused by major incidents, but by the trivial disruptions that are encountered daily. When we lack organization or the confidence to say no, our days become more stressful and disruptive. Responding repeatedly to chaotic situations becomes a habit or program; hence, we are creatures of habit. It is our modus operandi. Because we cannot erase old habits, we require new and more effective programs that do not exist in our subconscious mind as dominant guidance system settings.

Change for the sake of change often complicates life. The requirements to reduce stressful situations are usually minimal. Mind power is applying simple responses to unexpected situations. The issue or situation does not change. It is how we respond that reduces the stress.

To demonstrate the effectiveness that one small change can make, we will execute the same computer program but insert an additional line of code numbered "30." This line instructs the computer to process *one action differently* and represents you learning one technique or changing one behavior in your routine, without making any other changes in your life. The result is:

A Defined Program:

The Program with line 30 added:

```
10 FOR A=0 TO 6.3 STEP.2
20 Y = RND(1)
30 Y = SIN(A)
40 LPRINT TAB(20 * Y + 20); "EVENT IN LIFE"
50 NEXT A
60 END
```

The Result:

```
        EVENT IN LIFE
          EVENT IN LIFE
            EVENT IN LIFE
             EVENT IN LIFE
              EVENT IN LIFE
               EVENT IN LIFE
                EVENT IN LIFE
                 EVENT IN LIFE
                  EVENT IN LIFE
                  EVENT IN LIFE
                 EVENT IN LIFE
                 EVENT IN LIFE
                EVENT IN LIFE
               EVENT IN LIFE
              EVENT IN LIFE
             EVENT IN LIFE
            EVENT IN LIFE
           EVENT IN LIFE
          EVENT IN LIFE
        EVENT IN LIFE
       EVENT IN LIFE
      EVENT IN LIFE
      EVENT IN LIFE
     EVENT IN LIFE
      EVENT IN LIFE
       EVENT IN LIFE
        EVENT IN LIFE
         EVENT IN LIFE
          EVENT IN LIFE
           EVENT IN LIFE
            EVENT IN LIFE
             EVENT IN LIFE
```

Small modifications produce noticeable changes but won't remove unpleasant events. Situations become less disruptive when you develop techniques that enable you to go with the flow. Introducing an effective response to deal with disruptions instantly changes how you feel. Rather than being at the mercy of a situation, you calmly acknowledge it and respond constructively. Good and bad events will continue to occur, but the loss of vital energy and time is minimized when you control how you respond.

People become discouraged by thinking that they are required to perform a complete makeover. In some cases, there may be numerous issues to address. It is not advisable to attempt multiple changes at once. Although numerous techniques are presented, it is impossible to remember all of them after your first reading. By gradually introducing new concepts, you are guaranteed to enjoy positive benefits. Glance back to page 64 and imagine how your life would be if you occasionally reviewed the processes and implemented another choice or action. It would be impossible not to enjoy more of what life has to offer.

Ignoring small details is comparable to searching the internet and omitting one character in the URL address. The construct of the system negates your efforts. The same applies when applying mind power. You cannot reach your destination when small but essential steps are omitted or skipped. Your breakthrough begins when you notice the small things that initiate positive actions and interactions or trigger internal and external conflicts. Your life will become more relaxing and exciting when you are able to see more options and opportunities.

Becoming aware of how you can create significant changes with small actions should motivate you to deal with situations sooner. Avoid focusing on the agony and frustration. Focus on the benefits of knowing that the sooner you address an issue, the quicker it is resolved.

Small changes can create huge benefits. What may appear as an insignificant issue could present new opportunities or become an instant battlefield. When a situation challenges your comfort zone, your guidance system settings cause you to react the way you have in the past, unless you consciously recognize what is transpiring and suppress that response. Your confidence level increases when options are available and decreases when choices are not obvious. A lack of options creates anxiety and causes you to feel threatened. Stress occurs when you feel threatened, scared, worried or upset.

To manage mind power effectively requires knowing when and how your guidance system settings work *for* or *against* you. This discloses where the killers hide. When life is going well, we tend not to worry about anything. However, when a mini-crisis occurs, our biocomputer autonomically executes a program based on our past conditioning or how we previously responded to similar situations. Our conditioning causes us to display one of two behaviors.

When presented with a problem, challenge, frustration or perceived antagonism, our first reaction may be to feel threatened. The mind explodes with a plethora of words that flood our thought processes, instantly raising our anxiety. We may hear or feel our heartbeat thumping in our ears. The threat creates a chain reaction and our instinct is to defend. The defense is dependent on our conditioning and ability to assess the situation.

Whether we perceive the threat as real or not, we lose the most remarkable power humans possess and revert to the basic animal instincts of fight or flight. Our defenses are reactions that include flight, fight, anger, withdrawal, silence, avoidance, verbal retaliation or other dubious behaviors. The issue does not have to be serious to generate anxiety; however, anxiety suppresses our mind power and reduces our mental capacity and ability to formulate constructive solutions.

Anxiety is a killer that adds negative energy to an existing problem, making the situation worse. The additional negative energy increases the sense of threat or frustration and our mental capabilities continue to deteriorate into a downward spiral. A constructive response requires a controlled thought process. An emotional response or raised voice could provoke an argument and escalate the situation.

Except for situations involving physical threats, exiting the scene is a flight-response that generally does not resolve the situation. There are situations when a break or time out is constructive, but not without informing the other party of your decision.

When an airplane loses control, the pilot must skillfully control the aircraft to maneuver it out of danger or the plane will crash. By comparison, developing skills to negotiate negative encounters increases your chances of suppressing killer behaviors that destroy opportunities and relationships. To place yourself in a position of power and effectively manage a conflict requires a rapid assessment of the dynamics and injecting a single alternative action to create a constructive interaction. Controlling your conditioned behaviors and influencing others is mind power in action.

Many believe that reacting negatively is part of our human nature. It is, and it isn't. A negative response is a developed or conditioned setting that your biocomputer executes before you can consciously contemplate an outcome for a situation. All parties benefit when a negative situation is neutralized early or turned into a constructive interaction. Introducing one new technique or action advances you to a level higher than you performed at last week, last month, or in similar situations. It is never too late to enhance your lifestyle, set new goals or improve your interpersonal skills.

When someone approaches with a problem, your response or reaction is regulated by your conditioning. Silently you may think, Uh-oh, this is going to be my problem. They're going to blame this on me. I'm in trouble or what is this going to cost me? The mind erratically races ahead, creating unnecessary anxieties. If your conditioning was negative, you developed a killer that demoralizes and discourages you and complicates many situations.

This killer can be instantly neutralized. When you perceive a situation as negative or a problem, your mind power is instantly compromised. The word *Problem* activates negatively conditioned responses in your subconscious mind that cause you to feel threatened. Instead of reacting, do not label the issue as a problem but immediately classify it objectively as a **Situation** or **It Is**—being neither good nor bad. This prevents your biocomputer from retrieving defensive programs and responding negatively.

When conversing with your boss, partner, friend, relative or a stranger and you hear the word *Problem*, immediately switch your thinking to, Okay, they perceive a problem—what is the real situation? At that moment, you instantly intercept your command center and prevent the subconscious mind from executing defensive actions. The flow of negativity is instantly suspended and the subconscious mind seeks to generate positive solutions.

It is at this moment that the subconscious mind accesses a power that animals do not possess. It is the power of imagination. Imagination is a mysterious energy that produces creativity and a flow of ideas that create options or solutions. The subconscious mind can be guided and prompted with thoughts like—how can I make this better? What can I apply immediately? With repetition, this prompting action becomes a habit. A newly created idea mysteriously injects a positive or encouraging energy into everyone involved, providing a catalyst for other positive solutions and open participation. Success depends on your ability to recognize that mind power is a combination of words and imagination.

When a situation is non-threatening and the outcome is uncertain, our mind is instantly activated by curiosity to seek additional information. Our curiosity explodes! We can't get enough! We sense that an opportunity exists and our mind eagerly explores multiple possibilities. We are excited. The diagram on the next page displays both scenarios—a threat and an opportunity.

Consider how your spirits soar at the mere suggestion of having a party, going on vacation or engaging in a fun activity. The excitement begins in your imagination. The subconscious mind rapidly dispatches thoughts and images to your conscious mind. Positive emotions are then triggered and the idea evolves into a sense of euphoria.

When a manipulative individual approaches and says we have a situation, or we need to talk, the energy changes. The level of enthusiasm you experienced from reading the previous paragraph, compared to the angst created by reading the first sentence of this paragraph, is a powerful example of how unstable your energy is and how it can be affected by words. Any negative thought or expectation is a figment of your imagination until the situation is clarified.

Others can hijack your imagination. Scam artists are experts at bypassing your defenses and channeling your thoughts to focus on fear or loss. Good leaders are the opposite. They rally their team by encouraging participation and new solutions from everyone.

Maintaining A Position of Power

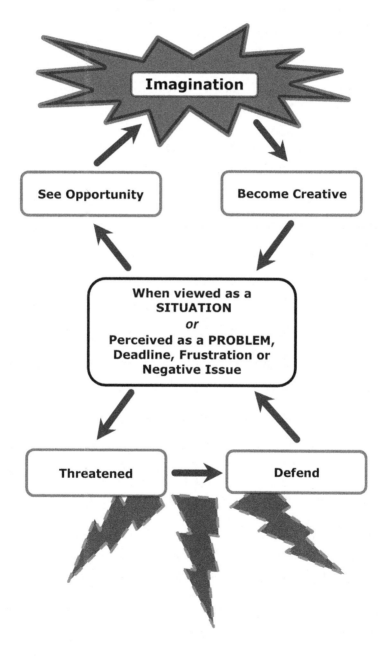

When threatened, we revert to animal behavior and we *React* without thinking of the consequences of our actions. When we identify the scenario as an opportunity, our human faculties enable us to *Respond* and generate constructive results.

Whenever we encounter a problem or situation, the power of words draws on our guidance system to process a response based on our conditioning. Our strength lies in our ability to respond constructively to situations.

A negative reaction is often caused by our interpretation of a facial impression, one or two words spoken by others or the first impression expressed by our self-talk. An awareness of this dynamic is a point of power. It enables you to recognize an opportunity, diffuse an adversary, assess your position, process your thoughts and respond constructively.

> *To see choice, is to MASTER a situation.*
> *Not to see a choice is when*
> *the situation has MASTERED you.*

The subconscious mind converses with you but it requires you to consciously interpret the sensory impulses that create feedback. Your thoughts and feelings are the feedback that constantly reveal your programming and whether that programming is compatible with your current situation, desire or goal. In computer terms, when subconscious programs and conscious desires are not compatible, they *do not compute*.

The feedback may appear discouraging, but it is valuable feedback signalling conflict and that change is required. An accurate interpretation of the sensory impulses is, I, your subconscious mind, can perform this but *you* must program me to override other programs that prevent me from helping you achieve your goal. Once a program is created, the subconscious mind protects it as being correct, including bad habits that are detrimental to your desires. New programs must compete with existing default programs that have become deeply embedded guidance system settings. The competition creates the internal conflict and the agony you experience.

Regardless of your age, whether you are 20, 30, 50 or 70 years old, whatever is occurring in life is your reality. Over the years your guidance system was programmed to effectively steer you to become whom you are today. The choices and decisions you made were based on your guidance system settings. What you do and how you respond to situations are reflex responses executed by previously established programs—better known as habits. Your guidance system settings continue to maintain your current reality because you are a creature of habit.

We operate autonomically. Old habits prevail until we consciously develop new habits. For example, think of an object, appliance or item that was relocated in your home or office, or a business that moved to a new location. As you entered the room or headed to that business, you autonomically proceeded to where the object or business used to be. By not providing a new instruction for your command center to guide you to the new location, by default your autopilot directed you to the old location. Many have experienced heading back to their old residence, even after a few weeks of living in a new home. Only when that "Oh $#!@" moment occurred did they realize where they were heading. This confirms that old programs are never erased and are ready to return by default.

Your biocomputer is a Global Positioning System (GPS) and requires a new setting to guide you to the new location of the appliance, business or new home. Although the subconscious mind had all the data to inform you of the new location, it remained a weak program unable to take precedence over the longer established habit. Since the old program (habit) could not be deleted, by default, the biocomputer executed the stronger program when your conscious mind experienced a lapse in focus. Several trips to the new location (repetition) are required to establish the new route as the dominant program or guidance system setting for the subconscious mind to autonomically guide you to the new location.

Changing your reality requires adding new settings to your guidance system. This cannot be accomplished without following the rules of the game or knowing how habit protection causes you to be a creature of habit.

Killers win by applying your mind power against you. Short-term results are often attained, but to ensure results remain permanent requires an awareness of how habits protect themselves and kill your efforts. You can perform anything differently once or twice but killers are programmed by the constructs of your biocomputer and follow the rules of computer programming. They can punt you back to the starting line before you realize what occurred.

You have to stay the course. Beginning a new diet, only to cheat on it a few days later or applying for a job and not continuing to search, does not develop new program settings. Your confidence and motivation diminish each time your best intentions fail to achieve a desired result. Following a series of disappointments, it is difficult to remain positive. A habit of accepting failure develops. Over the years, you have developed multiple habits that prevent you from achieving success. These habits are killers.

Killers have unique yet identifiable traits that enable them to instill internal havoc by creating worry, fear, doubt and other negative thoughts and feelings. Whether your goal is personal, social or business, an internal opposing force ignores the importance of your intentions and destroys your enthusiasm and ambitions. Failing to draw upon the power of your mind leads you to failure and disappointment.

You respond and perform according to your program settings. Like all computers, your biocomputer cannot detect whether the active program (habit) is good or bad. When the command center receives an instruction from the subconscious mind, it responds until the instruction changes or is intercepted. When listening to music you don't enjoy, you can replace it with another selection or turn it off. The song that you stopped playing is not erased or discarded. It remains accessible in your music library.

A similar storage system governs the programs and habits in your subconscious mind. An on-off switch does not exist for the programs you no longer desire. Conscious vigilance is required to intercept and prevent them from replaying. If an undesirable habit is not replaced with a new program or a deliberate choice, by default, the old program is activated.

A music device allows you to physically remove a song by erasing, discarding or destroying it. When you delete a program from an electronic device, even after multiple scrubbings, forensic scientists can usually recover the data. Your subconscious mind is extraordinarily sophisticated and old habits or programs remain dormant. Memories are merely archived, like the songs in your music library or old data in your computer device.

The disappointing reality is that old habits don't require practice to re-establish themselves. For years, they were the dominant programs and can return with ease. Old habits are programs that kick into action, like riding a bicycle after an absence of many years. When an old habit is dormant, its power doesn't reduce to zero. The moment it is reactivated, it performs at its former intensity.

This is proven by those who quit their diets or exercise programs and quickly gain back their weight or smokers who quit, only to begin smoking again. Killer habits retain their ability to perform and can instantly reclaim their position as dominant programs. Making changes requires two critical actions. The first is developing a process to create new programs or habits. The second is protecting new habits to ensure they remain the dominant programs. You must prevent the killers from returning like zombies.

Destinations and goals are synonymous. You have choices but it is up to you to make them. The power of attraction is activated by mental discipline or mind power, not physical force. As we often hear, insanity is repeating the same action and expecting different results. If you do not choose or act, that is a choice. When no action is chosen, your behavior defaults to accepting the situation as it was and is.

The power is in your mind. Most diets, exercise programs and study programs offer excellent outcomes. If one were to say that a diet or exercise program did not work, there is a high probability that the person who quit the program did not apply the power of their mind. They also did not select a program compatible with their lifestyle and fell for the bait of a trendy option or quick fix.

Achieving success begins with you. The saying, If it is to be – it's up to me, is excellent advice. If your focus is not on activities that are different from what you were doing, your time and energy are wasted, and you are setting yourself up for failure and disappointment.

Developing a new habit or program requires the same orderly input process as developing a macro or installing a computer program or app and setting the parameters for your personal use. Your biocomputer requires the same conscious effort to program its settings. Once set, your biocomputer remains on autopilot and executes your guidance system settings.

> *We cannot manage Results.*
> *We can only manage our Actions.*
> *Our Actions are our Behaviors.*
> *Behaviors are a choice,*
> *Therefore, we choose our Results.*

The conscious mind is where we make assessments, choices and decisions. Although we can apply mind power and override our subconscious mind consciously, the conscious mind has severe limitations and is easily overwhelmed or distracted. The limitations of our conscious mind enable killers to instantly regain control and nullify our efforts. The exercises in the next chapter will demonstrate the limitations of our conscious mind.

Chapter 7

Limitations Of The Conscious Mind

Life is experienced in our conscious mind. Our reality is the conscious awareness of what we experience now, or in present time. A dictionary meaning of the word consciousness is *the state of being awake and aware of one's surroundings*. The time frame of our conscious reality is limited and extremely short.

We live in a present moment and our experience is created by what we see, think, feel and do. The activity may be passive or physically intense. A present moment can range from cheering ecstatically at a sports event to silently watching a sunset or the activity outside your window. The experience is accentuated by your emotions that are stimulated in that moment.

Any activity that occurred a moment ago is in the past or history and stored as a memory. An emotion cannot be stored. The details of an event are recalled from memory. The emotions that the memories generate are experienced in the present. You can remember how you felt at the time, but the sensations you feel are emotions occurring now.

Future events cannot be experienced until the time arrives unless you vividly visualize the event in your imagination. Whether it is in ten minutes or ten days, the anticipation of a future event is an emotion experienced in the present time as the event occurs in your imagination. By the time you finish reading this sentence, the sentence resides as a memory. You can experience it again by rereading it or recalling the words from memory.

The activity that occurs in your consciousness, present time, is either a current event unfolding, an idea recalled from memory or an event flowing from your imagination. The experience is enhanced as your biocomputer instantaneously activates your emotions based on your conditioning or guidance system settings of similar events.

Both the conscious mind and subconscious mind control the command center, but only one at a time, and in the present moment.

Mind power is a conscious act that enables you to intercept the command center *and* the subconscious mind. Should you become lax or the capacity of your conscious mind is exceeded, the subconscious mind autonomically reclaims control by executing a previously developed habit or program. Repeating a recalled behavior confirms that we are creatures of habit.

Based on the events occurring in the moment, the subconscious mind autonomically executes a continuous stream of instructions from the programs stored in memory. Should multiple instructions conflict with each other, the command center falters or stalls. The conflicting instructions require clarification by you consciously or the subconscious mind will select the strongest established program (habit). Although the details of the conflict are rapidly conveyed to the conscious mind from the subconscious mind, the busyness of our lives consumes our conscious capacity. It masks these critical messages, causing us to miss the tipoff or clue that the subconscious mind provides. Without conscious action, the habit prevails.

Every second of every day, our subconscious mind sends us messages that range from general observations to critical alerts of dangers or new opportunities. The critical alerts can be suppressed by the habit protection system of killers that causes diversions and distractions in our conscious mind. The pre-existing habit, idea or belief is a seasoned killer that retains subliminal control. Your new choice or goal requires immediate protection within a finite time frame.

With practice, techniques become skills that we autonomically utilize without thinking. Developing a new skill is the programming of a new habit. The next exercise demonstrates that *conscious thought* is unnecessary when a habit exists, but conscious focus and action are required to perform a new task. Unless you deliberately choose to overrule the subconscious mind with instructions through the command center, the subconscious mind remains in control.

If you choose not to complete this next exercise, you will miss experiencing the conscious process required to overrule your autopilot and guidance system settings. The subconscious mind guides you based on its programming. These two steps are critical for understanding mind power and developing habits.

On lines 1, 2 and 3, sign your name three times as quickly as possible. Do not stop, read ahead or think about doing it.

1. _____   4. _____

2. _____   5. _____

3. _____   6. _____

Did you sign your name or did you continue reading? If you continued to read, a default program in your subconscious mind, *a killer*, has killed your first chance to break a pattern of failure. It is the same type of habit or program that prevents you from succeeding in other areas of your life. Your subconscious mind did not receive a clear instruction from you *consciously* to indicate that this was a crucial step. Without conscious action, a new process cannot be introduced and you remain defeated. Suppressing killers requires a decision that is first initiated in the mind. If you are determined to succeed, you can reverse this defeat by going back and signing your name now. ☺

Whether your goal is to achieve a desired weight or acquire money or status, nothing will materialize if you do not follow the rules. The act of doing does not begin with physical effort—it originates in the mind. Those who signed immediately made a conscious decision to pick up a pen and participate in the exercise. Their conscious action overruled their subconscious program to continue reading. They made it happen by applying mind power.

The next step demonstrates that your immediate power for change is in the current conscious moment and that your subconscious mind is useless without a conditioned or developed program. On lines 4, 5 and 6, we will repeat the exercise. This time sign your name as quickly as possible...but **with your other hand,** your non-dominant hand. Sign your name three times, <u>as quickly as you can</u>. Do it and observe the results.

When you analyze the two columns, it is obvious that the signatures on lines 4 to 6 are not as neat. You had to consciously apply extra attention to your non-dominant hand, specifically to the holding of the pen and the process of forming each character. Your subconscious mind has an existing program for writing with your dominant hand, but not your non-dominant hand. Until you develop a program, through repetition, the results remain the same.

It is humorous to observe the dynamics when this exercise is conducted in a group situation. The participants are seated and relaxed when instructed to perform the first three signatures. There is hardly a physical stir as they casually reach out and sign their names—One. Two. Three.

However, when instructed to sign their names with their non-dominant hand, their physical comfort is disrupted. At first, they sit up straighter. They transfer the pen to their other hand, then look at the pen to determine how it should be held. Unsure, they glance at each other for silent reassurance. Confused, yet continuing, they adjust their posture. Finally, they adjust the position of their workbook and with an intense focus form each character as carefully as they can.

Your signature, as it appears on lines 1 to 3, is the result of years of practice—or repetition. To sign your name as you normally do, it became a program in your subconscious mind.

This exercise demonstrates the progression from incompetence or not knowing to achieving what we desire. There was a time when you were unable to write, nor did you know the alphabet or the process for forming each character. At best, your childhood signature was similar to those on lines 4 to 6. This time, you had the advantage of a memorized alphabet and the spelling of your name.

The signatures on lines 1 to 3 were executed by programs in your subconscious mind. Lines 4 to 6 were performed by you consciously. You did not have to consciously think of the spelling or focus on the formation of the characters when you signed on lines 1 to 3. Your subconscious mind instructed your command center to perform these actions autonomically from developed programs in your memory banks. With *time, practice and repetition*, you improved the speed and style of your signature. Repeatedly signing your name for years reinforced a program in your subconscious mind to perfect your signature.

Developing a new habit requires the same process until conscious effort is no longer required. Habit development requires step by step instructions, the same as learning a new language, a computer application or inserting a new contact in your smartphone—one character at a time.

Life becomes less stressful when the subconscious mind is programmed to autonomically process and perform the actions required to achieve a goal or complete a task. If you were to perform every action consciously, you would become exhausted, exerting enormous amounts of effort instead of coasting or going with the flow.

Undesirable habits or conditioned inefficiencies are killers that consume your energy. To overpower them, you must apply excessive energy just to complete a normal task. You consciously battle killer after killer as your biocomputer easily performs exactly as it has been programmed. Any effort to introduce an action that differs creates a conflict within that causes you to feel frustrated.

Suppressing an old habit simply requires creating a new dominant habit. This involves a specific conscious process. Each step must be performed consciously and repetitively, as you discovered when you attempted to write with your non-dominant hand. The process is repetitious, and the slightest lapse in focus makes you vulnerable to attack.

If you were asked to sign again, your natural inclination would be to pick up the pen with your dominant hand. However, if you were instructed to sign with your non-dominant hand, you would have to consciously suppress your conditioned behavior (Page 56) or you would instinctively pick up the pen with your dominant hand. Our behaviors are the result of repeating programs stored in our subconscious mind. These programs remain in control until we consciously provide new instructions or establish new settings. Some of your habits are the killers of your desired achievements and ultimate success.

Applying mind power is a dedicated action that occurs in the conscious mind. Any change or action must first occur here. Regrettably, your conscious mind is severely restricted in the number of tasks it can perform at any one time. This leaves all other actions and behaviors to be performed by your biocomputer. As your awareness of killer programs increases, you will know precisely when to consciously intercept them. This timing is crucial because of the limited capacity of your conscious mind.

The next exercise demonstrates the finite or limited capacity of the conscious mind, proving that most of our behaviors are executed at the subconscious level. The exercise requires a pen and paper, a memo app on your phone or a tablet to record a series of alphanumeric characters. It is critical to follow the instructions precisely to experience your mind's limited capacity. Below is a list of alphanumeric characters. Read each line and look away. Without glancing back, from memory, recite and record the characters on your paper, or enter it into your phone or tablet. If using a pen and paper, set your pen down after recording each line. If keying your response, remove your hand from the keypad or screen.

The objective is to identify the number of characters you can recall without refreshing your memory. Continue the exercise until you cannot complete a line *without* looking back to refresh your memory. The moment you look back is the result that is important in this exercise. Don't be concerned if you are unable to remember more than one or two lines. Depending on your current stress level, the number of characters you recall will differ each time you perform this exercise. Glance once at the list and copy each line as instructed:

261

3,X85

2A7,4B4

6,9A4,1Z3

86,92R,327

47S,341,K86

4,3A4,2K8,1P7

As you perform the exercise, a point is reached when you cannot remember the complete line and have to glance back to refresh your memory. The number that requires refreshing is generally between the 4-digit number and the 10-digit number.

This exercise demonstrates that you are restricted in the number of details or actions that you can consciously perform, recite or manage at one time. In scientific terms, this is referred to as cognitive overload. Although this exercise may seem trivial, an awareness of your conscious capacity is a foundational attribute for effectively managing mind power and your thought processes.

These two exercises conclusively demonstrate that it is far more efficient and effective to create new autonomic programs in your subconscious mind than to rely on forcing your will and consuming the limited capacity of your conscious mind.

The conscious mind of an average person is limited to simultaneously managing between 4 and 11 individual actions. Each character temporarily occupies a memory spot in your conscious mind, like RAM (Random Access Memory) in a digital computer. As the number of characters increases, your ability to recall them becomes less until it shuts down. The range is not static and adjusts according to your level of stress, interest, energy and determination to complete a task. Your abilities are limited to performing a finite number of tasks consciously. It is your subconscious mind that performs all other functions. Similar to the RAM function in a computer, your conscious mind is the processing space for assessing situations, making decisions and initiating actions.

As the madness of our activities increases, so does our stress. Your efficiency and effectiveness diminish when you have too many things on your mind. The following examples demonstrate scenarios when the conscious capacity of your mind reaches the point of overload:

> ➤ You leave a challenging meeting or confrontation and are frustrated or upset. Within 15 or 20 minutes, your brain explodes with a plethora of responses as you think, I should have said...; or why didn't I say this instead? The confrontation created excessive anxiety that overwhelmed your conscious thinking capabilities. Your inability to think and respond under pressure caused you to feel threatened (Page 69).

> ➤ On your return from a store to purchase a specific item, you realize that you purchased several items, but not the item you specifically set out to acquire.

> ➤ You are engaged in an exciting conversation and have a brilliant snippet to share. To avoid being rude, you wait

until there is a break in the conversation. When you finally have an opportunity to speak, you cannot remember what you were going to say.

➢ You are involved in a task or project and require an item from another room. As you enter the other room, you momentarily forget what you required. A second or two passes before you recall what the item is. Sometimes you don't recall the item until you have returned to your task.

➢ Feeling overwhelmed by your tasks, you decide to prepare a To-Do list. As you jot down the tasks that require attention, you are surprised by how few there are.

These examples demonstrate that your life and conscious awareness exist only in the present moment. Unless you develop programs and habits for your subconscious mind to autonomically perform, like those for signing your name, your effectiveness and achievements will be restricted by what you can consciously perform. The creation of a plan or a To-Do list is a simple but effective way to amalgamate every activity so it can be viewed as a single task. The anxiety of remembering multiple tasks is removed and so is your stress.

To successfully operate within the constraints of your conscious mind requires the prioritization of each task. When the thought of a task occurs, you can relax because you know it is on the list to be completed. If it is not on the list—add it. Reviewing and updating the list as new tasks arise is critical, or you will be tossed back into the madness of disorganization.

Multitasking is simple. The skill of multitasking is not a conscious action but the execution of conditioned programs (habits). After a task is consciously chosen, the subconscious mind executes autonomic programs for you to perform the activity. You then consciously begin a second task. When your conscious focus on the second activity is no longer required, the subconscious mind accepts control and performs that task. As one becomes more proficient, the number of tasks performed simultaneously increases until an event interrupts the process and requires immediate conscious attention.

At that moment, the conscious mind resumes control to initiate corrective action.

The task that has your conscious focus is the task that consumes your conscious thoughts. After the interruption is rectified by you consciously, the subconscious mind is unimpeded to resume executing the other tasks.

For example, as you decide to pour yourself a coffee, your phone rings. You consciously decide whether to answer it or not, but it is the subconscious mind that manages the rest. The subconscious mind provides the autonomic instructions to glance at the display to identify the caller and press the button to answer the phone. If the caller is a familiar person, without consciously thinking you say, "Hello." However, if the caller is unknown to you, your actions to pour your coffee may be suspended momentarily as your conscious mind contemplates a response.

As your conscious mind engages in conversation, your biocomputer picks up from the interruption and guides your arm to reach for a cup and the coffee carafe. Imagine that the previous user did not replace the top of the carafe correctly and as you begin to pour, a major spill occurs. Instantly, your conscious mind attends to the spill. Your subconscious mind may volunteer a few conditioned expletives, silent or vocal, but it is your conscious mind that kicks in as you act and say to the caller, "Hold on, or I'll call you right back." As soon as you regain control, your biomechanical actions continue from a subconscious level. If the caller did not hold, you consciously look at the phone and press a button to call them back.

Activities occur daily that challenge our conscious mental capacities. It is common to be challenged when dealing with frustrating customer service representatives. On occasion, we imagine that they are specifically trained to frustrate us by overloading our conscious capacity with illogical explanations until we give up and go away. It would be heartwarming to think otherwise but that would be a stretch.

Our limited conscious capacity is a liability when we encounter a personal confrontation. Objectionable comments trigger the subconscious mind to autonomically generate defensive thoughts based on our experiences and past conditioning. It is not so much the message we hear that creates the mental overload but the perception our imagination creates about what is implied. The person's tone of voice may imply an accusation or insult and be perceived as an attack. Controlling your thoughts and emotions is required to avoid a negative response, as displayed in the lower portion of the diagram on page 69.

When you are aware that a situation is sensitive yet choose a tone of voice or words that ignite unfavorable responses, be prepared for the consequences. The other person operates within the confines of their conscious limitations, and like you, their subconscious mind contains their conditioned responses. If your communication consists of inflammatory words, tones or gestures that provoke a situation, you are courting a natural disaster involving the laws of physics. Your approach to a situation and the response received validate Newton's Third Law of Motion—for every action, there is an opposite but equal reaction.

When you recognize that a person has become upset by your actions or statements, realize that their conscious capacity is compromised and that for an undetermined length of time they will be at a disadvantage to provide a constructive solution. Your awareness of the situation places you in the best position to introduce damage control. The uniqueness of individuals complicates the challenge. Some recover in seconds. Others require time to calm down. A few may never be receptive to further interactions with you.

Unfortunately, upsetting an individual is a tactic that is often intentionally used in debates or as interviewing techniques by authorities, prosecutors and defense lawyers. Their intent is to agitate an internal enemy that lies waiting to undermine your ability to make reasonable decisions, present yourself rationally or communicate effectively. This killer is anger.

When you are upset or angry, your conscious capacity is overwhelmed by emotions. This reduces or destroys your ability to consciously process a rational response. By default, the subconscious mind directs the command center to respond according to your past behaviors or guidance system settings. It may be a negative response or none at all. All parties are in a position to recognize the dynamics and modify their responses accordingly. Too often, the realization occurs a moment too late and damage control, clarifications and apologies are required.

We have the power to prevent situations from escalating. Our awareness provides an excellent opportunity to apply our mind power and demonstrate self-mastery. Without being insulting or patronizing, we can be an agent of influence and clarify misinterpreted messages. This result is achievable because the conscious mind operates linearly. A simple—I'm sorry, I didn't mean it that way—often reduces the intensity of the conflict.

To experience the restrictions of your conscious thinking processes, spell your name and state your phone number simultaneously. You may think you are capable of doing this, but under closer examination you will realize that you are merely stating single letters and numeric characters in the order they would be written. You are limited to stating one character or digit at a time. To confirm, count from one to ten without interruption as you sound out one of your computer passwords. You will quickly realize that this is impossible. These exercises prove that, unlike the subconscious mind, the conscious mind is severely limited and can only perform one function at a time.

Recognizing the limitations of the conscious mind is a critical juncture for applying mind power. On page 75, reference is made to the command center having two controllers—the conscious mind and the subconscious mind. There are other forces that are able to hack in and control your command center through your conscious mind. For example, one is easily distracted while counting items or cards when a jokester starts reciting numbers out of sequence. The moment the person counting has a microsecond lapse of focus, they lose count. The conscious mind does not have a firewall or anti-hacking device. The jokester successfully hacks into their command center and disrupts the counting process.

Internal killers that reside in your subconscious mind are masters at protecting their programming. Program protection is effective and highly efficient because the construct of a habit consumes your conscious capacity through distraction and subtle diversions. Due to your inability to retain two thoughts at the same time, your conscious focus shifts to the distraction and your best intentions are crowded out and simply vanish.

Awareness of this human limitation is valuable when providing instructions to others. Their desire to perform a task correctly creates anxiety and stress for them. Their stress induces an internal conversation which further reduces their conscious capacity to process your instructions. They may look confused or not hear or understand what you are saying.

Achieving a new goal requires the conscious guarding of your command center to ensure your conscious focus remains on the new course and suppresses the built-in protection responses of old habits and external hackers (Page 56).

Implementing a simple To-Do list frees your conscious mind to enjoy the present moment. Just as a plan or blueprint is necessary when constructing complex projects, To-Do lists are valuable assets for planning and executing activities.

The physical mind is distracted in multiple ways. When shopping, driving or performing any task, the moment you answer your cell phone, the conscious focus on your current task is momentarily disrupted. Most jurisdictions in North America introduced distracted driving laws to reduce accidents caused by that momentary lapse in attention created while driving and operating a cell phone.

Parenting is a challenge. Parents expect kids to process requests and information at the same speed as they do. It is unrealistic to expect a younger person to have the same mental processing abilities and comparable memories as an adult. Yet, when we are stressed or in a hurry, we expect kids to perform at the same speed as we do.

Communicating with one or several individuals is challenging as you compete with the conscious limitations of multiple human minds. As a team leader, manager or coach, it is impossible to be aware of the conscious capacities and capabilities of your clients, subordinates, co-workers or superiors. Remaining cognizant of the limitations of their conscious minds enables you to conduct presentations that engage them. For example, if you are not presenting your information in a concise and engaging format, the conscious thoughts of the attendees become:

> ➤ How much longer is this going to be?
> ➤ I need to hurry or I'll miss the 4:20 bus.
> ➤ I need to pick up my kids at daycare.
> ➤ The garage closes at 5 and I need my car.
> ➤ This is $#@%# – now I have to stay late to finish that quote.
> ➤ I need to pick up milk on the way home.
> ➤ Who's at home to let the dog out?

In addition, if the above examples were to represent seven different people, it demonstrates that although everyone shares the same physical space and time, each of our realities is different and exists in our conscious minds.

The conscious mind requires constant management when communicating with others. It is common to mentally compose a response rather than listen to the complete conversation. The composing process occupies our conscious capacity and we miss valuable information. This proves that we cannot simultaneously talk and listen. The urge to reply is a communication killer.

The conscious capacity of our mind is a point of power. Yet, we often overload our mind by dwelling on irrelevant issues and re-hashing internal arguments with people we were upset with months and even years ago. They may have long forgotten who we are, but as we go about our activities, we keep mulling over past encounters rather than reliving pleasant memories, planning for the future or simply enjoying the present.

When the conscious mind's capacity is consumed with issues or crises, it is impossible to be fully aware of our situations, modify habits, manage tasks or communicate effectively. Introducing trendy or quick fixes may appear to be an option but as you will see, change is only successful when appropriate change is introduced. Introducing the right change is a process that we will explore in the next chapter.

**A new idea lasts only
for a moment.
Record it quickly
or it fades
like an apparition.**

Chapter 8

The Cycle of Change

Change provides benefits and positive growth, yet at times change is a killer. The Greek philosopher Heraclitus is credited with stating—change is the only constant in life. Change for the sake of change can be dangerous. Many do not understand the old saying—be careful what you ask for. Its meaning will become clear as you learn more about the power of your mind.

For a change of pace, you may choose to go to a trendy happening or event. Unfortunately, when dealing with serious matters like relationships, family, health, money or earnings potential, random or trendy changes have the potential to complicate your current situation.

Chapter Six, pages 62 and 64, demonstrated the effect of introducing one small action to create a difference. On occasion, individuals indiscriminately introduce change simply to have variety or because they believe that anything would be better than their current situation. As you may have discovered from your past experiences, not every change was beneficial.

It is impossible to introduce the right change without an awareness of what requires improvement. Our weaknesses are preyed upon daily with promises of weight loss, low effort exercise programs, performance enhancement devices and get-rich-quick schemes presented as guaranteed winners.

New offers of gadgets to increase your metabolism, burn fat, increase thinking power, monitor your activities, earn money quickly and other flashy and catchy promotions are intended to stimulate deep-seated cravings buried in your subconscious mind. The stimulation causes one to act, enroll or purchase. As referenced by the Hawthorne Effect (Page 28), new concepts, routines and gadgets that catch your interest do work temporarily, but you are back to that discouraging starting line within three to six weeks.

Should you fall prey to the enticement of a process devised by others and not suited to you, your actions and efforts are destined for defeat. As your enthusiasm evaporates, you abandon your efforts and return to the way you were. Discouraged, you begin to believe that you can't improve, yet deep within remains an internal yearning that you are not living your life the way you desire. Until you overcome the killers that hold you back, you remain a hostage.

Disappointment and frustration are often the result of not being aware of what is holding you back, what you are doing wrong or what is required. That is the moment when you are *unconsciously unaware*. It is the first stage in the cycle of change. It is a state of mind when you are unaware of your incompetence. You are blind to your situation. You are unaware of the fact that you do not know that you do not know what to do. A seminar attendee once asked, "Is this like being stupid and you don't know it?" Amid the laughter I replied, "Yes, but there is a more constructive explanation."

If you are struggling to complete a task, it is an indication that you have not developed an internal program to perform the task required to achieve your goal. Goethe is credited as saying—what I know, I don't need. What I need, I don't know.

Ironically, to begin the process of change, we are often unaware of our shortcomings until the second stage when our self-awareness evolves into an "Aha" moment or something is brought to our attention by an external source. The message can be painful to accept or acknowledge. Throughout life, we develop programs or habits that jeopardize our performance and well-being. The programs evolve so subtly and perfectly that we remain unaware that our actions are impeding our success. We retain a construct within the subconscious mind that is our ego, a compilation of experiences or programs that reflect whom we have been conditioned to be. The ego is a self-executing program that is not receptive to input that contradicts its construct. The ego is not entirely your true self, and at times is a fraud that prevents you from being the authentic you. You were programmed to be someone, but not the person you sense you are. Any actions or thoughts that can adjust your guidance system to become your true self are threats to the fraudulent ego. Identifying and developing new programs to suppress the ego require a systematic approach.

We have already identified that results or outcomes are the products of actions or behaviors. By assessing what we can and cannot do, we become aware of what is required. *Awareness* is a point of power and the second stage of the cycle of change. Awareness enlightens and promotes purpose (Page 53), the second element for establishing focus. With a new focus, behavior modification may involve taking courses to acquire academic, scientific, business or technical knowledge or locating a person experienced in what you are striving to achieve and engaging them as a coach or mentor. The sooner you act, the sooner you achieve success.

We constantly receive feedback from friends, strangers, customers and anyone with whom we interact. Constructive feedback is often dismissed because the ego feels attacked by what may be implied. The defense programs in the subconscious mind that protect the construct of the ego instantly deny, argue or dispute the feedback (Pages 56 & 69). This does not imply that the ego is correct, only that the feedback is not compatible with the programming of the ego. If feedback does not bolster the ego, the ego dismisses its value. If the feedback generates an intense conflict, emotions are triggered and the autonomic response is to defend or ignore the feedback.

As tough as it is to accept, a negative reaction to the feedback often identifies the exact barrier to address or the action required. The negative reaction is a killer's defense and program protection that deflects and distracts you from seeing and acting on opportunities that could change your behaviors and subsequently, the outcome.

At this stage, the ego and subconscious mind have colluded to become your enemies. If you are serious about improving, you will recognize that although the feedback may not be enjoyable, it is extremely beneficial. It creates an awareness of our behavior or our conditioning. Reflective questions are provided in the Appendices to privately explore the constructs of your ego and conditioning.

As you become aware of the cause of a situation, it is often an "Aha" moment. It is a pivotal moment for identifying elusive killers that continually undermine you. The purpose of the autonomic protection system is to circumvent or obscure any attempt that would uncover these valuable clues.

The third stage of change creates an awareness of your incompetence. It does not mean that you are going to change. You have advanced to realize that you are ***consciously incompetent*** and may or may not know what is required to change your situation.

Frustration increases as you acknowledge your incompetence. Your efforts to push on are defeated by subliminal killers that continue to protect the ego. One killer may respond in an arrogant mode as you hear yourself say—I don't need that, or it's good enough. Other killers are distractions that divert your attention from exploring or implementing actions that would improve your situation.

When subliminal programs conflict with change or a new choice, the subconscious mind acts like a traitor as it remains loyal to your old conditioning. Killers attack by overloading your conscious capacity with distractions and futile diversions to waste your time and effort. One such diversion may involve directing your attention to a quick fix or gimmick that is guaranteed to fail within three to six weeks. When the failure occurs, your disappointment and discouragement cause you to quit or cease making any changes. The killer program remains protected and in control. You are back at the starting line.

It is imperative to recognize the setback. Your increased awareness should generate the realization that continued conscious action is compulsory to suppress the killers in your subconscious mind. It is up to you to provide the appropriate programming so the subconscious mind can adjust your autopilot and shift from being a traitor to becoming a warrior fighting for you.

The fourth stage of change is ***Action and Determination***. This is where new processes, actions or behaviors are introduced. During this step, the mental battle increases as your subconscious mind detects new actions as a serious threat and directs the killers to fight harder for control. That internal conflict is the agony you sense. Although it may last seconds or continue for days, it is a defining moment to apply mind power. Only you or the killer can be victorious, not both.

After carefully evaluating your goal and the skill sets required to achieve it, an effective plan of action is essential. During the implementation of a plan, your subconscious mind continues to be a traitor and sabotages you with a constant array of distractions. As you vigilantly continue to focus on the new goal, the repetition of your efforts magnetizes a setting on your autopilot to become a new program. The subconscious mind gradually shifts to execute the new setting autonomically. The battle is easier when you are committed to a goal.

The fifth stage is the realization and awareness that you are performing satisfactorily and achieving positive results. At this moment, you are *consciously competent*. Intense conscious effort is no longer required. You realize that you have sufficiently influenced your subconscious mind to perform new behaviors routinely and the agony of effort is gone. To your surprise, previously unpleasant activities are no longer agony and can be surprisingly enjoyable.

The sixth stage is the final transition. The new technique has become a habit. Your repeated actions developed a *new dominant program*. You rarely think about the doing as the subconscious mind autonomically performs the process. Your proficiency and confidence increase. Depending on the goal, this stage can be achieved quickly or it may require several years to master a complex set of skills.

The seventh and final stage of change is the moment when you no longer need to think about the actions required. You have become *unconsciously competent* and unaware of your new skill. You are often not conscious of your actions until someone compliments you with—you did a great job handling that; or Wow! you look terrific! What have you been up to? When this occurs, silently congratulate yourself as you are now unconsciously competent and are becoming the person who you strive to be.

The seven steps of change are depicted in the flow chart on the following page.

The Cycle of Change

Subconscious Mind
Existing Behavior

To perform a task or achieve a goal,
a new program or habit is required.

*1. – When you do not know that you do not know,
you are Unconsciously Unaware.*

*2. – An event occurs that creates an
awareness of your inabilities.*

*3. – You become consciously aware that you are
incompetent and that alternate actions are required.*

*4. – Action and Determination.
You consciously fight the killers by
holding steadfast to your new action.*

*5. – With practice, you become aware that you are
competent with a new technique.*

*6. – Through repetition, the new technique becomes a habit, new
dominant program, and conscious effort is rarely required.*

*7. – You perform without conscious effort as you are unconsciously
competent. Your autopilot / guidance system performs
autonomically as a habit.*

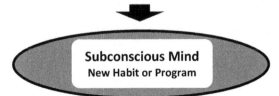

Subconscious Mind
New Habit or Program

The following two examples demonstrate how awareness is the precursor of change. The first occurred as a result of direct feedback, and the second was identified by a five-year-old who recognized his own behaviors.

Feedback, whether supportive, malicious or constructive creates awareness. When I was in my late twenties, an individual once asked me, "Aren't you concerned about your hands?" Unsure of what was implied, I inquired, "What do you mean?" She responded, "Well, as a professional, aren't you self-conscious about your hands when presenting documents and pointing to details?" Wow!! This "Aha" moment was not comfortable. I had never paid attention to the fact that I was a nail biter, and my fingertips looked terrible. Before that moment, I was unconsciously unaware of the impression my hands created.

The newly created awareness triggered several subliminal responses. What transpired during the next few days was that each time I was about to raise my hand to my mouth, an awareness of my behavior flashed into my conscious mind. A second awareness was created when I realized that the behavior was a reaction to an irritation caused by the roughness on one of my fingernails. A nail file was located and the situation was rectified. Nail biters may not recognize this cause and effect as it occurs at an early age. The action to smooth the roughness by biting or nibbling the rough spot is repeated often and quickly becomes a habit. This may not be the case, however, when nail biting is the result of an emotional condition.

A week later, I was in a meeting when I felt a strange sensation at the tips of my fingers. When I looked at my fingers, I realized that I had fingernails that needed trimming. No specific effort was implemented to achieve this. An awareness caused me to assess my personal grooming and my subconscious mind responded by directing my command center to alter my behaviors. A lifelong habit was changed within a few days with minimal conscious effort.

The second example demonstrates that self-awareness is achievable at any age. When my son was five years old, I purchased a video recorder. He and his sister clowned around while I recorded them. When the video was played back, the kids were full of laughter until my son snuggled in beside me and appeared sad. When I inquired what was wrong, he said, "I can't say my ors." Confused, I encouraged him to repeat what he said. In exasperation, he replied, "I can't say my ooor's!!!" I realized that he was referring to his "Rs." He recognized from the video's auditory feedback that he did not pronounce the letter R properly and did not enjoy hearing how he spoke. As a five-year-old, his observations created an awareness to recognize what he wanted to change. This proves that we can explore and develop an awareness of our behaviors at any age.

By carefully assessing situations, you can implement a methodical process to create change. Unfortunately, every change that you initiate will be attacked by internal or external killers. To counter the attacks, you require a vigilant defense and a savvy escape technique. These are the topics of the next chapter.

Chapter 9

The Power of Suggestion

This chapter reveals the techniques others employ to attack your mind, mislead you and cause you to instantly lose control. The rapid speed at which the brain processes information is beneficial yet poses enormous risks. The mind's susceptibility to the power of suggestion enables misleading information to infiltrate your thought processes and causes you to conduct yourself as if the information is accurate or essential.

We tend to think that we are in control but were never taught that our mind is often used against us. A lack of awareness creates a passivity that undermines us as we struggle to achieve our goals. When passive, the command center is unprotected and vulnerable to attacks from external sources or our own counterproductive habits.

No matter how careful you think you are, the next exercise demonstrates how quickly your mind can be influenced. The instructions will confuse the subconscious mind, and you will respond opposite of the request. As you read the instructions, pause and think about them, but do what is <u>specifically requested</u>:

Do not think of a grey elephant. [pause]

What transpired in your thoughts? What did you think about? There is a high probability that you reread the phrase and focused on the words, grey elephant, and wondered what you should do next. Several of my seminar participants, attempting to be clever, stated that they switched the grey elephant to a pink elephant or a different object. In doing so, they had to instantly acknowledge the grey elephant before they could alter the color or visualize an alternate object. If only for a nanosecond, the processing action of the brain focused on the words or imagined the physical form of a grey elephant. Your mind was tricked into thinking of a grey elephant when the instructions clearly stated—*Do not think* of a grey elephant. The words *do not* are non-action words that the mind, your biocomputer, cannot process. The word *think* is an action word that your command center executed. To apply mind power for success and goal achievement, you must choose your words carefully.

The fact that the command center is easily duped into following external instructions explains why people fall prey to scams and sales pitches or are conned into acting against their will. Although the mind responds instantaneously, you have the power to intercept and prevent any implied suggestion. To defend against unwanted attacks, you must be aware of them and immediately instruct your command center to execute a defensive action.

This technique requires an understanding of the *quantum leap*. A quantum leap instantaneously intercepts the thought processes within the mind. In the earlier example of the phone call announcing unexpected visitors, it was a quantum leap that subliminally unleashed a mysterious energy that enabled you to tidy your place.

The term *quantum leap* is described as an abrupt, sudden or extreme change of matter, a situation or property *without a logical explanation*. It is based on research by Max Planck, a theoretical physicist (1858-1947), that describes how the energy change in atoms does not follow a set path or pattern. Without explanation, the energy instantly jumps to a new state of energy.

Scientific explanations and theories are valuable but most of us are not scientists. Your power lies in understanding how the power of your mind can be shifted by a quantum leap. A quantum leap abruptly alters the instructions to your command center or prompts the subconscious mind to dispatch an alternate command.

When a question or imperative statement is asserted, the specific words initiate a quantum leap and channel the power of your mind. For centuries, metaphysical instructions encouraged the application of a quantum leap as noted in the biblical writings of John 4:35. The instructions were—*Do not say that there are four months until the harvest but see that the fields are now ripe for harvest.*

In the example of not thinking of the grey elephant, your thinking process was influenced by the words you read on the page. The words, grey elephant, were implanted by the process of a quantum leap and are now permanently stored in your memory banks. Your inability or repeated failure to achieve a specific goal can be linked to external interferences or subliminal programs that cause you to repeat your behaviors. To free yourself from the enemies that keep you captive, you must *manually* (consciously) intercept their incoming attacks.

A quantum leap intercepts your thought process, or that of others. It shifts the focus precisely to what is being said or thought and forwards instructions to the command center to respond exactly as the words suggest. In Chapter 7, you learned that the conscious mind cannot simultaneously focus on two issues. Your point of power is your ability to focus on what you desire, rather than the negativity or barriers that distract and consume your thought processes.

A Quantum Leap

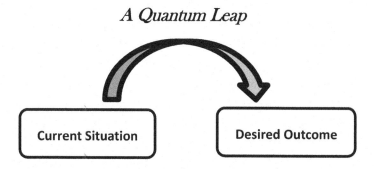

Current Situation   Desired Outcome

Skillful application of this powerful technique enables you to intercept and redirect thoughts, actions, conversations and your energy. The quantum leap will be referred to often. It is an action that instantly alters your thoughts to maximize your mind power.

It is the instant effect of a quantum leap that enables the subconscious mind to protect its existing programs (habits). New goals, ideas or actions that are not compatible with existing programs are guaranteed to be attacked or dismissed. Program protection is the ability of the subconscious mind to autonomically implement a quantum leap to dissuade, distract or introduce doubt. Any doubt or distraction causes you not to proceed with your new choice as that would override your current conditioning. This autonomic function is a killer—but it can be neutralized.

Subliminal attacks are internal conflicts that generate the sensations of agony, reluctance or doubt. After consciously instructing the command center to perform an action or focus on a new goal, a momentary lapse in focus provides an opening for the subconscious mind to override your conscious request by defaulting to the undesirable existing habit (program).

> *There cannot be any uncertainty.*
> *Focus only on the outcome that you desire.*

It is imperative that you consciously and continuously counteract your subconscious mind's loyalty to its existing programs until a new dominant program or habit is established. It is the process of repeatedly deflecting interruptions or quantum leap distractions that enables new programs to become firmly established as new guidance system settings. Not only does the agony of your physical efforts disappear, but you sense an exhilarating feeling of achievement.

A quantum leap can be your best friend but when used against you, a lethal enemy. Others can alter your mood or influence an activity intentionally or unintentionally through their words, facial expressions or actions. In the exercise of stating your name and phone number, you experienced that your conscious mind cannot simultaneously process two independent instructions or thoughts. An inability to focus or concentrate when people are talking is an example of how your conscious thought process is easily disrupted. The slightest interruption (quantum leap) becomes an instruction that your command center follows. This is the same as being instructed to not think of a grey elephant. Your thought processes are easily ambushed by auditory, visual or sensory interferences.

Learning to apply a quantum leap is a powerful skill to develop. A quantum leap is extremely effective when combined with the power of a question.

What does your mind do when you are asked a question?

If you were reflective, you paused and contemplated a reply, even if it was for a moment. Or you glanced back at the question and continued to read. The voice in your head was prompting you to evaluate if you missed anything. If you didn't contemplate the bold print above, you glanced back after you read the next two sentences and evaluated what was happening in your mind. What was the conversation in your head?

Continue exploring by observing your thoughts when you read the following questions. Pause after each question.

> How old are you?
> What do you use for an ID Card?
> Are you reading these questions?
> What is your last name?
> Are you alive and breathing?
> Is your mind answering these questions?
> Are you smiling?

It doesn't matter whether a question is reasonable, logical or ridiculous. The brain responds instantaneously to a question and processes an immediate response, regardless of your intention to verbalize the response or not. The answers are conveyed from your subconscious mind to the conscious mind instantaneously.

Continue the exercise, but this time *__do not answer__* the questions with your internal voice. Pause after each question and ensure that you do not utter or imagine a response:

> Do you have a pet?
> Do you continue to read or pause after each question?
> How long did you pause?
> What is that mark on your left thumb?
> Did you look?
> What is the first word of this sentence?

Without a doubt, silently in your conscious mind you responded to most of the questions. The answer is not verbalized but is expressed in the mind. This exercise shows the speed at which your mind processes information and proves that *the mind cannot ignore a question,* unless a second quantum leap is instantly applied to divert your thought process.

The quantum leap has unlimited practical applications. It is the quintessential action for self-coaching, influencing others and directing your mind power. A quantum leap can quickly and diplomatically diffuse an unpleasant discussion by introducing an alternate topic. The simple act of introducing a question can instantly place you in a position of power and control. As you progress through the following chapters, the quantum leap will become a powerful tool. Each chapter provides an opportunity to enhance the application of mind power and modify your current situation.

You proved that a question tricks the subconscious mind to respond, even when you are directed not to respond. An interrogative or imperative command is effective for self-coaching. If you have not finessed this technique to arouse curiosity or intrigue in general conversation, others may object or resent your direct questioning. A question can circumvent our conditioned resistance. Whether we respond or not, the answer is processed in the subconscious mind and becomes a subliminal instruction to the command center.

The subconscious mind performs more efficiently in a relaxed state. Since ancient times, relaxation has been taught through controlled breathing. Meditation and relaxation are effective techniques for slowing the breathing process. It is common to observe a parent coaching a distraught child by saying, "Slow down, take a deep breath, now tell me what happened." A conscious instruction from an external source (parent) calmed the child by intercepting the child's thought process and command center, enabling the child to respond. A calm, direct command has the same impact as a question, whether it is directed to yourself or others.

A relaxed approach is more effective than an aggressive approach. When people feel relaxed, they participate positively and do not feel threatened. The tone of our voice and the choice of our words either encourage participation or create resistance, silence, distrust or conflict. By carefully listening to an individual speak and observing their body language, you can formulate a response to encourage or discourage their participation.

When people say they have to walk on eggshells around him or her because he or she is so volatile, they obviously lack an awareness of how their presentation style, words and expressions may be antagonistic or provocative. Again, Newton's Third Law of Motion (Page 84) provides an explanation—if a person was not upset when first approached but became agitated by the delivery of the message (words, tone and body language), there must be a cause and effect relationship between that presentation and the negative reaction. A relaxed approach and an awareness of the words we choose and how we express them enhance our effectiveness. This combination also gains the trust of those with whom we interact.

Our approach can create positive energy or tension and conflict. When experiencing a volatile interaction, it is beneficial to evaluate your presentation, body language, words and tone of voice. On reflection, you may realize that your presentation was provocative and, therefore, perceived as judgmental or a passive-aggressive attack.

As quickly as the grey elephant entered your mind, messages (choice of words, body language, tone of voice) are implanted in the minds of those with whom we interact. Body language also conveys acceptance, judgment or dismissal. For everyone involved, a quantum leap instantly unifies all this input internally, resulting in each person forming their own unique impression of the other person or situation. Our perceptions are based on our interpretations and conditioning and may be completely accurate or totally incorrect. These perceptions are labels or settings on our guidance system.

Society is obsessed with labeling everything—to the extent that it interferes and prevents us from being objective or open minded to new people, concepts, ideas and products. The human trait of reasoning is lost when the mind is not trained to be objective. When you judge or label a situation or people at the onset of conversations, meetings or activities, a prejudged mindset or prejudice is instantly created (label) and retained as fact. A prejudice activates a quantum leap to instantly create or reinforce the setting on your guidance system. Your behaviors correspond to this setting.

A label is a digital app or macro that triggers a quantum leap to execute a program or conditioned response. Observing a situation as *"it is"* (from a neutral position) allows one to remain calm and objective. It enables the subconscious mind to be free of prejudices that interfere with the exploration and development of a constructive solution for the issue or situation at hand.

Labeling does have its advantages and can serve as an app or macro for your biocomputer. The example of the phone call advising of your friends' unexpected visit demonstrated how a quantum leap can trigger a burst of instant energy. The subconscious mind was attacked and positive energy was generated with the speed and impact of a dropped bomb! When we label a situation negatively, like being embarrassed by our housekeeping, the subconscious mind autonomically implements appropriate actions and injects adrenalin to create the required energy to rectify the situation. Our overall success depends on our ability to create programs (labels) that autonomically trigger this instant energy to work for us and provide positive results.

The killers that reside in the subconscious mind as habits and programs continually activate quantum leaps to protect themselves. To recognize how quickly you can be distracted, recall a time when you were working on a project or attending a social function and were interrupted by your electronic device. An incoming message or text caused your device to ping, flash or vibrate. The notification, message, advertisement, reminder, tweet or social media posting instantly caught your attention and disrupted your focus or activity. It was the effectiveness of a quantum leap that shifted your attention from your activity to the incoming message.

The message may have been an important reminder for an appointment or meeting. But if it was non-essential and you were not disciplined to ignore it, the *compulsion to respond* becomes a killer. The irresistible urge to check or respond escalates until your thoughts and feelings totally consume the conscious capacity of your mind. Whatever the distraction, you must initiate a conscious action in order to return to your original activity. The disciplined response would be to ignore the interruption knowing that your subconscious mind will remind you to check the message later. Without discipline, your life is at the mercy of the next distraction—the quantum leap of a call, tweet, text or beep.

It is the power of the quantum leap that interrupts a conversation when either you, a friend or an associate receives a casual text or message. A quantum leap generates that irresistible urge for people to constantly glance at their device to check if a new message or post has arrived. There are times when we are expecting an important call and advising the other person in advance is a courtesy. The repetitive checking of devices creates a habit of rudeness and disrespect for others. Not only is it a disruption, but a strong indication that one is looking for an escape or a more interesting option than the existing conversation or situation.

Many individuals feel so compelled to immediately respond to distractions that their lives have become scattered (Page 62) and resemble a hamster spinning on a wheel. Until you develop a habit to ignore distractions and stay focused, your mind power will continue to be compromised. That habit is discipline. Discipline is attained through mind power.

Goal achievement requires mental strategies to manage and defend against distractions. In 1931 Nicholas Murray Butler stated that there are three categories of people when it comes to taking action. Some watch things happen, others make things happen and the rest will forever wonder what happened. Effectively applying the quantum leap is a powerful technique to catapult that mysterious energy toward the achievement of your goals.

The power of a question instantly creates a quantum leap and can turn negative thoughts into positive energy. For example, when you feel discouraged, reflect on an enjoyable place or an event you attended; or recite, what activity or events do I enjoy? *[pause]* Repeat the question until you recall a pleasant memory or imagine a future activity that causes you to feel good. It is the quantum leap that triggers your subconscious mind to imagine a pleasant event. A *word of caution*—when thinking of an enjoyable time, ensure that you do not choose an event where the person, place or issue is the primary component of a negative situation that you are striving to improve. Select a favorite childhood memory or an event that you enjoyed. Instantly, your mind is in a positive place. You may notice that it brings with it a slight smile.

A quantum leap is a powerful tool when working with others or making a presentation. Influencing the thought processes of your audience requires preparation. When an individual does not actively participate, it is an indication that they have lost interest and tuned you out. A question directed to them instantly engages their mind to respond. The next time you are watching TV or listening to a radio station with advertisements, notice the number of ads that begin with a question. Advertisers only have a few seconds to capture your attention. They are skilled in applying the quantum leap to make their kill shot.

The power of the question is extremely effective when you are developing and practicing scripts for specific situations and conversations. However, if the questions you introduce sound patronizing, condescending or like a police interrogation, the recipient will feel managed or think you are attempting to be someone you are not. With practice, your conversations and questions will sound natural.

Individuals, politicians, governments and corporations influence the masses by incorporating the laws of mind power. It is the power of the quantum leap that implants a suggestion or effectively applies reverse psychology. Although not ethical, promoting false or misleading information is a persuasive tactic. The results are as effective as instantly implanting psychosomatic symptoms in others, merely by mentioning that one does not look well.

You now have the advantage of knowing that the mind is capable of being tricked. Self-coaching is the art of inducing a distraction, via a quantum leap, to instantly intercept your current thoughts. You can choose discouraging and negative thoughts or instantly change your total physical being by thinking positive thoughts.

The following challenge is provided to demonstrate the speed and power of a quantum leap and its ability to disable your analytical and critical thinking skills. If you do not solve the challenge on your first attempt, don't be discouraged. Understanding the process to resolve the issue is more important than the solution. Here is your challenge:

Step 1: In your mind, imagine a plastic or glass water bottle with a capacity of 20 to 22 liters as seen in standard water dispensers. The opening is 4 to 5 cm (2 inches) for the water to fill and drain. In your mind, see the bottle and imagine that it is empty.

The bottle is empty. Pause – *imagine it empty.*

Step 2: Inside the 20 to 22-liter bottle is a living and healthy 6 to 8 pound goose. In your imagination, visualize that it is alive, healthy, and unharmed—but *it is entirely confined in the bottle.*

Imagine the goose in the bottle.

Your challenge is to remove the goose from the bottle without injuring the goose or damaging the bottle. You cannot cut, reglue, melt or reform the bottle in any manner. The bottle is to remain in its original unaltered condition.

How do you remove the goose from the bottle without hurting the goose or damaging the bottle?

Your answer:

_____

_____

_____

_____

_____

_____

The solution is revealed in a later chapter. Understanding why you can or cannot solve this challenge is the purpose of this exercise and is pivotal for developing mind power.

The next four chapters explain the straightforward but often overlooked processes of the subconscious mind. You will discover how devious killers develop and cause your subconscious mind to remain a traitor.

Imagination is more important than knowledge. Knowledge is limited. Imagination encircles the world...

Albert Einstein (1879-1955)

Chapter 10

Overriding the Subconscious Mind

The previous chapter focused on the instant effect of a quantum leap. In this chapter you will observe how the conscious mind can override the command center. There are specific words that command action or cause you to falter through indecision or procrastination. It is imperative to identify words that weaken or cause you to surrender your power. The power of your mind is a combination of words, thoughts and sensations that simultaneously controls you and develops new settings in your guidance system. Many search for mysterious or mind-altering methods to develop mind power. It is the simplicity of the process that is overlooked.

The ease by which your mind can be influenced by words should both delight and alarm you. The command center performs best when it receives unambiguous instructions. An instruction can originate from the subconscious mind, conscious mind or external sources. As you progress, it should become apparent why this knowledge has been referred to for centuries as the secrets of the mind.

Achieving your goals depends upon your ability to bypass the negative conditioning that your subconscious mind accumulated during your lifetime. Overriding the subconscious mind requires the understanding that repetition is the equivalent of the magnetizing process of digital recorders. In the absence of an *OFF* switch, the subconscious mind continuously records every event that you experience, whether real or imagined, and innately processes the information to formulate programs (habits).

The amount of data contained in your memory banks is phenomenal. It increases with each passing second. As information enters your mind, it is immediately compared with what has been previously recorded. The processing system provides a preliminary assessment that identifies whether the new input is compatible with the previously stored data, programs and your ego. If the new data is not compatible or is a threat to the established programs, the program protection system is instantly activated. This does not mean that your pre-existing programs are correct or operate in your best interests. Nor does it mean that the new information is good or bad, only that the new data is not compatible with your current programming.

If what you are sensing or imagining is an unjustified or incorrect perception, a program is still created and recorded. Although false, it is true to you and becomes a fully executable program. This program is comparable to a song in your digital library. The program is accessible to play, or plays as the default program, until it is replaced with an alternative program.

The subconscious mind provides a constant stream of visual, auditory or sensory activity to your conscious mind. The flow of thoughts, feelings, pictures or words forms an internal monologue. Because of the limited capacity of the conscious mind, the feedback being streamed is comprised of your strongest and most often repeated behaviors and thoughts.

The streaming continues unless it is consciously interrupted by a new topic or command. An example is when you are daydreaming and are abruptly interrupted or choose to return to your original activity or reality. The daydream was streaming from your imagination, but it was an action in either your conscious mind, an external stimulus or a subliminal program that intercepted and brought you back to conscious reality.

If you do not take conscious action, whatever flows from your subconscious mind, or is activated by an external stimulus, becomes your current conscious experience, even if it is a daydream. Your power is in your choice to go with the flow of the random monologue or apply a quantum leap to focus on a new topic.

Here lies another critical tipping point in managing mind power. You may classify it as a secret, but it is common knowledge. The subconscious mind controls or processes programs but it *cannot make judgment decisions*. The subconscious mind is restricted to executing what was programmed by you consciously, imagined or was subliminally accepted from external sources. Judgment and choice are conscious actions. Although a habit response may appear as a subliminal choice, it is actually a default program established by previously repeated choices.

Your success lies in your ability to program the subconscious mind to autonomically execute behaviors that will lead to the achievement of your desired goals. When a new choice, action or behavior is recorded in the subconscious mind, it does not immediately become a habit as it has not been repeated a sufficient number of times to become a dominant program or default response. The existing default program retains control until it is displaced by a more commanding program or a deliberate conscious choice (Habit and Program Protection–Page 56). The conscious mind is a control mechanism that can intercept and control the power of your subconscious mind.

When we become upset, the reflex response to lash out is a preset program or setting in our guidance system. Yet it is our conscious mind that has the power to intercept that behavior and calm ourselves down. Control is achieved by our choice of words that issues commands to the command center. If we experience a situation where we perceive a comment to be antagonistic, we can choose another response other than the conditioned response of becoming upset.

Physical computers, smartphones, intelligent assistants (IA) and other electronic devices are comprised of keyboards, microphones, cameras, scanners and touch screens for input and Esc, Delete, Enter and Pause keys to program or intercept computing processes.

It is impossible to erase a subliminal program in your biocomputer but you can intercept it by issuing a conscious command. New programs are developed by voice-activated instructions and mental images that are enhanced by the intensify of your emotions.

The next three exercises should become life changers as they demonstrate how your words and thoughts influence your actions. By following the instructions explicitly, you will identify the subtle thought process of how words influence your biocomputer. As demonstrated in the previous chapter, it is the simplicity of the process that enables others to hack into and control your actions, thoughts, plans and at times even your life. Not completing these exercises will impede your ability to apply the techniques presented in the remaining chapters.

The **First Exercise** expands upon a process originally described by Paul Thomas (Thomas, 1979) in *Psycho-Feedback*. To perform this exercise, select a light object to hold—a pen, pencil, business card, USB stick, plastic straw or any item that is smooth and can be lightly held with two fingers.

> **Step 1** – As lightly as possible, hold the object vertically by your thumb and middle finger.

> **Step 2** – As you hold the object vertically, focus your eyes on the top of the object and relax. Take a few slow deep breaths.

> **Step 3** – As you attempt to open your thumb and middle finger to drop the item, silently repeat the words, "I can drop it. I can drop it. I can drop it."

The Result – If you are focusing specifically on the object with no other thoughts rambling around in your mind, your fingers will not open and the object remains in your hand. If this does not occur, repeat steps 1 to 3 until the object remains in the same position. It may have slipped a bit, but it remains in your grasp. *Do not proceed* until you can repeatedly say, " I can drop it," and the object *does not drop*.

If this is not working, you may be impatient, not taking the exercise seriously or you doubt its importance. These are a few of the internal killers that prevent you from learning new processes that would ensure the achievement of your goals.

The next step demonstrates that specific words are the essence of mind power and the coding requirements for the subconscious mind to execute any command.

Step 4 – Continue by holding the object vertically and repeating the words, "I can drop it. I can drop it. I can drop it." As you are repeating the words, "I *can* drop it," *immediately switch* to saying, "*I will drop it, I will drop it, I will drop it, I will drop it.*"

If you performed the steps exactly as described, the object stayed in its original position until that precise moment when you mentally switched the words from—I *can* drop it, to I *will* drop it. You may have noticed that the object began to slip as your thoughts began to change before the new words were *verbalized*. If you recognized the difference—congratulations! The speed that thoughts travel to autonomically command the biomechanics of your fingers is significantly faster than your ability to verbalize the words. The object began to slip the nanosecond that your thoughts shifted as impulses were autonomically dispatched to your arm, hand and finger muscles via your command center.

Repeating this exercise until you *see* and *feel* the effect that one word can have on your physical actions is a quintessential step for mastering the power of your mind. If this did not occur, repeat the exercise slowly and precisely, following the instructions word for word. A rushed or casual approach undermines the focus required to control the multiple biomechanical steps with a single mental instruction. If the object drops before you issue the command, you are not controlling your thoughts and an autonomic response from the subconscious mind takes precedence. Practice this exercise until you specifically notice that your hand does not release the object until you consciously initiate a specific instruction to drop the object.

The second critical realization is that the words, I will, are a direct command. *I can* is an information statement rather than a command. Practice this exercise until you distinctly notice that the physical shift or action results from the *words you choose– silently or aloud*.

The result is that the object drops only *on command*.

Exercise #2 – To further prove that you control your actions by thoughts and words, grip one or two fingers with your opposite hand and firmly squeeze as you gently apply pressure to pull your hands apart. Continue squeezing as you repeat, "I can let go. I can let go. I can let go." Keep a firm grip of your fingers and continue pulling as you say, "I can let go, I can let go," and quickly switch to, "Let go. Let go. Let go." Observe what transpired.

Instantly, your hands separated. Your conscious mind instructed your subconscious mind to grip your hand or fingers. As your grip held, you voiced the phrase—I can let go—but nothing happened. Only when you consciously instructed your command center to "Let go," did the command center receive the necessary impulses from the subconscious mind for the muscles in your fingers to release the other hand. Practicing this exercise is a constant reminder that you can control your mind.

Exercise #3 – If you are in a train, plane or vehicle, this example is not appropriate, but you can perform it at home, in your office, on a park bench or wherever your movements will not interfere with others.

Your instructions are—Try to stand up.

You may be confused as to what to do. You may have reread the instruction with some curiosity but continued reading as you remained seated. That was not the instruction. Written above is an instruction that explicitly requests you to—Try to stand up.

An internal conflict is created in your mind. Your command center is not receiving a clear message and cannot fulfill your request. To overcome this, make a conscious effort to stand up now.

Notice that you had to consciously stop the reading process, decide what to do with the book and then instruct yourself to stand up. You will remain seated until you make a conscious choice to act.

If you did not stand up, your biocomputer was controlled by one word. The word *try* creates confusion between the subconscious mind and the command center. *Try* is not a command word. To stand up requires a specific instruction, program or command. That command involves the words—*I will stand up* or simply—*Stand up*—as you proceed to stand up. In my seminars there were those who thought they could outsmart the process by saying, "I'll stand up as I say, 'I'll try to stand up.'" It worked because they initiated a *compound command* with two actions:

(1) "I'll stand up;" and,

(2) "*as I say*" (the words), "I'll try to stand up."

The simplicity of the command is the key. For example, close this book and look away for thirty seconds.

Are you continuing to read? Without making that conscious choice to close the book and turn away, your command center will not receive the required instruction to interrupt your reading. No alternate action occurs until the command center is intercepted with instructions to redirect your head and hands.

The force that kept you reading was the result of a killer program. Its survival depends on diverting your thought processes to prevent you from performing the new request. The killers are programs in your subconscious mind that function the same as programs at SpaceX or NASA that calculate the possibilities and probabilities of a spacecraft colliding with objects. So too, your biocomputer processes the possibilities that a new idea or technique could usurp its existing programming and activates its program protection to distract and discourage you from complying or proceeding with any changes. This is a powerful realization. Either you win or the killers (habits) win. If you consciously chose to close the book, you initiated the first step toward overpowering your killers.

When you state, "This isn't going to work," you are correct. You issued an instruction to your subconscious mind as to what is correct. As mentioned earlier, the mind does not process correct vs incorrect. When a workable process does not work, this is because the person issued negative instructions or no instructions at all. In this situation, the outcome is a self-fulfilling prophecy. For the naysayers who insist that they followed the instructions but they didn't work, their mind power was used against them. Their subconscious minds processed instructions faster than their conscious minds. They issued non-executable instructions to their command centers that were generated by their doubts, denials or other limiting commands.

The intricacy of this process is the mystique of the power you are seeking to control. The subconscious mind controls your breathing, vision, heartbeat and all autonomic functions of your body including the ones that became habits. Some of these functions can be temporarily halted. You can hold your breath for a while, slow your breathing or initiate a deep breath on command. Your eyes blink autonomically, but you can force them to blink, hold them closed or attempt to keep them open until the safety mechanisms of the autonomic nervous system override your conscious efforts. Through meditation and relaxation, you can lower your heartrate. You can override reflex actions like catching an object as it falls or catching it when it is unexpectedly tossed to you by consciously letting it pass and fall to the floor.

To drink from a beverage container, you do not look at the object and then formulate the instructions to extend your arm, open your hand and grasp the container nor do you go through each of the biomechanical movements that are required to bring the container to your mouth, take a drink and swallow. No different than signing your name, the thought of having a drink activates an app, macro or program that contains each of the biomechanical movements required to perform the task. Should you choose to have another drink, your conscious choice instantly causes the subconscious mind to instruct the command center to repeat the biomechanical functions required to perform that task.

These are the fundamental processes required to develop mind power and discipline. If you are still unsure, reread the instructions on the previous four pages. When you can undeniably say that you are capable of mentally intercepting actions that your subconscious mind controls autonomically, then, with the techniques provided in the following chapters, you will be able to achieve any practical and reasonable goal that you desire. You will also be able to defend against seasoned killers that prevent you from succeeding.

Your mind power increases proportionally based on two factors. One—your awareness of the power of words and how they are expressed. Two—your awareness that your command center completes the biomechanical actions required to execute new or preconditioned behaviors requested by your subconscious mind, your conscious directives and any external input.

The subconscious mind has the advantage of issuing instructions by means of neurotransmitters to create action. Consciously, we are restricted to our imagination and the limitations of our verbal communication. For the subconscious mind and command center to execute our instructions accurately, the instructions must be relayed with action words or imperative commands. When we provide instructions to our subconscious mind or command center, or others in general, our language can only convey three types of messages. Only one creates action. When we communicate verbally, we can only.

1. **Inform** – Statements like, *I can stand up, I can drop it,* are non-action or declarative statements that only provide

information. The statements are similar to the sky is blue, the water is warm or the building is tall. A response or action is not required. This explains why the object did not drop or you did not stand up when an information only statement was conveyed to your command center.

2. **Convey Humor** – The objective is to recount a humorous incident or joke to create laughter. For humor to be successful, the message must convey a situation that the audience can relate to from their perspective, conditioning and values. Each member of an audience will either respond with laughter, smiles or disdain or will consciously suppress their autonomic reflexes to withhold their response. Unfortunately, your subconscious mind has no sense of humor and processes all input as actual and correct.

3. **Create Action** – Action is achieved by issuing an imperative command or question. When you say, "I will," the subconscious mind instructs your command center to immediately execute a biomechanical program to activate the motions that will accomplish the task. Your command center requires clear instructions, the same as when you said, "I will drop it." The subconscious mind is a computer that only processes exactly what is inputted. Initiating a question tricks the subconscious mind into processing a command in the form of an answer. The answer instantaneously becomes a command as it is an autonomic response to a question. (See examples on page 101).

The clarity of your words directly impacts your level of commitment to comply with a request. When you agree to do something, your entire being believes and is committed to completing the task. When you respond with, "I'll try," you provide yourself with a standby insurance clause to avoid a commitment. Subconsciously, you may feel that you will not be blamed if someone inquires why their request or instruction was not completed. Your reply would simply be—I said I would try. When you hear the word *try* from others or in your self-talk, insert a quantum leap or a question to redirect yourself or the person to focus on completing the task or request.

For every goal that you desire to achieve, it is imperative that the instructions to your command center be specific and unambiguous. When you tell yourself that you will try, your subconscious mind does not recognize these words as a command and your autopilot will continue guiding you according to your existing guidance system settings.

For example, when I am requesting a service provider to complete something and I hear them say, "I'll try to do it" or "I'll try," I immediately and pleasantly respond with, "I know you will try your best, but can you assure me that it will be completed by X time?" The reaction from the person can range from a pleasant smile to a look that can kill. They sense that I am forcing a commitment from them as they think, "What if I can't?" Happily, most people respond with a laugh and say, "Yes, it will be ready" or "Yes, I can."

Naysayers proclaim that positive mind power and affirmations do not work. For them, they do not work because the naysayers restrict their biocomputer from processing them. Internally, their subconscious mind protects the programs that they believe are true. When they refuse to objectively explore options, their killers hold them hostage in a state of unconscious incompetence. Their conditioning prevents them from becoming aware of the cause and effect of the words that instill action. For these naysayers, what they believe to be true will remain their dominant program.

Words have an instant effect on the programming of your subconscious mind. Your mind operates in various modes, with some modes enabling the development of new programs and habits with less effort or resistance than others. In the next chapter, you will explore the various states of mind activity that create favorable conditions for programming your mind.

Chapter 11

The Programmable Brain

Referring to the brain as a computer is a modern concept. The brain is an electrochemical entity that executes a myriad of autonomous body functions. It develops programs or new guidance system settings based on input received through the senses. As amazing as the subconscious mind is, it can also be manually programmed. To suppress killer programs requires an understanding of how programs form. Digital computer programs are written in code and perform exactly as they are written. A coding error results in an output error, or in computer terminology, garbage in—garbage out. The same applies to your subconscious mind. The programs in your subconscious mind that execute counterproductive behaviors are akin to the garbage in—garbage out programming of digital computers.

A magnetic-like feature of the subconscious mind allows it to collect endless amounts of data from any source. Harmful programs develop for one critical reason—the recording function of your subconscious mind is continually in the *On* position. Its magnetic capability creates the same hazards as accidentally leaving a recording device on when you thought it was turned off.

Your subconscious mind collected and recorded everything you imagined and experienced in life and retained each incident or thought as a memory. A casual event registered once as a memory is generally not a significant factor if it is not recalled or reinforced by dwelling upon it. It remains stored but more difficult to consciously retrieve or remember. Memories established with intense emotions, or recalled and replayed often, solidify into dominant programs and guidance system settings.

Whether programs are for your biocomputer or an electronic device, the quality, accuracy and value of the stored programs or data are irrelevant to their execution. The subconscious mind, or biocomputer, processes any and all executable programs.

Your current conscious experience is influenced by external stimuli and memories autonomically streamed from the data stored in your subconscious mind. If your conscious mind is not intensely engaged in an activity, a continuous flow of random memories captures your imagination and conscious thinking process. Without any noticeable interruption, you consciously follow the ideas that become your current thoughts and imagination. The recalled memories trigger emotions that further intensify what you are experiencing in your imagination. It may evolve into a pleasant experience, or it may not.

For example, as you perform a task, the thought of an unrelated upcoming event flashes into your conscious mind. It may be an exciting date, meeting or appointment or a family gathering that you are dreading to attend. As you consciously become absorbed with that event, your subconscious mind prompts your imagination to recall past interactions or creates dynamics that *may* unfold. The vividness of your imagination calls on the command center to add emotions that intensify the imagined scenario.

When the imagination runs rampant with thoughts of worries and fears about what *might* occur at the upcoming event, it autonomically corrupts the programming process and the guidance system settings. A vicious cycle is created. The imagined expectations generate other unpleasant dynamics with supporting emotions and destroy your current peace of mind for days or weeks before attending the event. Sadly, the repetition of the scenarios in your imagination strengthens the negative memories that are your program settings. Each time the event is recalled or imagined, the emotions experienced in conscious or current time become more intense.

The coding process that develops subliminal programs can be manipulated by your imagination. The most incredible mystical resource that you possess is your imagination. Like consciousness, imagination is not restricted to the images of what you imagine, but also the emotions that make these images seem life-like. It is comparable to a dream that feels real.

The autonomic process that formulates programs is non-judgmental and can be indiscriminately used against us. It is our ability to trick the subconscious mind with a question that enables us to use imagination as a powerful programming tool. We can interrupt the flow of negative thoughts by inserting an alternate idea via a quantum leap into the imagination. When repeated often, we can use this technique to establish new guidance system settings that support our goals and desires.

Programming the subconscious mind is fast-tracked when you simulate a dream process in an altered state. It was your imagination and the power of specific words that instructed the command center to act when you stated the words—*I will drop it,* or *Let go.*

When you recognize the cause and effect relationship between a thought in your imagination and a corresponding physical action, it becomes an "Aha" moment, like realizing the solution to a puzzle. The intangible connection and sensations are what some refer to as *the magic.*

Einstein described the imagination as a powerful element of the human mind. James Allen, *"As a Man Thinketh"* (Allen, 1903), referred to a person's current situation as one correlating directly to what they constantly dwell on in their mind. The act of *dwelling on* is a process of the imagination. A hypochondriac is a perfect example. By repeatedly thinking about feeling ill, a hypochondriac begins to think they are ill as their well-being shifts to that of their imagination. It works both ways. If one can feel ill simply by thinking one is ill in the absence of a verifiable medical condition, then dwelling on thoughts of feeling good can also cause one to feel better. Dwelling on an idea is the process of energizing the law of attraction.

The French psychologist and pharmacist, Émile Coué (Coué, 1922) stated that when the power of the imagination is combined with willpower or effort, it becomes an unstoppable force. Due to its popularity, his technique came to be known as *Coué's Law.* Coué believed that it was easier to train your imagination than your willpower. He stated that *when the imagination and willpower are working together, an irresistible force is the result.* Coué concluded that when the imagination and willpower are in conflict, the imagination always wins.

As you become more aware of how subtly you can and have been programmed, it should become increasingly evident how your subconscious mind and thoughts sabotage you. The concept of the law of attraction generally prompts one to associate it with receiving financial gain. Regrettably, without your conscious awareness, the subconscious mind has multi-tasked and recorded every idea that you have ever imagined, including self-denigrating and counterproductive thoughts. When an opportunity is detected at a subliminal level and corresponds to a desire or a pre-recorded thought, the subconscious mind prompts you to explore or ignore the idea. This prompt is the magnetic pull of the law of attraction as your autopilot guides you to achieve your goal or comply with a killer program setting. The opportunity may be to your benefit or not, but the prompt corresponds exactly to the ideas implanted into your memory banks.

When your best intentions or current desires conflict with established programs, the dominant programs in the subconscious mind activate program protection maneuvers or distractions to regain control of your command center. What this means is that if an opportunity occurs that matches your new desire, the program protection of old memories or programs kicks in and intercepts your command center. The result is that it distracts you from noticing the opportunity or prevents you from acting.

Conscious intervention is required if you are to free yourself from the power of undesirable programs. Although an old program may be dormant, it conflicts with your current desire and, like a recording in your music library, it is ready to destroy your intentions. This is a program that causes your subconscious mind to remain *a traitor* and prevents you from achieving your goal. As Coué stated, the imagination always wins.

For example, if you are invited to make a public presentation but have a fear or dislike of public speaking, your imagination formulates a picture complete with negative sensations of what public speaking means to you. The sensory impulses that instantaneously flood your command center cause you to say and imagine, "I can't do that, or No way" or other negative and discouraging thoughts.

Your fear will prevail until you consciously develop a habit or a desire to speak in public. Each time you refuse a public speaking request, the imagination and old programs of fear, a.k.a. the killers, win and become stronger programs. You begin to win the battle when you prepare for the next invitation and imagine yourself delivering a satisfactory presentation. Programming the brain or retraining the imagination requires repeatedly imagining what you want and not what you don't want. Instructions for shortcutting the programming process are explained in the next chapter.

Prior to Coué revealing the correlation between will power and imagination, no one could rationally explain the power of the mind and it remained a mystery deeply rooted in mysticism and religion. History is rife with accounts of people burned at the stake for heresy, dabbling in magic or participating in activities that were contrary to the laws and beliefs of the country, region or local religion. For centuries, religious leaders skillfully applied the concepts of mind power and coerced or manipulated the masses into remaining submissive. It wasn't until the 17th century that brave philosophers began writing and speaking against religious and political suppression. They encouraged people to be free thinkers in order to improve their lives without religious and political restraints.

Unfortunately, modern-day commerce giants continue to attack our insecurities through our minds for financial gain and to control our behaviors. As technology evolves in the 21st century, our desires and behaviors are monitored and recorded by highly sophisticated intelligence devices embedded in browsers and shopping websites. From the data gathered, they stream a plethora of advertising and propaganda to engage our imagination. Their intentions are to attract us to participate in anything from surveys, personal comments, games or videos to providing general feedback. The unsuspecting masses are conned into providing free research that was previously a major expense for corporations.

Your programming is performed by you consciously, by external entities or by past conditioning that runs rampant in your imagination. Whether you imagine a new process to modify your behaviors or mindlessly reiterate a fear, worry or desire for a material object, a program is reinforced each time it is imagined.

Whatever you think of or imagine *once* becomes a ***permanent*** record or memory. A thought pondered or imagined a second time is recalled from memory. When combined and repeated with intense emotional stimulus and vivid imagination, it becomes a dominant setting on your guidance system. As with the hypochondriac, ideas do not have to be true or even real. When an event that never occurred is dwelled upon, a false memory develops and years later, one may intensely believe that the event actually occurred. This condition is commonly known as *false memory syndrome*. A false memory develops when you imagine and accept a concept or event that has no basis of truth but feels true—to you. It becomes a construct and another guidance system setting.

> **What happens in your head,**
> **Stays in your head.**

Subliminal programming occurs when you unknowingly enter a relaxed state of mind and do not consciously contemplate the input your subconscious mind is receiving. For example, your mind could be drifting off while watching a TV program or while listening to a talk show of the radio as you are driving. Without your conscious awareness, this information is still being subliminally recorded in your memory banks. At some later point, you may offer information on a topic gleaned from the TV or radio program without any awareness whatsoever of the origin of your information. Your subconscious mind autonomically draws from all data stored in its memory banks.

When you observe others on social media having a great time or on vacation, the photos are frequently posed or staged. Any feelings of envy or jealousy are based on your *perception* and *imagination* that they are having a wonderful time. These emotions influence your reality, whether the people are having a great time or not. They could be having a terrible time but that is rarely posted as they want you to think that their lives are AWESOME. Nor are you aware of the financial situation their vacation or party may have created for them. Their staged lives are registered as fact in **your** memory. Each time you think of the fun they are having while you are not, disappointment is triggered in your imagination by false or inaccurate memories.

Imagination has the power to instantly intercept your guidance system. If you are driving and remove your hands from the steering wheel, the vehicle gradually veers off course and requires slight but specific correction. Your imagination is the same and can drift off course as random memories stream from your subconscious mind through your imagination and into your conscious mind.

Like an undesirable melody or commercial that randomly surfaces, a random thought can also suddenly surface. It could be a comment about your performance or behavior stated by someone recently or years ago. These random thoughts become instructions for your command center to activate positive or negative behaviors and emotions. Whatever the thoughts, they continue to be reinforced in your memory banks. Because of this, it is crucial to remain cognizant and focus often on what you desire, rather than what you don't want. The most often repeated thoughts will randomly return like that undesirable tune. It is always important to decipher whether the thoughts flowing at random support or negate your plans.

Science has not determined why a particular memory surfaces at any given time. A memory revealed in the imagination cannot be silenced or stopped but it can be replaced. Your imagination serves as a display screen and speaker for your biocomputer. It continuously reveals what is being processed. It may be an intense memory that totally consumes the capacity of your conscious mind, or if relaxed, a constant chatter that flows similar to background music, only with words, images and thoughts that can trigger emotions.

Emotions and external stimuli are significant influencers. They can be positive or negative and their impact varies depending on your conditioning. There isn't a consensus or authority that deems which emotions are the most important.

The intent here is not to be misled by lists claiming to identify the *most* influential or *actual* number of emotions. Your power increases when you recognize the effect emotions have on your behaviors and conditioning. Positive emotions include—Desire, Faith, Love, Sex, Romance, Hope and Enthusiasm. We also experience the negative emotions of Fear, Jealousy, Hate, Revenge, Greed, Superstition and Anger.

We can all recall situations when we experienced these emotions or observed them in others. Merely reminiscing about an unpleasant situation has the power to spontaneously activate our emotions. Long forgotten memories randomly surface when you least expect them. Even though a memory is long forgotten, it is never erased from the subconscious mind.

Suppressing killer programs requires an awareness of when your imagination and emotions are triggered unexpectedly and inadvertently reinforce counterproductive programs. Memories and flashbacks occur throughout your day—at the mall, with friends, watching TV, commuting or while engaged in activities.

Advertisers are elite masters of deception who subliminally implant effective killers and assassins into your subconscious mind. In short, advertisers are hackers and mind programmers. Regardless of the products or services they are selling, the medium of choice often conveys sexual connotations via pictures, posters, videos or billboards. The image of an attractive person with revealing sexual features is quickly captured by your subconscious mind and instantly instructs your command center to turn your head or pause to observe. The advertisers have succeeded and hit their target—you. They created a *subliminal memory* and often a conscious awareness of their identity or product by intercepting and commandeering your senses. You are part of the animal kingdom, and *sex* is an innate stimulus that is often used as a weapon against you.

Love is a potent stimulus that has driven people to perform ridiculous and illogical acts, including murder, in their attempt to declare their love for someone. We are more receptive to ideas when they are presented by someone whom we find attractive. When we are lost in a daydream, longing to be with a specific person, or reeling from the pain of rejection, these thoughts are in our imagination and trigger the emotions we experience. These thoughts and feelings are stimulated by love.

It is common to experience an instant attraction to a particular person. The emotional stimuli of physical desire and attraction can place individuals in peril when they are unaware of the character or the intentions of the one to whom they are attracted. It may be too late by the time they realize that they are heading into a life of dishonesty, cheating, abuse, addictions or crime where future troubles are guaranteed. Considerable discipline is required to remain grounded and alert when intense emotions ambush your conscious mind and common sense. The younger and less experienced have not developed an awareness to recognize these consequences. Yet older and experienced individuals also make and repeat dangerous and thoughtless choices. We have heard of victims falling in love with their kidnappers, terrorists and other unsavory characters. They willingly abandon their values and beliefs for those of their captors. The term, love is blind, is a legendary cliché that is not only true but often misunderstood. When love is the active emotion during an assessment and decision making process, love makes people blind to the *consequences* that could transpire.

The burning *desire* for fame, power, money, popularity or a cause kindles an inner power that drives people to be excessive or fixated. Many successful people have lost their families and friends because of their fixations and unbalanced approach to achieving their goal. In the past, I associated this only with individuals who achieved greatness, built large companies or made millions of dollars based on their dedication and ambition to achieve a goal. During one of my corporate assignments, an individual took offense that I would suggest that there could be anything more important than money. In his culture, people believe that money is uppermost, and his every waking moment was dedicated to making more money. He expressed that his wife, children and friends were there only to support his efforts. His fixation on earning money is an example of the power of *desire*. The concepts presented in this book do not encourage this unbalanced or obsessive approach to life. However, as explained in Chapter 5, desire is the fuel that energizes motivation.

Love, sex and desire are not the only emotions that influence our programming. An emotional connection to a *cause* may begin subtly but become all-consuming. Whether the cause involves politics, religion, environment, human rights, working conditions, terrorism or conspiracy theories, leaders and promoters excite their audiences through emotions and provocative statements. Should you be invited to a presentation on a specific topic, be aware that as casual and friendly as the lecture may be, you are being targeted at a subliminal level. It is common for groups or organizations to insist that their message is the right one. When you recognize that excessive emotional energy is being applied to heighten their message, or you are feeling emotionally excited, it is best to listen, observe and follow Descartes' 17th century advice to doubt everything and assess the input objectively.

Cults are notorious for casually but methodically attracting and inducting new participants. Cults often prey on those seeking higher learning. If you are exploring a group that reveres a leader who has all the answers or advocates a process to progress through multiple levels to attain success or enlightenment, you may be at risk of becoming a victim of a cult. If there is the slightest suggestion or pressure to leave your family, friends or provide financial gifts—*be concerned*! Learning the techniques provided in this book increases your awareness and enables you to be more observant of your surroundings. Internalizing the concepts enhances your independence as you become a free thinker and break free of those who insist on what they believe is in your best interests.

Fear is a persuasive stimulus and motivator. Fear ignites that mysterious energy as it autonomically induces intense behaviors of avoidance or other conditioned responses. Salespeople, presenters, managers, religious leaders, politicians and partners who cannot convince you with their message, engage techniques that promote a sense of potential loss or make you feel inadequate or guilty. They know that fear and intimidation work and skillfully apply them. It is unfortunate, but for reasons of greed or manipulation, dictators, evil natured people and those intent on controlling others, seek and develop these skills. Instead of humanity and societies evolving, they regress.

Fear is often viewed as a negative stimulus. It lends itself to misinterpretation. In an upcoming chapter, you will learn how the emotion of fear provides valuable feedback. Fear is a motivator and when recognized as valuable, it can provide an instant awareness of knowing when, where or how to respond.

Music is a pleasant yet powerful stimulus. Be it music videos, concerts or the beat on the dance floor, music resonates through your body with impact and pleasure. As you sense the intensity of the music, accompanying messages are registered in your subconscious mind. Training camps, gyms, workout sessions and advertisements rely on music to reinforce their message. History is riddled with stories of fascists training with patriotic music or cult leaders and brainwashing centers captivating their audiences with rhythmic music and chants.

I experienced a powerful transformation when I chose to participate in a firewalk. A firewalk involves walking across fifteen feet of red-hot burning coals in bare feet. The preparation involved listening to rhythmic music while chanting phrases to psyche myself up. It was not until I was totally psyched that I could proceed. Then, at an amazing moment, it felt as though I was being pushed onto the hot coals. I proceeded to walk to the end as I focused on the *cool green grass* that awaited me. The experience confirmed my belief in the power of the mind and verified that it is the mind that overcomes extreme physical challenges. I do not recommend assessing your resolve by performing a firewalk. You can experiment and prove the effectiveness of mind power techniques by applying them to the life challenges you encounter daily. With practice, the techniques transform into fine-tuned skills and will remain with you for the rest of your life.

Mental stimulus is not entirely activated from within. *Friends* are as powerful as music and a major source of programming or conditioning. It is common for friendships to develop into business or personal relationships and they often replace the importance of family. As you proceed, you will realize that your friends have implanted strong messages into your subconscious mind. Frequent or excessive recommendations from friends develop into subliminal programs and conditioned behaviors that gradually suppress your free will to decide for yourself. Throughout life, in high school, university or college, the workplace and social circles, individuals constantly seek advice that ranges from what to purchase to the serious decisions involving personal relationships.

Personal power is lost when decision making is turned over to a friend. The resource of a confidential sounding board, words of advice and cautions are valuable input, providing the person consulted remains objective and able to play the devil's advocate.

Their assistance can be extremely beneficial if their advice is governed by your values and desires rather than their own values or opinions.

Seeking advice is not the issue. The killer is a lack of confidence that creates a compulsion to constantly seek the opinions of others. Regardless of the seriousness of your inquiry, the advice of a good friend often influences your decision. The Appendices (Pages 335-373) contain reflective questions designed to develop your independence and reduce your dependency on others.

Mind programming or conditioning is stimulated by an exposure to or membership in *Clubs, Societies, Associations* and *Support Groups*. The unified focus of collective interests is valuable. Regrettably, there are organizations that maintain control through the enforcement of rigorous rules. Remaining alert and assessing a group's intentions allows you to evaluate whether the group makes you stronger or expects you to be submissive and remain a follower.

Mental conditioning and programming can occur within support groups. Their intent is to assist individuals coping with loss, sickness, addictions, war, racism, bigotry or any other shared experience. When seeking support, again, caution is advised. You are vulnerable when at an emotional low or during a troubled time.

Support groups offer valuable encouragement for those requiring assistance during troubled times. Unfortunately, in rare circumstances, unscrupulous coaches and guides prey on the unsuspecting and the vulnerable. What may appear as a gesture of support, could be a scheme to convert you to a religion or a cult, support a cause or lure you into an insincere friendship that exploits your time and finances. These unscrupulous individuals are masters at implementing the techniques described in this book. The importance of identifying how your mind power is used against you cannot be sufficiently emphasized.

When multiple stimuli and emotions are combined, a force is created that is difficult to repel. Presentations that include hype and music are designed to influence you at a subliminal level. The combination of the power of friends, groups, causes and music has a compounding effect and rapidly establishes new memories in the subconscious mind. When the stimulus of a charismatic leader or romance is added, the risk increases as your awareness and logic diminish.

If you do not remain neutral or objective, you may surrender to the enjoyable sensations and go with the flow. Although the moment may be enjoyable, you are at risk of becoming a blind follower. The experience may have been so enjoyable that you felt it was the missing component of your life. It may be some time before you realize what transpired, or never, and remain convinced that what you chose was of your free will. It may be, but it could also become a significant source of stress and future disappointment, particularly if your choice affects your finances, partner, children, career or extended family.

As disciplined as we strive to be, the stimuli we have no control over are *Alcohol, Drugs and Narcotics*. The danger of alcohol, drugs and narcotics is that when they are consumed in excess, our mental processing abilities are impaired until the substance wears off. Even then, the ability of the conscious mind to make logical decisions remains hazy. When impaired, the awareness required for personal control and discipline is compromised yet the subconscious mind continues to record the details of the event, regardless of whether it is enjoyable or a threat to your well-being. Occasionally, in deceitful situations, narcotics are administered to the unsuspecting. Developing mind power is not limited to attracting opportunities; it also increases your awareness to avoid many of the dangers that we regularly encounter.

Remaining alert in every environment places you in a position of power. You can observe and evaluate input without accepting it and deflect negative input with finesse. Stimulating ideas are often unexpectedly presented. You can explore or ignore an opportunity when you are mentally alert and in control.

When the input to your subconscious mind is not monitored or controlled, you are not protected. There is the danger of becoming that proverbial ship without a rudder as you casually go with the flow. Being aware of the input and quality of the programming that your subconscious mind is exposed to is in your control. When you think of your success and what is reinforced or added to your guidance system, what do you choose in the following scenarios?

> ➢ To be successful in terms of what you consider success...are you associating with people who assist you and encourage you? What self-doubts, ideas or external comments are you hearing and mentally repeating?

> ➢ To develop a new skill—are you associating with people who also focus on self-improvement?

> ➢ To improve or attract a relationship—do you watch reality shows and listen to sad songs, or do you focus on options that would improve your relationship or attract a like-minded partner? What ideas are you reinforcing as autopilot settings to engage the law of attraction?

> ➢ To expand your activities or pleasures—do you wait and see what is on TV, or hope a friend will initiate an activity? Or do you seek out activities that you enjoy and make plans to do more of these activities?

Your brain is programmable—either by you, autonomically, or by others. Each program (habit) is reinforced by the choices you make. Developing programs that benefit you is achievable when you train your imagination and program your subconscious mind to work in your favor. This is the topic of the next chapter.

Chapter 12

Training Your Imagination

Controlling the internal and external forces that compete for control of your mind may seem challenging and daunting. If so, you will find this chapter most encouraging. The mind processes information instantaneously or autonomically. Applying mind power requires the orderly execution of a few basic instructions. Unfortunately, it takes longer to read and understand the instructions than it does to implement them. Adjusting or resetting your guidance system can be fast-tracked by a process called *autosuggestion*.

When first practiced, the process may seem confusing to some or too simplistic to others. Within days, you will realize that you can control your thoughts and intercept your command center when counterproductive or bad habits (programs) are active or about to be activated. To confirm how quickly you can acquire the tools to apply mind power, the following is a review of what you have experienced to this point.

Without your conscious awareness, you have explored and identified the interconnectivity of 20 crucial constructs, aspects and mental processes required to control mind power. They are your conscious mind and its limitations, the subconscious mind as a programmable biocomputer, habits as programs, the command center as a hub that you can consciously intercept, imagination, the quantum leap, awareness, habit protection, the power of the question, goals, focus, life balance, false memories, thoughts, action words and the effect that stimuli and emotions have on each component or function. The mysterious energy of your mind is interconnected to these aspects and can be altered, controlled or influenced by you. Your success depends on how you apply the concepts to suppress the killers that control you.

The mystery of the energy of mind has been explored for centuries. Hypnosis and animal magnetism were documented in the works of Franz Mesmer in the 18th century. Mesmer believed that we are drawn together by a strong magnetic force; hence, the term mesmerize. It was not until 1925 that Hans Berger, a psychiatrist, discovered that the brain produces measurable brainwaves.

Brainwave activity is measured in frequencies or cycles that range from 0.5 to 50 cycles per second or higher. Brainwave activity above 40 cycles per second is classified as gamma brainwaves. There are four frequency ranges that are easy to identify. Although we rarely think about them, three of the four types regularly occur during our daily activities.

The four cycles are identified as Beta, Alpha, Theta and Delta. When one is awake and active, brainwave activity is in the range of 14 to 40 cycles per second and is referred to as the **Beta** or our conscious state. In this state, we are alert as we consciously interact with our environment and people.

As we relax, our brainwaves decrease to a range of 9 to 13 cycles per second. This range is the **Alpha** or Altered state. It is in this range that the subconscious mind is highly susceptible to suggestions or influence.

Relaxing deeper, we enter a **Theta** state or deep sleep with brainwave activity in the range of 5 to 8 cycles per second. In this state, one may not consciously recall what occurs, but words and sounds that are audible and sensed can be implanted in the subconscious mind without resistance.

As brainwave activity drops below 4 cycles per second, we enter the **Delta** range or a state of unconsciousness. This state is described as clinically alive but unresponsive to any stimulus. A measure of 0.0 indicates that one is clinically brain dead.

The subconscious mind is highly receptive to suggestions in the Alpha or altered state. It is the frequency range during which your subconscious mind can be manually accessed and programmed to develop new guidance system settings. This is not a secret. The remainder of this chapter and the next provide explicit instructions for creating and reinforcing new programs to replace the subconscious settings that keep you on autopilot. Remember, the old setting is not erased and is still in your program library ready to return should you not remain vigilant and in control of your mind power.

We pass in and out of Alpha brainwave frequency (altered state) multiple times a day. Some examples are:

> ➢ Upon awakening and prior to falling asleep. You may sense you are awake, but when you attempt to get up, you find that you cannot, nor can you drift back to sleep. You are aware of the sounds around you and can change your thoughts or focus but you remain in a drowsy state.

> ➢ When deep in thought, daydreaming or nodding off as a passenger, in front of the TV or listening to a presentation. You are relaxed and your thoughts may be following the activity or drifting to other topics.

> ➢ During meditation or any deep relaxation that calms the mind and body.

> ➢ When in a state of deep and sincere prayer. This is not the panicky prayer recited when you experience a scary situation and call out to a deity as your bike or car slides out of control.

Entering an Alpha state and focusing your thoughts are the basic processes of self-hypnosis, biofeedback, self-suggestion and autosuggestion. For simplicity and continuity, this relaxed state will be referred to as *autosuggestion*.

A few of the exercises you completed demonstrated that you could bypass the subconscious mind and consciously manipulate your autonomic responses. You proved that the conscious mind is limited to performing a finite number of tasks while the subconscious mind can execute an unlimited number of processes. For this reason, it is critical to establish program settings that are compatible with and relevant to the achievement of your goals.

The exercises in this book and the questions in the Appendices provide guidance for identifying programs that undermine you. It is impossible to identify every program that exists in your subconscious mind. Fortunately, many of the programs (habits) that are not compatible with your goals and desires are identifiable. Some programs are more detrimental while others are more elusive and require patience and persistence to identify. When they are identified, they can be suppressed but not removed. Rather than attempt to find all the programs in memory that impede your success, it is easier to retrain your imagination and develop new programs that focus on what you desire.

Retraining your imagination is fast-tracked when you apply autosuggestion. It is a process that channels your mental energy and imagination to memorize new guidance system settings. It is the simplicity of repetition that causes memories to evolve into dominant programs (habits). This enables the subconscious mind to begin executing the program using the same unexplainable process that causes you to randomly hum or sing that irritating song or jingle from a commercial. Your newly created goal and image in your imagination and the irritating melody are both programs that reside in your subconscious mind. The program recited most often and with an emotional intensity is the one that evolves to become a dominant guidance system setting.

If the destructive habits developed over time and without your conscious awareness, imagine how much more progress you can make toward your desired goals by developing constructive programs. Every program requires an initial thought to be embedded into your memory. With repetition, that singular thought will develop and grow like a vibrant plant.

The process to embed and reinforce a memory can be fast-tracked by entering a state of autosuggestion and vividly imagining the successful completion of your goal or desire. The process maximizes the subconscious mind's innate susceptibility to accept suggestions, hence the name autosuggestion. As you enjoy a relaxed sensation in the realm between sleep and total consciousness, your thoughts are controllable, and you can focus and imagine anything you desire.

Regardless of its label, visualizing, fantasizing or repeatedly imagining a scene or situation with added emotions, creates a dominant memory, no different than a false memory. In time, the new memory becomes an autonomic setting enabling your subconscious mind to prompt you to consciously act. This occurs when opportunities are within range to advance you one step closer to a goal or when critical action is required for your safety. The subconscious mind prompts you to notice an opportunity, but it is you who has to physically act—as the required action will not be mysteriously performed for you.

This is the process Coué referred to when he stated that, *"it is easier to train your imagination than to continually force your will power."* Retraining your imagination is the process of combining your imagination with a form of autosuggestion to create memories that evolve into programs and settings on your guidance system.

Should you dwell on or imagine negative situations or possibilities that might never occur, then malicious programs are developed and reinforced—no different than false memories or illnesses conjured up by a hypochondriac. An upsetting situation that triggers an emotional response causes a harmful program to become more powerful. When you allow your thoughts to drift randomly, you *unconsciously* activate the autosuggestion process and random negative thoughts develop or reinforce programs that undermine your desires and intentions.

Mind power is not effective unless it is applied to a specific goal or challenge. Many err by describing, dwelling or excessively focusing on a negative situation, or what is blocking them, rather than focusing on a constructive solution or what they desire. They fail to apply the power of a quantum leap to escape the undesirable draw created by the protection system of an existing habit or situation. A vicious loop is created. The subconscious mind continues to reinforce the problem rather than generate a solution. The reinforced guidance system setting ensures one remains in their unpleasant situation.

When I coached individuals, they often expressed a dislike for their current situation. When asked, "How would you like it to be?" the typical response was, "I don't know, anything would be better than this." It is this lack of clarity and commitment to what is desired that ensures killers remain in control. If you do not initiate a conscious decision and choose a specific goal, your actions are that of a lab rat running on a wheel. If you do not decide what you want, you unconsciously accept and continually *make do* with what you attract.

If you are stressed and want to get away for a while, you would not approach a travel agent and ask for a ticket to an unspecified destination. When the agent inquires, "Where to?" you wouldn't reply, "I don't care. I just need to get away from here." The agent might respond, "Well, we have an inexpensive flight leaving shortly to this war-torn, high crime country. Would that provide the change you seek?" The impact of this undesirable reality should tell you that you have choice and must decide where you want to go or need to be. This is the essence of living a successful life.

Before activating or applying autosuggestion, it is critical to identify your current situation and what you desire. A situation that requires improving must first be described from your perspective. Your perception may not be accurate as to whether it is good or bad, but it does identify your *reality—it is* exactly as you describe it. Altering your present reality begins in your imagination. It requires you to first identify and visualize the *goal* or desired *outcome* in your mind.

When you completed the self-assessment on pages 39-40, the answers to what makes you happy were identified. They provide an excellent starting point for your future success. This is one aspect of mind power that will enable you to:

> ➢ Attract or improve a relationship or social life.

> ➢ Attract or improve financial opportunities.

> ➢ Improve health, weight and physical well-being.

> ➢ Start a business.

> ➢ Find a new job.

> ➢ Improve your skills in a sport or an activity.

> ➢ Develop confidence and improve public speaking.

> ➢ Enhance communication skills and personal power.

> ➢ Achieve anything that is practical or reasonable that you desire.

If the situation that impedes you is challenging, review your responses on pages 43-44 under blocks and barriers. Without describing or referring to your current situation, in one clear sentence, describe the situation the way *you would like it to be*. The following examples provide guidelines for creating unambiguous instructions for your subconscious mind to work in your best interests.

Example 1: Instead of saying, "I hate my job; or My job is too stressful; or My boss is a @&#%$," say, "I attract the perfect job for me; or I like my job and manage the challenges with ease." Do not say, "I can manage the stress," because stress will then become your grey elephant and energize the law of attraction to increase your stress. A command like, I develop skills to manage challenges, instructs your subconscious mind to generate ideas, options and solutions to manage your challenges more effectively. Not only will you manage your challenges better, but you will enjoy a greater sense of job satisfaction.

Example 2: Rather than saying, "Why can't I attract a partner? Relationships suck; or I am unhappy here," say, "I attract the perfect relationship for me; or My relationship gets better and better every day." Describing a relationship negatively rather than how you want it to be becomes a grey elephant that activates the law of attraction to increase the negativity and make the situation worse.

Example 3: Carefully evaluate what you repeatedly say to your subconscious mind. Instead of saying, "I need more money. Things are tight. What am I to do with my debts? Where does the money go?" say, "I attract and efficiently manage my money; or My finances improve daily." Do not repeat words of limitation like need, debt or shortage as these specific words become grey elephants and commands that reinforce negative programs. Repeatedly stating negative descriptors guarantees the law of attraction will increase your needs, debts and shortages, ensuring you remain in your predicament. Action words like manage, save and attract abundance magnetize your subconscious mind to attract what you describe. Your words are biocomputer coding that reinforce subliminal programs to attract the circumstances you describe.

The power of a single word (Page 64) cannot be overly emphasized. The cause and effect of words that generate action, as in the example of dropping an object (Page 112), is a founding principle of mind power. Reiterating or dwelling on a negative situation is a mental trap that keeps you hostage. This is the construct of mind power that James Allen identified (Page 121) when he stated that our reality is remarkably similar to our thoughts. To force your will focuses on overcoming a negative condition instead of channeling your energy toward a desired goal. Clarifying and repetitively stating your goal programs the subconscious mind to autonomically adjust your behaviors and actions. To obtain favorable results:

> *Do not try to tell your subconscious mind*
> *how to do something.*
> *Clearly state or visualize what you want.*
> *Rely on a quantum leap.*

Imagination is powerful and solving the challenge of removing the goose from the bottle will prove to be most enlightening. Once imagined, an idea is solidified as a permanent memory. To remove the goose from the bottle requires an understanding of how the goose entered the bottle. If you were not able to identify the solution, don't be disappointed. During the thirty years that I presented this example, fewer than five participants solved the problem. Over 2,000 participants attempted this challenge before the first participant recognized the answer. The exercise demonstrates how individuals, and the masses, are subliminally influenced by the power of words and suggestions.

If you read and followed the instructions precisely, here is what transpired. One, you were instructed to begin with an empty bottle. Two, you were then instructed to visualize a goose in the bottle. Three, when it was time to remove the goose from the bottle, you couldn't do it.

Here is the solution. First, one must consider how the goose got into the bottle. Some responded that they could *not* remove the goose from the bottle because they couldn't figure out how the goose got into the bottle, yet they could see the goose in the bottle. Your conditioning and rational mind argued that it was impossible to remove it unharmed. The reality is—the goose and the bottle never existed. The event took place in your imagination and was created by the words written on these pages. As you consciously followed the instructions, you initiated a quantum leap that instructed your command center to imagine a goose in a bottle. Your belief that the goose was there, even though you were unaware of how it got there, prevented you from developing a solution to remove it. The action is comparable to a hacker placing a virus in your computer, but in this case, the computer is your subconscious mind.

Your imagination performed flawlessly. If you used a quantum leap to place the goose in the bottle, then a second quantum leap was required to remove the goose from the bottle. Imagine the goose out of the bottle—and the bottle is empty.

The exercise demonstrated two critical processes. First, the mental process of imagination does not exist in the physical world. Second, in your imagination you accepted a situation that you *believed* was true and acted upon that belief. Understanding this construct is crucial for mastering mind power.

You can imagine yourself performing any activity, whether it is possible or impossible. Advertisers, politicians, salespeople, clerics, friends, family or anyone wanting to influence you, thrive on *hacking* this vulnerable aspect of your mind. It is the cause and effect of words that makes the power of suggestion, a question and reverse psychology effective. When an emotional stimulus is added to accentuate a perceived gain or loss, the impact of the message increases and is more difficult to deflect.

If you could not imagine the goose in the bottle, a deceptive killer, better known as distraction, prevented you from initiating the visual component of imagination. The visual aspect of imagination is a crucial component of mind power. Your mind accepts all input as fact. The ability to strategically embed specific ideas is a technique for training your imagination and influencing others.

If you were unable to remove the goose from the bottle, you should be concerned about how quickly you can buy into or believe all that you are told or shown. What you see, read, hear or process may not be accurate or in your best interests. Deciphering whether the information is distorted, embellished, fake or fact requires evaluation. New ideas and explanations, either accepted voluntarily or involuntarily, form memories that develop and support a myriad of combinations of performance settings that dictate your behaviors through your autonomic guidance system. Without becoming stuck in time as the unwavering skeptic, it is critical to evaluate what one accepts as truth by verifying the facts.

The goose in the bottle proved that you could accept a thought, idea, belief or concept and instantly *believe* it to be true. If you can recite a bad situation, relationship, job or money issue, then you are equally capable of introducing a quantum leap and imagining yourself in a harmonious relationship, an enjoyable job and a favorable financial situation. By applying this process to each aspect of your life while in a state of autosuggestion, new memories are placed in your subconscious mind that perform like mental magnets. When recalled or repeated often, they become the influential settings on your guidance system that energize the law of attraction to prompt you to notice new opportunities. Consciously affirming and performing physical actions are necessary, but when combined with the practice of autosuggestion, the time required to develop new programs (habits) is significantly reduced.

To successfully utilize the power of autosuggestion, it is imperative that you follow the instructions carefully and do not skip any steps. Pay careful attention to the words you express because the moment you say, "This is not working," those specific words instruct your command center to slip into neutral, and you are drawn back to your old or existing behaviors (Page 56). Remind yourself often of the goose in the bottle or the grey elephant and that the slightest suggestion or deviation of thought will throw you off track. The command to drop an object was thwarted by *one word* that was an information word rather than an action word (Page 112).

Your success or achievement depends on whether your focus is on the existing behavior that restricts you or on a new behavior that leads you to your desired achievement. The power is there but requires you to manage it and remain focused on the solutions and actions required to achieve your new goal. Any reflection or dwelling on the specifics of the situation you wish to change, or what you perceive is restricting you, sabotages your efforts and turns the power of your mind against you.

To successfully apply autosuggestion, you need a quiet place to concentrate until you are comfortable with the process. You can begin in the privacy of your home. As you become comfortable with the process, you can activate autosuggestion while travelling on a train or plane, sitting on a park bench, waiting for a meeting or appointment or before making a presentation. To begin:

1. Close your eyes and take a deep breath. Exhale slowly as you relax and enter a state of meditation, relaxation, prayer, self-hypnosis or autosuggestion. Take a second deep breath and exhale slowly.

2. State that you are engaging the process of relaxation or autosuggestion to reinforce or develop a new program. This command directs your subconscious mind to follow your instructions the same way you instructed it to drop an object. It is the biomechanical equivalent of physically turning on a recording device.

3. Initiate a quantum leap to visualize and simulate your desired outcome. This step requires a clear and concise statement of what you desire. Keep the description short, simple and easy to recite. Imagine you are active in the image as if it were a vivid dream.

4. Add emotions and feelings as you imagine your desired outcome until you sense your actions feel real, and your goals are manifesting.

5. Imagine yourself implementing efficient and effective actions that achieve your goal by saying, "I achieve this by—*increasing my efforts to...; I attract a new job in the field of...; I notice and attract opportunities.*" Identify the specific action(s) that you will initiate or perform differently to channel your energies toward achieving your goal.

6. Repeat the imagination process until the activity feels real—as if you are experiencing the event in real life. If this sensation is not achievable during the session, end the session and repeat it another day. The ideas you embed in your subconscious mind become guidance system settings that can be repeated and reinforced autonomically, consciously or during autosuggestion.

7. On completion of your session, it is critical that you tell your subconscious mind that the autosuggestion session is over and you are energized and returning to total consciousness. This is the closing step equivalent to turning your recording device *Off*. Take a few deep breaths and open your eyes.

The following guidelines will enhance the effectiveness of each session.

1. Ensure you have 20 to 30 minutes to perform the exercise. Later, you may practice the process as you are falling asleep.

2. If distracted by background noises, you can play *soothing* music on low volume to mask the interferences. Do not play music that has an upbeat tempo, a strong beat or lyrics.

3. Focus on one goal or issue at a time. Ensure your desired outcome is clearly defined and is not just *getting better* unless you are already doing well in that situation. For example—each and every day I get better and better at accomplishing *[task or goal]*. Perform reality checks to confirm if your goal is realistic and achievable.

4. **It is critical to end the session.** Do not leave your session without stating that the session is over. Ending the session is the equivalent of turning off a recording device, logging off your computer, ending a phone call or a computer programmer placing *Stop* or *END* to instruct the computer to stop processing a program. Your subconscious mind is a computer and recording device. Your voice, imagination and feelings are programming tools.

It is difficult to perform an autosuggestion session if you cannot locate a quiet place where phones, family, friends or pets will not interrupt you. Turn off your phone, TV and music as the slightest distraction complicates and defeats the process. Manage the process as if you are in a recording studio where background sounds are blocked to prevent interference with the recording session.

It is not advisable to practice autosuggestion before bedtime until you are comfortable with the process. By bedtime, you are often too tired to concentrate and are likely to fall asleep thinking about what requires change rather than a desired outcome.

Managing a busy schedule amidst the madness of society requires an abundance of energy. The relaxation exercise is effective for taking power naps, providing you are not overtired. With practice, the technique can be effortlessly applied in the noisiest environments to re-energize yourself when short bursts of energy are required to remain alert. You can train your internal clock to wake you in twenty minutes, two hours or at a specific time. This is achieved by looking at the current time and as you relax and close your eyes, say, "I will wake up refreshed in twenty minutes," or at a specified time.

The time required to establish a new program depends on your commitment to practice the process and the strength of your killer programs. As you go about your daily routine, you will become aware of situations when you know you are doing better, or someone compliments you about how well you managed a situation. That is excellent feedback and a time to take a deep breath and silently say, "*YES! I am my best friend and coach! Every day and in every way, I get better and better*"(Coué). You are performing at the level of being unconsciously competent.

The simplicity of this process is a double-edged sword. While it is easy to create a visual memory of yourself achieving a goal, the illusion of mind power lures one into thinking that by focusing on a goal it will mysteriously appear. An ancient text once stated that faith without works is dead. Action is required when opportunities are noticed. Taking action reinforces a pattern or guidance system setting that causes you to transition from an observer to a doer. The agony of your efforts evaporates and the act of doing becomes satisfying and at times, exciting and enjoyable.

Once you have implanted a new memory of seeing yourself doing, being or achieving your goal, the next step is coordinating your actions to achieve or fulfill your visions. Old programs (habits) do not voluntarily concede or surrender. Multiple killers have been efficiently programmed and are combat ready to ambush every idea, plan or intention that conflicts with your existing programs. You may feel overwhelmed as you move forward and experience continued attacks. Fortunately, you have powerful tools at your disposal. Learning their function and ease of application will guide and protect you from the pitfalls and traps that send you back to the starting line. It is time to become aware of the traps and pitfalls.

The goose in the bottle is an example of how your mind can be hacked and hijacked. You don't need to be a neuroscientist or a psychologist to find and subdue these invaders. To further enhance your ability to apply mind power requires an awareness of the invaders that influence your subconscious mind and behaviors. This is the focus of the next chapter.

Chapter 13

Hackers, Hijackers and Renegade Thoughts

Digital computers are constantly at risk of being hacked or embedded with virus programs that destroy and steal their data. Your biocomputer is exposed to the same risks. It can be hacked and destructive programs can be formed by external sources. When your command center is intercepted by a quantum leap, your mind power can be used against you. Inevitably, your behaviors, decisions and overall success will be jeopardized. This is an ongoing hazard. In the absence of physical on/off switches, firewalls and anti-virus programs, learning to protect your biocomputer is invaluable.

The repetition of or overexposure to sounds, pictures, and activities induces a complacency that causes you to ignore stimulus that is entering and programming your mind. Your past thoughts, desires and idle wishes function as magnets or guidance system settings and continue to affect your behaviors and choices. Scenarios that you wished and yearned for in the past continue to be processed subconsciously in your imagination and mental monologue. They could be a curse if they materialized today. We encounter that dreaded saying again—be careful what you ask for.

The programs and idle thoughts in memory are active requests for the law of attraction to fulfill. Those who take the time to identify memories that are still active will find this most rewarding. If you are unaware of what is being processed in your mind, you allow hackers, hijackers and renegade thoughts to develop virus programs that sabotage your success.

Subliminal programs are formed and implanted as easily as you accepted the goose in the bottle or the thought of a grey elephant. The danger is that these programs become hidden killers that prevent you from achieving what you really desire. Until you become aware and take action to subdue these attacks, your efforts will be continually undermined.

A hack or hijacking occurs when your mind power is applied against you. When you are passive or indifferent, the speed and power of words, visual effects and random thoughts hijack your command center. In the example of dropping an object, the moment you noticed the object begin to slowly slip through your fingers demonstrated that *thoughts* travel faster than you can consciously process instructions. Your thoughts can be hacked by external sources or by the random thoughts that continually bombard your consciousness.

You may experience this when you are relaxed or engaged in a mundane task. You may hear a word or notice an object and your mind immediately associates it with a past, present or future event. We will call that event "A." Soon it causes you to think of "B" and then "C." There is no limit to how many times your thoughts will bridge to another subject matter. Your random thoughts continue until you realize that you are drifting and say, "Hey, how did I get to thinking about that?" Again, this proves that your conscious mind cannot remain idle and memories and imagination form a constant stream of activity. The train of thought may be harmless. Unfortunately, the repetition of negative thoughts develops or reinforces detrimental programs that undermine you.

Protecting yourself from hackers, hijackers and renegade thoughts requires constant attention to two essential rules:

Rule # 1: Your subconscious mind or guidance system is continuously programmed by your thoughts, imagination and external input. Regardless of whether you agree with the input or are consciously aware of the input, it becomes a permanent memory. Your future behaviors and choices are at risk of being influenced by these memories.

Rule # 2: Your words, or the words others use to influence or control you, either provide general information or create action. A past goal that did not materialize requires a careful assessment of the words you chose, those planted by external sources and random thoughts from your imagination. The evaluation will undoubtedly identify that action words were not applied in your favor, including those from your imagination, and were streamed through your command center and used against you.

The rapid processing of your mind that enabled you to place the goose in a bottle is the power you surrender to external hackers and internal killers. Any thought or worry of an outcome that is unlikely to occur or fixation on a negative comment created by you or uttered by others, has an instant adverse effect on you. The negative or limiting thought that is active in your conscious mind is the one that maintains control of your command center. The negative result is assured, just like your inability to remove the goose from the bottle.

Each time a memory or thought is processed consciously, it is emotionally energized and increases in strength. Repeated often, it becomes a subconscious program that can be autonomically activated. It is like a skill that you have become unconsciously competent at performing. The original suggestion may have originated as a fleeting thought, passing comment or an idea imagined years ago.

Understanding the speed at which thoughts are processed is critical for managing mind power and communicating with others. To effectively apply mind power requires controlling the negative thoughts that constantly hack your conscious mind. At times, a carefully selected and forceful statement is the firewall required to protect your biocomputer.

External sources constantly attempt to hijack and hack your subconscious mind and implant programs or direct instructions that affect your behaviors. For example, recall the first time you decided to use your favorite expletive or expression. The odds are that you cannot identify the exact time or circumstance as you did not make a conscious decision to remember or repeat it. It was only after you heard the expression multiple times that it became a dominant program, and subsequently, part of your current behavior. Indisputably, you were programmed by an external source as described in rule #1 on page 148.

Coaching and motivating others are the acts of intercepting another person's thought processes (hacking) with words that generate impulses for their command center to initiate action. When a boost of energy or enthusiasm is required, you can motivate yourself with a command by applying a quantum leap to initiate it. The command may be a simple thought prompted by you or others.

In Chapter 5, you observed that it did not matter how exhausted you were or how much you were looking forward to a quiet evening, merely hearing that your friends were stopping by sparked a mysterious energy that overcame your lethargic state. You were instantly energized and socialized late into the night. You did not stand back and ponder what you should do. A single thought caused the subconscious mind to detonate your autonomic guidance system into action.

Your subconscious mind already knew the disarray of your home. Your command center was receiving instructions amplifying your tiredness when the call was received. The impetus of the action was the nanosecond impact of a quantum leap suddenly overtaking all processes and instantly instructing the command center to act. The command center instantaneously accessed the subconscious mind for a "how to fix program" (habit) to correct the situation. The instructions were efficiently executed by your biocomputer to make you and your home presentable, but not by you consciously. The killer that was controlling your command center was instantly suppressed and replaced with a program of action.

Although you are not aware of the fact, you are already controlling the power of your mind, but only in limited circumstances. You know that you can temporarily turn off a default program, like an expletive or expression when it is inappropriate. You consciously monitor your choice of words or topics around your parents, at funerals or weddings or with your employer and clients but let loose as soon as you return to a relaxed environment. These are deliberate (conscious) choices that you know are not difficult to perform but require focus and attention. You have proved that you can do it. Applying mind power to achieve personal, career and financial goals requires similar protocols and discipline.

We can consciously initiate bursts of enthusiasm or energy to complete tasks and meet deadlines. Success is achieved more quickly when the subconscious mind is programmed to autonomically implement behaviors that generate specific outcomes. Additional instructions for activating the powers of your mind and self-coaching techniques are included in Appendix O.

Caution is advised as we delve further into the dynamics of who controls your mind. We are constantly at risk of hackers and hijackers ruthlessly preying on us. Various organizations and businesses engage in deceptive advertisements or employ presenters to conduct seminars and presentations for the sole purpose of entrapping and manipulating people. Protecting yourself requires an awareness of how your mind can be hacked. Hackers employ all the processes and techniques described in this book. In addition to subliminal programming that delivers hidden messages and agendas, presentations often refer to the processes of *reprogramming* or *deprogramming* to break free of barriers that prevent one from achieving success or a rewarding lifestyle.

It is imperative to remember that memories cannot be removed or erased. They can be neutralized so that they are no longer the active or dominant program or detrimental to your well-being. The terminology of reprogramming and deprogramming is misleading because it implies that habits can be erased. Digital computing devices can be erased, reprogramed or deactivated but your biocomputer retains all programs. The deprogramming or reprogramming process involves the creation of new and stronger programs that become the dominant programs for the subconscious mind to execute.

The techniques of deprogramming or reprogramming are frequently used by cults and religious organizations or countries where dictatorial leaders place the non-compliant in rethinking programs. Their agenda is to have you think and believe in their idealisms. The process to convert followers is often conducted by charismatic leaders with support from friendly and over-enthusiastic volunteers. As explained in Chapter 11, this method produces an emotionally charged environment. The stimuli of a cause, desire, fear, friends and music are combined to inhibit your objective reasoning and create a pleasant emotional experience. Regardless of how it is described, it is a form of brainwashing.

Most presentations offer great value and skills training; but it is wise to remain cautious and evaluate each presentation. It is important to remain aware of situations that make you susceptible to being programmed or brainwashed. Free seminars and presentations that provide life skills training, religious guidance or ways to be successful in business often include high doses of smiles, hype and enthusiasm, relaxation techniques or mantras while others employ upbeat music or singing and dancing. The excitement reduces your rational thought processes and you are consumed by the sensations of feeling good rather than thinking and remaining objective.

As your comfort level increases, your susceptibility to the power of suggestion and autosuggestion is activated and your subconscious mind cannot resist recording the new ideas and concepts. It may be weeks or months later, after one has become involved and relaxed, that secondary agendas are introduced to develop greater benefits *if* you join their organization or advance to second or third levels of instruction. All of these will likely involve additional fees, tuitions, donations or investments. The following warning is warranted.

> *Be wary of groups with charismatic leaders or venues where excessive enthusiasm is displayed. This includes cults, religious gatherings, political rallies or organizations persistently recruiting new members. Reprogramming is a dangerous form of mind control and brainwashing used by groups to influence and control you for their gain, under the guise of benefiting you. Be careful of groups that insist on reciting phrases, mantras or slogans. The hypnotic and repetitive processes establish programs in your subconscious mind that cause you to accept them as true. Their mission is to retrain your imagination.*

Regardless of the label or description, reprogramming and deprogramming are processes that apply autosuggestion, emotions and repetition to develop and alter your beliefs. As bizarre as it sounds, you could say that to initiate change we must brainwash ourselves with stronger and more dominant programs to achieve our goals. The benefit of self-coaching is that *you retain control through conscious choice (free will) of the type, number and degree of the changes you want to make.*

When attending gatherings that involve reciting scripts or concepts, it is critical to evaluate what you are requested to recite and what is expected of you. You may be encouraged to increase your interactions with members of the organization and spend less time with family and friends. As you become emotionally connected to the activities and members, requests for volunteering and financial or property donations to support their cause are often introduced. Reverse psychology is heavily applied. They offer the option of participating or not but in reality, promoters depend on peer pressure and your insecurities to ensure your compliance. Should you offer resistance, additional intimidation or coercion is sure to follow.

Desktop computers, laptops, tablets, smartphones and automated appliances have operating systems like Windows, Android or iOS. Devices contain keypad input, interface screens, scanners, artificial intelligence components and consoles that provide audio and visual feedback to warn when programs encounter processing conflicts. They pause when conflicts occur to enable manual corrections. They continue to operate when hacked but malfunction or distribute data to unauthorized sources according to their programming or agenda. The hack is not visible on the screen to ensure its presence remains hidden.

Your biocomputer does not have the traditional components that display processing and input. Instead, it has a unique but intangible feedback system that submits audio, visual and sensory feedback. Learning how to interpret this feedback enables you to quickly identify programs that are counterproductive and impede your success. Some programs are easier to detect while others are more elusive and require patience and considerable exploration.

Hackers and hijackers can easily control your mind when you consider how quickly the grey elephant and the goose in the bottle became your thoughts or how a jokester can confuse a person counting items. Autosuggestion is a form of self-hacking that intercepts and establishes new beliefs and programs. It is a self-induced process for fast-tracking the creation of memories that become guidance system settings.

Caution is warranted because the subconscious mind is constantly at risk and programable, whether you are in an Alpha state or not. There are multiple ways for killer programs to become embedded in your subconscious mind and control you without your *conscious* awareness or approval. Each experience or encounter at work, with friends, family, social activities, watching TV or passing through a mall is added to the memory banks of your biocomputer.

The feedback that requires deciphering is identified by specific *aspects* of your mind and being. To compensate for the deficiency of not having an anti-virus or firewall for the subconscious mind and programming process, you possess 12 innate aspects that provide invaluable feedback. Managing these aspects is vital to becoming a free thinker and channeling the power of your mind to attract success. When ignored, your subconscious mind becomes vulnerable to being hijacked by random invaders that implant subliminal programs or instructions. Do not think for a moment that this is insignificant.

Applying mind power is difficult without an understanding of these aspects. Developing a relaxed vigilance to monitor your subconscious mind and guidance system settings enables you to take control of situations as they happen. To avoid seriously compromising the 20 constructs that make up your sophisticated biocomputer system, these aspects cannot be ignored.

Of the 12 aspects presented, mastering the first three is essential to effectively control the power of your mind. They are the primary feedback monitors that reveal how you have been programmed and can be used to form the programs that become *you*. The first three aspects are:

1. Self-Talk
2. Solar Plexus
3. Simulation / Visualization / Imagination

All three are autonomic processes within the human mind and body. They continually transmit audio, visual and sensory or kinesthetic feedback to your conscious mind, creating and displaying your conscious awareness and reality. Consider them your feedback and control panel. When not monitored or controlled, the data that they process become the coding for your biocomputer to develop or reinforce rogue programs.

Your point of power lies in managing or preventing inappropriate input from interfering with your efforts and sabotaging your goals. When your actions or intentions for change are challenged or stymied, it is at this critical juncture that you are able to apply your mental powers to move forward and remain unwavering with your new choices and actions.

There are nine other aspects that significantly influence and program your guidance system settings and behaviors. They are often overlooked because they are camouflaged or masked by habit, familiarity and indifference. They are:

4. Self-image
5. Believing
6. Beliefs
7. Values
8. Attitude
9. Emotions
10. External Killers
11. Cycles
12. Goals and Plans

When you become aware of the influence each aspect has on your behaviors, your mind power and personal success will increase exponentially. The feedback from one or several aspects can identify where action is required. Monitoring and analyzing these aspects will enable you to channel that irresistible force to defend yourself when your mind is hacked or hijacked by renegade thoughts or external distractions. It is now time to learn how to apply your power so that you can benefit from each aspect.

**Very little is needed to
make a happy life.
It is all within yourself,
In your way of thinking.**

Marcus Aurelius (121-180 CE)

Chapter 14

Your Power—Use It or Lose It

Controlling the power of your mind is a serious matter. Either you control it or it controls you. You've learned that your conscious reality is a small fraction of linear time and occurs in the realm of your conscious capacity. It is in this realm that you can attract, control or influence your reality and the world around you. It is also the battleground where the world subtly influences you or beats you up.

Part of your conscious reality is a monologue that is audible in your head and articulates a continuous commentary. That monologue or voice is your thoughts. It autonomically becomes the commands that direct your biocomputer to initiate new actions or continue with your current behaviors. The words may be yours or recalled memories of what others have said. This aspect of your biocomputer system (conscious mind—conscious capacity) is your *self-talk* or inner voice and your conscious moment of existence. It is an auditory summary of your reality.

Self-talk is the primary input device that can override your biocomputer and the imagination. The words that you say, whether consciously chosen or autonomically expressed, send direct instructions to your command center to coordinate the required action. Each statement is an auditory explanation of your programming or conditioning and a disclosure of your guidance system settings. To identify your self-talk, close your eyes to avoid visual distractions and listen to the conversations that you hear in your head. You are listening for the verbal monologue and not external sounds. Take a moment to clarify this difference.

Your words, voice or monologue may have led you on a never-ending trail of comments or questions—what am I listening to? What am I saying? No, that's an external sound. What's the difference? Oh, my voice is describing or identifying the sound. That unending monologue is your self-talk and conscious thoughts.

When uninterrupted, the stream of words carries on indefinitely and without boundaries. You can recall events from the past, evaluate current activities, imagine the future or drift into a daydream that encompasses all of these. The words flow endlessly, one thought after another expressing situations that are good, bad, real or imaginary. As you reflect on the words or thoughts, you might think, "Why did I think about that or where did that thought come from?" If you experienced this—fantastic! This is normal and if you can identify that monologue, you can identify memories that evolved into killers that prevent you from achieving your goals.

Your next challenge is to bring your self-talk to total silence. Close your eyes again and stop the monologue for twenty seconds. Do it now.

You will realize very quickly that silencing the voice or monologue in your head is an impossibility. It may feel like a runaway train that you cannot control. Self-talk is estimated to flow between 1,000 to 1,400 words per minute. The average person speaks between 200 to 400 words per minute. If you are speaking at 400 words per minute and your audience is mentally processing information at an average rate of 1,200 words per minute, you cannot know what each person is thinking with their remaining 800 words per minute. The mind processes information faster than we can talk.

Those who carelessly ignore the power of self-talk will suffer severely for their miscalculation. As your awareness increases, you will notice that the descriptions and commentaries in your self-talk are manifesting or maintaining your reality. Your self-talk foretells the reality that the law of attraction is manifesting in your life. Once you begin to notice that your comments are remarkably similar to how your life unfolds, you will have made a major personal discovery. This is the same discovery James Allen presented in 1903 (Page 121). Attracting opportunities and noticing coincidences are directly linked to what you say to yourself.

Retraining your imagination requires the ability to control your self-talk. If you choose to ignore the explanation of this process, you will never know how your self-talk evolved into the enemy within, and without mercy, it will continue to kill your efforts to succeed.

The exercises of dropping an object, standing up, not thinking of a grey elephant and imagining the goose in the bottle might seem trivial. It is not the physical action that requires your focus but the mental process that created the results. Not understanding this cause and effect undermines your ability to manage the power of your mind.

Of the twelve aspects, self-talk is the one that can instantly bail you out of most predicaments. Words, when skillfully applied, perform like magic. When improperly or carelessly expressed, they become your greatest nemesis. In 1839 the English author, Edward Bulwer-Lytton, coined the phrase, *The pen is mightier than the sword.* His message was that the written word has power, just like the text on these pages influences your thought processes. In the early twentieth century, Florence Scovel Shinn was a dynamic new thought teacher. She focused on the importance of being aware of the words used in our thought processes and the effects words have on our behaviors. If one word prevented you from dropping an object, imagine the impact that multiple words can have on situations—they can undermine you or improve your life.

Self-talk can be a conscious choice, a thought from memory, stimuli from observing an event or an interruption by an external entity, like a jokester confusing you while you are counting items. The words in your mind, either yours or others, form your self-talk and issue instructions to your command center. Your behaviors match those expressed in your self-talk. To achieve a new goal or identify an internal killer, you must understand the construct of program protection (Page 56) and the cause and effect of your words to drop an object or stand up (Page 112). The moment the conscious effort of your thoughts or self-talk stops, killers attack. You instantly return to your old ways and continue as if none of your efforts ever happened. These killers are the enemies within that effectively kill diet and exercise plans, undermine your courage to stand up for yourself or prevent you from acting on new opportunities revealed by the law of attraction.

Self-talk is your source of energy. Yet as psyched as you can be, you can be easily attacked and mentally pummeled when you least expect it. For example, think of a time when you were excited to meet someone or attend a function. Your conscious capacity (self-talk) was bursting with the excitement of what was to unfold. Shortly after your arrival, you encountered a person who made a comment that spoiled your excitement and enthusiasm. Deep within, you wished that you had never come and the search for an exit felt like an eternity.

Your mind and emotions were attacked. You may have been cornered by someone who complained about their life, the government, their job or relationship or expressed comments that were not uplifting or enjoyable. Their words consumed your conscious capacity, or self-talk, and prompted your command center to activate negative emotions that instantly killed your energy and enthusiasm. Your reality was abruptly changed.

Occasionally, the only way to stop an attack or bombardment from an individual is to activate their awareness by stating, "Gee, that sounds like it upsets you a lot. What have you done to deal with the situation?" The power of the question (quantum leap) immediately intercepts their complaining (their self-talk) with a prompt to do something about their situation rather than complain. Do not believe for a minute that you can change them or that they are impressed with you. All you can do is derail their negative tirade and stop them from venting at you and destroying your happiness. As they glare at you with murder on their mind, use the pause or silence to diplomatically introduce a new topic or wisely make your escape.

When unpleasant situations extend for longer periods of time, causing you to suffer through negative bombardments, it requires discipline and inner strength to stand firm. You may be required to temporarily surrender and protect yourself as you endure a meeting, event, family gathering or social encounter by silently reciting a previously prepared action phrase or assertion like, *Deep breath. I am calm. I will soon be out of here.* As soon as you are away from the situation, immediately breathe deeply and repeat one of your prepared command phrases. Otherwise, your self-talk will continue to replay the negative conversations and your reality will remain unchanged, even though you are physically removed from the scene.

If you don't control your thoughts, the negativity of others will overtake your self-talk and activate negative emotions that drag you down. This is the reverse of psyching yourself up. Negative social interactions psych you *down* and destroy experiences that should be enjoyable.

Killers hide in the depths of your mind and when ignored, they surface whether you want them to or not. They are the enemy, your devil or demons. But don't despair. They are simple to identify when you monitor your self-talk and apply the power of the question.

To identify a block or barrier, ask yourself a question relating to the issue. For example, Why can't I achieve/gain/access...(your goal)? What is stopping me from....? What is holding me back from...? It is extremely critical that you ensure your question is not a compound question and focuses only on one issue.

The moment you ask the question you will instantaneously sense, hear or see the answer in your mind and imagination. The response in your self-talk may be your inner voice; the voice of a friend, parent or old acquaintance; or someone you despise. The answer is there but it is a *subtle response* that is easily missed. The thought or answer exists only for a microsecond, and it is critical to identify it and the words that immediately follow.

The instant your answer surfaces, a killer activates a quantum leap and flips your thoughts into a tirade that contradicts that first response, rationalizes why it cannot be true or belittles its legitimacy to convince you to ignore the original response. The tirade from the killer continues until you agree and *convince yourself* that the first response can't possibly be the right explanation or that it is utterly ridiculous. The words of your self-talk that agree with the rationalization are the instructions you send to your command center to dismiss the explanation and continue as you were.

By agreeing with the second response or rationalization, you guarantee the protection of the killer program. This is the essence of how bad habits survive. They retain their power until you develop a stronger program (habit) that triumphs over them. At times, an answer is not immediately disclosed to your consciousness but may reveal itself days later when you least expect it. It may become an "Aha" moment or a realization of disbelief. It may seem unreasonably simple or unrealistic, yet it is the exact cause or issue that requires attention.

A trap that one falls into is following the long explanation that negates that first and immediate response. The incredible survival trick that killers apply is explainable. Think of a time when you were asked a question but preferred not to insult or hurt the one inquiring by providing an honest response. The moment you heard their question, instantaneously, the first and true answer flashed into your mind, but you mentally processed and expressed a different reply to remain diplomatic or kind—but not truthful.

When searching your subconscious mind for killer programs, any thought that shifts you away from that subtle first response is the critical moment for identifying real answers from bogus ones. This is how your subconscious mind remains a traitor and protects existing programs. When you question your subconscious mind about a specific cause of a behavior, situation, barrier or challenge, the moment that you identify the difference between that first subtle response and the overpowering tirade of explanations that follow, you will discover the exact program or conditioning that is holding you back. It is in that first microsecond response that the truth is revealed.

It is impossible to suppress that first response from your subconscious mind. You proved that you cannot mentally withhold the answer to a question (Page 101). However, that first response is easily missed or overlooked. If you choose to rationalize your thoughts and feelings with the tirade of bogus responses that follow, then a killer is protecting itself and you will not benefit from that vital feedback. The dismay or discomfort you experience when you hear that first answer is great news. It may not be enjoyable for the ego but it identifies your conditioning and reveals your killer. Mastering this technique requires an awareness that your self-talk is a component of your imagination. Without deliberately taking control, your imagination (self-talk) bolts off like that runaway train.

Another example is when you are reading a book or lengthy article. If your conscious attention is not focused on the topic, your mind begins to think about other issues or events. When you realize that you are reading the words but not processing what you are reading, you have to reread several paragraphs or pages. Your focus shifted to other issues instead of the article. Your consciousness is vulnerable and was hijacked by other thoughts from your subconscious mind that commandeered your self-talk and imagination to follow them instead.

The subconscious mind controls the act of reading. Reading is a learned behavior or skill. The mental process to comprehend what you are reading requires conscious *willpower*, yet the thoughts that distract you come from your *imagination* and switch your conscious focus into a state of daydreaming. This is what Coué implied when he stated, "*It is this that we call imagination, and it is this which, contrary to accepted opinion, 'always' makes us act even, and above all, against 'our will' when there is antagonism between these two forces.*"

It is your self-talk that provides the greatest power and control of your mind and life. Self-talk is the input device for programming your subconscious mind and controlling your current behavior. In addition, self-talk is a system that provides audio feedback for all the other aspects that we will explore.

As you explore these aspects, you will realize that your self-talk is a running commentary of what you think, see, hear, smell, touch, taste and sense. When self-talk discloses an objection or disagrees with what you are doing, thinking or whatever is coming at you, it is an audio warning no different than a buzzer on a control console. The feedback may be valuable or disclose that a killer is protecting itself and preventing you from proceeding and achieving your current goal or desire.

Left uncontrolled, your past, present and imagined thoughts become killers. Worrying, fretting and dwelling on negative issues are killers that use your self-talk to maintain their dominance of your subconscious mind. Repeating negative comments about your partner, job or situation conditions your subconscious mind to notice those traits rather than focus on the many positive traits that you enjoy. The reinforced programs not only dictate your behaviors, but they cause the law of attraction to work against you. Your negative statements activate negative emotions about how you feel and the type of day you are experiencing. Your point of power is knowing that your self-talk is vulnerable and easily manipulated. A major step to managing mind power is to identify, interpret and replace the random words and thoughts that control you, kill your efforts and wreak havoc with your emotions.

Silent killers, internal or external, attack and commandeer your self-talk without warning. When you realize that you have been ambushed, you can regain control of your thoughts by introducing a quantum leap through the power of a question. As you already experienced with the examples provided, your words can instantly affect your thought processes and physical behaviors.

Programming yourself to succeed at a chosen task is totally dependent on *your words* and self-talk. The moment you stop consciously talking, verbally or silently, the dominant thought from your subconscious mind supersedes your willpower and becomes your self-talk. The example of asserting a single word to drop an object is a command that channels or directs your mind power. If you did not perform this exercise or achieve the result described, (Pages 112–113) it is imperative that you repeat the process until you experience how one word influences your physical actions. Without sensing the physical release initiated by the command of your words, the upcoming information may be of academic interest but will have no lasting value.

Your will, or the voice that you control in your head, is your touch-screen, keyboard or input device that directs your command center while simultaneously programming your guidance system. Random thoughts and imagination are the audio feedback that disclose *exactly* what your subconscious mind has recorded or is conditioned to reinforce. These words and thoughts instruct your command center to activate the behaviors that are stored as programs in your subconscious mind. Without an awareness of the difference between random thoughts and your chosen self-talk, you become complacent and submissive to the random and uncontrolled chatter.

Choosing to consciously suppress these random thoughts instantly alters your reality. This is a tipping point that places you one step closer to overpowering programmed behaviors that impede your success. The moment conscious effort stops and your command center does not have a new instruction to execute, an old habit slips in and regains control. This is *guaranteed* (Page 56).

The simple command required to drop an object or stand up is the same *command process* required to perform any task or achieve a goal. Your actions are regulated by the dominant instruction forwarded to your command center—either by you consciously, your subconscious mind or external sources. The voice in your self-talk that disagrees with your goal or intentions is a killer.

It is common for athletes, performers, public speakers and anyone expected to perform in high stress situations to psych themselves up. Psyching yourself up is performed by consciously projecting your self-talk to overload your command center until your emotions peak. When self-talk and emotional intensity are high, you are psyched.

An awareness of what you mentally recite, or what others say, is your clue to identifying killers. Killers and negative commands that destroy enthusiasm and energy are phrases like:

> ➤ *I can't do it.*
> ➤ *It's not working.*
> ➤ *I'm scared I will [do, say...]*
> ➤ *I'm depressed.*
> ➤ *It's just not me.*
> ➤ *I'm having a terrible day.*
> ➤ *I have a terrible (relationship, job, family, etc.)*
> ➤ *I can't take much more of this.*
> ➤ *This is killing me.*

The list is infinite. Focusing on negative and destructive thoughts will only cause you to feel miserable, when in reality you have total control. Religions explain these negative thoughts as the devil or the temptations of evil. Call it the devil if you will, but the only demons and enemies you will encounter are the ones that were programmed during your lifetime, with or without your knowledge or approval. You now have the power and the techniques to suppress your demons or your devil. The enemy is within and will control you unless you talk back and take control of your thoughts.

When one expresses loss or limitation, it is unreasonable to expect, attract or see opportunity or abundance. It does, however, present an opportunity for you to apply mind power and change your circumstances. Like a sniper, it is imperative that you annihilate the killer (enemy, devil or demon) the moment it is identified by intercepting it with a prepared and practiced phrase, assertion or command. Instantly, the negative self-talk (the enemy) is defused.

The benefit of having an assertive phrase on standby enables you to instantly implement a quantum leap when killers unexpectedly appear. When I hear someone say, "What a rotten day," in my mind and without hesitation, I immediately state, "That's his/her day—I'm having a great day." I have repeated this statement so often that it has become an autonomic response and I do not have to consciously think about it. Do not allow external negative statements to take over your self-talk or activate non-encouraging thoughts that destroy your well-being.

Gaining the attention of a person you are communicating with or coaching is achieved by activating a quantum leap in their self-talk. It redirects their thought processes to a specific topic or reinforces a procedure. Trainers and coaches also know that by repeating positive commands, their students and athletes absorb and register the instructions in their subconscious minds.

It may seem noble to focus on positively developing and supporting individuals. Unfortunately, not all people are respectful coaches or are aware of the malicious impact of their words. As the subconscious mind cannot distinguish between good or bad input, incredible harm and psychological damage occurs when individuals speak ill of their partners, parents berate their children or pass on unfounded prejudices or siblings belittle each other. Bullying in all forms and venues has the same destructive impact on the targeted individual. Instantly, the power of a quantum leap registers the message first in one's self-talk and then in their subconscious mind. With repetition, a cycle of negative programming begins that develops insecurities, lack of confidence, low self-esteem, hatred, disrespect and a litany of negative behaviors.

Your self-talk can undermine you in conversation. Rather than directing your self-talk to listen and follow the conversation, you may have developed a habit of racing ahead and attempting to compose what you want to say next. When you recognize that you have missed part of the conversation, your anxiety increases as you are often too embarrassed to ask the person to repeat what they said. In the end, you may have missed valuable input or an enjoyable learning experience.

When you lack confidence, dealing with negative situations can be difficult. Not only do you have to overcome your lack of confidence that is a killer, but you also have to battle your adversary who is likely to be confident and intimidating. As you prepare to state your position, killer programs intent on protecting your old habit of avoidance behaviors, overload your self-talk. The overload of data clogs the command center often causing you to clam up. You are unable to act or respond effectively. Although it takes courage and determination, resolution only occurs when you decide to act. Your adversary is never going to put your needs first.

Mind power incorrectly applied causes you to become your own worst enemy. There are situations when you sense that something should work or what is required to make it work, yet you sabotage the process by saying, "This isn't going to work." That statement instantly dominates your self-talk as an information statement, not an instruction that the command center can complete. Instantly, a self-fulfilling prophecy is created. It is impossible to succeed when the command center does not receive a clear instruction to act. The result is that the information statement in your self-talk or imagination of "This isn't going to work," takes precedence. From a computing perspective, it does not compute. To resolve this conflict, a quantum leap or question is required to activate the subconscious mind to work in your favor. Ask, "What do I need to do to make this work?" As you repeat the question, your imagination responds with options and new ideas. The subconscious mind may not provide the solution immediately or directly, or it may provide other options.

Self-talk acts as a magic wand for initiating the law of attraction and implementing a quantum leap. It is a silent force that will amaze you. As your awareness of your self-talk increases, new opportunities that were always there but went unnoticed by you will now become obvious. Should you claim that there is no connection between self-talk and recognizing opportunities or state that it does not work, reflect on what you just stated or attracted. For thousands of years, it has been known that *"By your words you are judged and by your words you are condemned."*

Self-talk is your steering mechanism, like the steersman of cybernetics (Page 19). No matter how skilled we become, if we do not maintain control of our steering mechanism (self-talk), the biocomputer reverts to processing what has been established as guidance system settings. Control is instantly gained when an action phrase is asserted with conviction or when a quantum leap is introduced with a question. For example, when you recognize that a friend or colleague is in a negative space, you have an opportunity to befriend them and casually introduce a quantum leap (question) to shift their thoughts to something positive.

Changing a difficult situation requires a prepared script for what you want to say to others or yourself. It is crucial to practice vocalizing the words out loud until you are comfortable stating your position. If you practice silently and do not verbalize the words aloud, when it is time to talk, your voice will crack, your confidence will disappear and by saying nothing, you will appear submissive or incompetent. Your larynx, commonly referred to as the voice box, is a muscle that requires training and conditioning to perform on demand. The repetition of your inaction and sense of frustration reinforces the ineffective behavior (program setting) of how you will respond or act in the future. This behavior or program is a killer of success and achievement. In addition to the verbal practice, you can reinforce the new technique using autosuggestion.

Reflect often on the exercise of dropping an object. One word *prevented* action and one word *created* action. Scripting several *action phrases, assertions* or *questions* in advance, prepares you to defend against killer attacks. For example, when you hear yourself or others say:

"It's not working. This isn't going to work."

> **Repeat**, *"What is required to make this work?"*

"It's not happening."

> **Repeat**, *"Why is this not happening? What am I missing? What action is required to make it happen?"*

"This is killing me."

> **Repeat**, *"What can I do to resolve this, peacefully? productively? quickly? or find an exit?"*

"I'm going to be late."

> **Repeat**, *"Okay, I messed up this time. Next time I will leave earlier."*

In the case of the last example, you cannot regain lost time. Beating yourself up adds a negative emotional stimulus that reinforces your undesirable habit. A chain reaction created by your berating words consumes your conscious capacity, diminishes your attention to other matters and increases your risk of being involved in an accident.

The questions require listening carefully to that subtle response that your subconscious mind will provide. If you are anxious, you'll miss the prompt. Breathe, relax and listen.

Negative words and phrases in your self-talk reinforce negative programs. Realizing that a single word can instruct your command center to drop an object or cause you to stand up, it should be alarming to note how destructive and limiting statements are that include the words can't, won't, unlucky, can't see or other negative and limiting phrases.

Any Negative Idea, Saying or Expression Becomes a lethal virus in your biocomputer.

Preparing phrases or commands is tricky as you do not want to state words that compromise your efforts. For example, stating words like problem rather than situation, or the word try. For financial gains, avoid words that refer to debt. Focus on surplus or being a better manager of your finances. To attract a partner, instead of repeating statements like, I wish I could meet someone or no one is available, focus on attracting a compatible person. To achieve a desired weight, do not repeat words that describe being overweight. The words *lose weight* and *weight loss* emphasize to your subconscious mind that you have excess weight or encourage weight to return after it is lost. Focus on phrases and words that indicate progress and that you are achieving your desired weight or enjoying your diet or exercises. For every goal you desire, there are words and phrases that become commands that either promote or kill your success.

Socially, the quantum leap is effective for changing or redirecting conversations to different subjects. Regardless of how intense a conversation is, a quantum leap easily diverts it to a new topic. This technique is effective and can be inserted with finesse to avoid an abrupt diversion. For instance, "Sorry, I know this is off topic, but this reminds me of the situation at X. Have you heard about it?" The question instills a quantum leap in the self-talk of others. As their curiosity focuses on the new subject, the previous topic fades away.

It is wise to prepare a mental first aid kit with commands like— Those are their thoughts. I am positive and focus on pleasant things. I feel refreshed. I am strong. I am out of here. I am free. These exact words are not the be-all and end-all, but it is valuable to prepare scripts that are clear and meaningful for what you need to remain positive and focused. Reflective questions for controlling self-talk are provided in Appendix A.

To develop a habit of evaluating your self-talk, examine the conversations in your head as you encounter situations, during your commute or when relaxing. The killers and negative programs reveal themselves when you listen closely to that first subtle response that is immediately heard after a thought, question or a challenge is encountered. Your ability to identify this subtle message is a powerful weapon to overcome the habit protection that killers utilize to prevent you from succeeding.

If you insist that you can't...
Guess what? ... You Won't.

Self-talk is extremely powerful and is the main interface for identifying and evaluating the other aspects that we will explore. To add to your skill sets, mind power is significantly enhanced when you listen to your intuition or sixth sense. This is the topic of the next chapter.

Chapter 15

Intuition —Your Sixth Sense

Self-talk was introduced first as it is the primary interface between the conscious and subconscious minds. Self-talk is not a stand-alone component and receives valuable feedback from the *solar plexus*. The feedback is that undeniable sensation often felt in your midsection. The solar plexus acts as a radar and mini-biocomputer processor that evaluates whether your conditioning, behaviors and thoughts are compatible with your actions or the events occurring around you. Deciphering the sensory impulses generated by the solar plexus is vital for using mind power. The solar plexus forms an intuitive component of your conscious awareness. When an unexpected event occurs, your will instantaneously experience physical sensations in your midsection immediately followed by a monologue of the event streaming in your self-talk. Together, the solar plexus and self-talk form an indisputable inner voice. Regrettably, many have never been taught how to interpret the sensory impulses that resonate from the solar plexus or listen to that inner voice.

For centuries, listening to your heart, soul and inner voice were essential principles in ancient Sanskrit literature and the teachings of Confucianism, Taoism, Buddhism and the Bible, to name just a few. The power of the mind is taught in various formats to encourage people to be free thinkers and explorers of the mind. This book is one example.

Sensory impulses that originate from your solar plexus are distinguishable. You may struggle to decipher the significance of the message, but you do know when you are curious or uncomfortable in a situation. People often say, "My gut tells me...; or I have a gut feeling that...; or I sense that...". The sensation may have occurred during a critical decision or moment of fear or when someone made an offhand comment or posed an indiscreet question. It is a similar sensation to when you are waiting for your number to be called on a raffle ticket, anticipating the results of an exam or meeting a person whom you do not trust.

Finding the Killers

The pleasurable sensation or discomfort is a sensory impulse triggered by the solar plexus that creates an awareness. One message may be an intuitive nudge from the law of attraction to act or explore a situation further. Other messages may reveal an old program that is preventing you from achieving a new goal, warn of danger or identify an opportunity that is right in front of you that you are not consciously noticing.

The following are examples of when your solar plexus or radar operated perfectly and provided you with valuable feedback to act or assess a situation further.

➤ You became nervous when a stranger approached you on the street, or a colleague approached you and you did not know what they wanted or would say.

➤ You became anxious when your boss or a person in authority said to you—do you have a minute?

➤ As you provided instructions to someone, it appeared that they were listening, but as they nodded their head indicating that they were following, deep within, you sensed that they had no idea about what you were explaining or requesting of them.

➤ Someone was explaining something that wasn't making sense to you. Your anxiety increased because you were afraid to say that you were not listening or did not understand.

➤ A salesperson made a statement and you sensed that the information was incorrect. Although you did not believe them, you did not consciously have an explanation but knew not to continue with the transaction.

➤ As you approached someone, you sensed that they were uncomfortable, but you did not know whether their discomfort was because of you or a different situation that they were experiencing.

➤ You were at work or at a social gathering and observed others conversing when someone made an insensitive comment. Instantly, you noticed by the facial expressions of the recipient of the comment that they were either hurt, offended or insulted. Although you were able to sense and feel what they felt, you were reluctant to act in their defense and later regretted your inaction.

➤ As you affirmed or expressed how you want to be, you felt uneasy and your self-talk ran rampant with contradictory statements that doubted or dismissed your statement.

Regardless of the activity, we continuously experience sensory impulses in our solar plexus. A relaxed sensation in our midsection is often accompanied by calm statements in our self-talk. When we are unsure of what action to take, our self-talk becomes consumed with words of anxiety as the sensations of angst in our midsection simultaneously increase. Mind power is compromised when our anxieties increase and our self-talk rants out of control. Like a deer in the headlights, we freeze and often do not know how to respond. We become consciously incapacitated, leaving our subconscious mind to implement default guidance system settings established by our past conditioning.

The solar plexus can be your ongoing coach or personal guide when establishing new programs (habits). The sensory impulses confirm whether an action statement, affirmation or assertion is becoming a guidance system setting option or if a killer is attacking your efforts. Any expression or statement that induces discomfort in your solar plexus is created by a killer protecting itself in its attempt to discourage and prevent your new action from proceeding. The sensation of discomfort or angst is an indication that change will occur if you persist with the process. The discomfort is the angst that prevents you from mastering diets and exercise programs, reaching financial goals, developing new habits or acting on the law of attraction. The moment you quit, the killer wins. You remain controlled by the habit or program that you desperately wanted to change (Page 56). The impulses and sensations generated by your solar plexus can be major game changers for success—if you evaluate the messages revealed by your self-talk.

The solar plexus has multiple functions. Just like emotions, it only functions in current or real time. It compares what you are doing with how you have been programmed. The sensation you feel is either a conflict or confirmation that you are following the rules of your conditioning, or an indication that you may be missing cues that the law of attraction is sending to fulfill one of your desires. Intuitively, the solar plexus is a radar that identifies opportunity or danger. As your awareness increases, your solar plexus will detect the level of honesty in others and their discomfort or lack of understanding in discussions. It is crucial to maintain an awareness of the dynamics around you and decipher the comments expressed by your self-talk. The marvel of the solar plexus is that with practice you can develop your radar to become your most trusted ally. Yet at the same time, you can be easily misled if you force your intuitive abilities rather than evaluate and let the energy flow.

The common term for the nerves sensed in your midsection is the solar plexus. Alternate terms are *celiac plexus* or *plexus coeliacus*. The solar plexus is connected to the brain via the *vagus nerve*, a complex network that binds a mesh of abdominal nerves around your vital organs. This is why the sensations in your midsection feel extreme when anticipation, fear or angst is experienced.

When it is time to act, you rationally know what you should do. If a change of a past behavior is required, you choose a new or alternate response. Instantly, because your biocomputer is an inanimate, non-thinking processing machine that is based on your programming, it will continue to protect its current settings by instructing the command center to activate the solar plexus to make you feel uncomfortable. The discomfort acts as a deterrent to stop you from executing the new or alternate action. Your solar plexus reacts with feelings of angst or fear and triggers your self-talk to issue commands that cause you to be indecisive. The sensory impulses ensure the protection of old habits. (Habit Protection–Page 56)

A moment of indecision enables the rapid and flawless execution of killer programs to autonomically perform before you can consciously intercept the process. When you detect a sensory impulse in your solar plexus, you can maintain control by intercepting your self-talk with a question, assertion or dedicated command. That new command instantly directs the biocomputer to trigger an overriding behavior. With repetition, your new choice will become a new guidance system setting.

This is a tipping point that requires assessment. Are the programs that cause us to act based on fact or are they garbage conditioning that we accumulated over our lifetime? Sorting through the garbage is a prerequisite for eliminating killer programs that prevent success.

Like the subconscious mind that cannot withhold an answer to a question, the solar plexus cannot lie. Unfortunately, based on your conditioning, you can be tricked. It truthfully identifies the conflicts you encounter or imagine in real time. The subconscious mind continuously compares the current event to your past experiences and conditioned settings. The assessment is autonomically revealed by the sensory impulses in the solar plexus and the simultaneous *flow of words* or explanations in your self-talk.

Unless you consciously override self-talk to alter or suppress the sensation, the reflex response instantaneously generates the words in your self-talk that become the instructions for your command center. This is a point of power that requires your undivided attention.

Sensory impulses from the solar plexus can be subtle and easily dismissed. Continuing to ignore the sensory impulses that identify an action should be taken develops a conditioned behavior or guidance system setting to avoid action when the feedback is uncomfortable. Hence, avoidance behaviors are programmed settings. When the sensory impulses are evaluated, that first subtle explanation in self-talk is often tough on the ego. The feedback increases in value when one develops a habit of regularly assessing their self-talk each time a sensation is triggered in the solar plexus.

Increasing your awareness of this process enhances your interactions with everyone—customers, team members, family, friends or your partner. With practice, you can develop an awareness to sense the needs or intentions of others, whether they are honorable or not. This is your sixth sense and by deciphering the feedback from the solar plexus, you attain an advantage over others.

In addition, the solar plexus, like self-talk, is used by the subconscious mind and the law of attraction to gain your conscious attention. It may be prompting you to act or warning of impending danger. The negative vibe that you may be sensing from the person with whom you are interacting is your ego objecting to valuable input that is attacking the killer holding you back. The discomfort in your solar plexus is the subconscious mind screaming a warning or telling you to pay attention.

With or without your conscious direction, the subconscious mind, self-talk and solar plexus create an irresistible force that can coax you to be brave or produce unjustifiable fears that prevent you from acting. Your ability to control your mind and overcome your fears is best described in the following well-known example. Imagine a rigid plank, one-foot-wide by twenty feet long placed on the floor or the ground. You are instructed to walk across the plank without touching the floor or the ground. The task appears easy and creates no issues or concerns.

However, if we place that same plank over a raging waterfall, between two tall buildings or across a deep chasm and invite you to walk it a second time, without handrails or safety lines, your reaction changes drastically. The angst in your solar plexus explodes and your self-talk runs rampant with words of fear and resistance.

It is the same plank that you walked on without touching the ground, yet the reaction of the average person would range from a minor concern to major trepidation, particularly if there is no compelling reason to walk that plank. This is a reasonable response. However, it is also the defining moment to realize that while your intent or will is *to walk that plank*, the thoughts and fears of consequences that you imagine, will cause you *not* to walk that plank. Your imagination wins every time.

Continuing with this example will prove beyond any doubt that your words and imagination (self-talk) and feelings (solar plexus) can change your life when mind power is applied to overcome fears and inaction. Imagine that a wild animal, a vicious dog or an escaped criminal is chasing you. You arrive at that plank situated over the raging waterfall, between the two tall buildings or across the deep chasm. Without a doubt, and with fear exploding from your solar plexus and your self-talk spiking, you would cross that plank at record speed, even if you had to crawl across it. Then you would quickly turn and pull the plank back or sideways to stop your pursuer from advancing.

The words in your self-talk and the sensations in your solar plexus constantly influence your daily choices and actions. By developing an awareness of what you say and evaluating the words or verbal commands that restrict or impede you, you can locate the programs or conditioning that have become active killers. This approach enables you to develop new programs or guidance settings that will supersede negative programs and direct you to the achievement of your goals. As stated, the new programs will now dominate but do not erase or remove old programs that remain ready to attack at any time.

The law of attraction is a stretch for some, but as your awareness increases, you will have to admit that some events are at times too much of a coincidence. The law of attraction makes no rational sense and causes us to make unexplainable choices. Consider the example of a situation that requires choosing between A or B. Rationally, the information may suggest selecting option A. As you proceed, you feel an anxiety in your solar plexus to choose B, even though you sense option B is not a better choice or that it could create immediate complications. Consciously, you cannot decipher why you feel as you do but you make a choice.

If there is excessive anxiety, it is caused by other programs or desires hidden in your subconscious mind. That means that if you make the rational choice (A) for the current situation, it may conflict and jeopardize the outcome of another goal that you strongly desire. If you make your choice based on your feelings (B), your choice may be less appropriate for this situation, but it may promote the advancement of another goal by providing or placing you in a better or possibly the only position to achieve it. As complex as the biocomputer is, your decision may be executing a previously held belief or continue a pattern of constantly making bad decisions. That may not sound encouraging.

Examining previous decisions and beliefs identifies hidden programs that attracted you to opportunities or experiences and guided you to where you are today. If a result later proves to be unfavorable, it may be the law of attraction projecting you into a position to achieve another desire. We have all heard of individuals who made bad decisions that resulted in losing their jobs, homes or finances. They often say, "I knew I shouldn't have done or said that." Yet, it was later revealed that because of that specific negative outcome they were in a better position to act on an opportunity that they would not have encountered had the negative situation not occurred.

If you do not evaluate who you are and what you desire, you are at the mercy of the law of attraction to deliver exactly what your guidance system has been programmed to do. Directing the law of attraction requires assessing your wishes and desires held from long ago and evaluating if those old desires are compatible or will interfere with your current life. Old desires that were once set with emotional intensity can remain as dormant guidance system settings. The exercises on pages 39 to 44 and the guidelines provided in Chapter 27 will assist you in assessing internal conflicts. As you review past failures and disappointments, your self-talk and solar plexus will confirm which explanations are truthful or bogus.

When you discover a conflict that continues to prevent you from succeeding, it becomes an incredibly powerful moment of knowing that you have the ability to adjust or reset your autopilot or guidance system settings. As you reflect on past outcomes that did not turn out successfully, you will also hear in your self-talk memories of options that weren't acted upon at the time. The sensory impulses and prompts that you did not follow were subtle inner messages from your sixth sense. If the past outcomes were not what you desired, your solar plexus and self-talk will provide a new awareness as to why you chose not to act. Your power lies in *knowing your true self.*

Think of your resistance when you first read the challenge to walk across the plank under perilous conditions. Compare that resistance to how you felt when you were being pursued under the same perilous conditions. The thoughts and anxieties that you experienced are conditioned fears held in your subconscious mind. As you sat in a comfortable environment and read this passage, your imagination performed as if you were in a real-life situation, only with less adrenalin rushing through your veins. It is this real-life sensation that you are looking to create when practicing autosuggestion to solidify the development of a new program, memory or behavior. The greater the emotional intensity that is applied in your imagination, the sooner a new program or goal will energize a memory setting to guide you to a new reality. This is what Coué stated—that it is easier to retrain the imagination than to continually force your will power.

The unique function of the solar plexus is to alert you to conflicts. It will become your most trusted friend and coach. The solar plexus acts as a radar. When there is a conflict between your intentions (desires) and the programs in your subconscious mind, an explanation will be revealed in your self-talk. Often, you will dismiss or doubt the thought or idea as it appears too absurd, simple, unrelated or could not possibly be the issue. Your doubt and internal debate will consume your conscious capacity. This diversion is the killer's program protection creating a barrage of explanations so that you ignore or miss those subtle first responses. Deciphering the difference between the killer's barrage and the subtle response often leads to an "Aha" moment when you realize how you have been programmed. Thoughts, experiences and memories from long ago remain as deep-seated programs that interfere with your current achievements. If they surface—they exist. This is a private journey. Only you can recall and evaluate your memories and maintain or dismiss their value to you today.

When you identify programs that undermine you, your personal power increases. As you continue to focus on your goal, the solar plexus will identify the blocks that require addressing. The solar plexus will become anxious or intense, offering warnings of conflicts ahead or gently nudging you, like an autopilot or steersman, to bring you back on course. An ongoing assessment will verify whether it is the right course, a distraction or a prompt by a killer compelling you to repeat an undesirable behavior.

Due to the intensity of some situations, whether at work or with a friend or partner, there may not be time for evaluation. Initiating a form of damage control to prevent the conflict from escalating may be the best option. Stories abound about ancient masters and leaders who made inappropriate decisions because they became emotionally upset over trivial matters.

You have a powerful inner mechanism that can lead you to attain self-mastery, but it requires you to control the power of your mind. You may not achieve the high level of enlightenment reported by gurus or shamans, but you can attain a level of self-mastery that enables you to be better today than you were yesterday.

When you have removed yourself from an upsetting situation, you can assess what transpired by questioning your subconscious mind, biocomputer or guidance system settings with—what triggered that situation? Why is this happening? How can I make this better? Questions open multiple subliminal channels where subtle responses are revealed. If an answer is not revealed immediately, several hours or days later an idea or memory will flash into your conscious mind and you will recognize the answer. The *cause* or *origin* of the response is often not logical or rational but it is your subconscious mind identifying the killer. Additional self-reflection may be necessary to decide on the changes specifically required.

Any distraction or inability to remain on topic is a definite clue that a killer does not want you to continue exploring that first response. The killer cannot reason and is simply an inanimate executable program that overloads the capacity of your conscious mind. Your thoughts are easily diverted to other topics. Mind power is the ability to remain focused and intercept the distractions in your self-talk with questions or carefully worded assertions that are confirmed and supported by the solar plexus.

Your next challenge is to disable the power that the barrage of rationalizations (that followed the first subtle response) has on your guidance system settings. *It is how a killer (dominant program) prevents you from achieving your goals and ensures your current situation remains the same.* The explanation may surface from long ago or seem ridiculous when compared to your current reasoning. Its existence must be acknowledged before it can be suppressed. During an autosuggestion session, or when the thought surfaces at random, you can dismiss its power by declaring or affirming how you want to be from this day forward.

Additional information is revealed when a **Why?** question is asked. For example, if the subtle response is—*because I am not confident*, follow up with—*why am I not confident?* The next response may be—*because of a situation that occurred in grade school.* As the exploration expands, a trap is set for you to fall for the explanation when your self-talk says—*but that was years ago! That is silly or ridiculous.*

That last statement contains words that inform rather than create action. It is the program protection of the killer attempting to distract and dismiss your efforts. By doing so, it preserves your guidance system settings for you not to be confident or change anything. The moment you repeat that explanation in your self-talk and your solar plexus agrees with it, you fall for the bait. The trap is—did you repeat the statement verbatim or did you refute it, affirming that it is no longer you and introduce a quantum leap to clarify who you are today and what you want to do, be or have? Dismissing the old explanation with action words versus words that inform has a profound and commanding effect.

The instructions that your command center completes are the ones that your solar plexus feels comfortable with and are confirmed by what you repeat in your self-talk. Whether your goal is to maintain an exercise program or New Year's resolution, start a new business or address a sensitive issue, your efforts can be subtly neutralized within two or three weeks. The following examples demonstrate how killer programs use your energies to kill your efforts and remain in control.

Example 1: When you began a new exercise program, your imagination provided emotional stimuli or excitement and you felt motivated. The plan motivated you to rush out and purchase the latest equipment, clothing and gear that made you look cool. The first few days were exciting and promising. Days or weeks later, when it came time to exercise, the mere thought of exercising was immediately attacked by a killer. The killer hijacked your self-talk with the words—I am too tired; I don't *feel* like it; or this time won't matter. The words expressed how you felt and instructed your command center not to act. As you *recited those very words* in your self-talk, your solar plexus agreed that you were tired, you didn't feel like doing the task and this time wouldn't matter. **BANG!** Your plan is **DEAD!** The existing killer program of you not exercising won. Instead of controlling your command center with a positive command or instructions to exercise, you repeated the killer's program protection words that enabled it to remain in control. As Coué stated, the imagination always wins.

Example 2: The same killers destroy your best intentions when you force your will to diet. A diet may forbid certain treats. As you reach for the forbidden treats, your new desire, a weak program, activates your consciousness or willpower and says—I shouldn't. But the killer, the dominant old program, quickly responds—*this time won't matter. It's just one.* The battle for control of your mind power is about to unfold. It will be quick and deadly. By immediately reciting a simple action phrase to overpower the killer statement of *this time won't matter* with—yes, it does matter—you win. If you consciously repeat the killer's words, they become the instructions forwarded to your command center. The killer wins the moment your solar plexus feels comfortable that *this time won't matter.* The treats are gobbled up and your diet is in its death throes or *D-E-A-D.*

Example 3: You have projects or issues to resolve that seem difficult to begin or if in process, your efforts are gradually diverted and the projects remain uncompleted. The importance of the project becomes irrelevant. Whether it is completing a major goal or assignment, following up on an opportunity, repairing an item or cleaning out a drawer, the objective becomes secondary. As you proceed to act, the mysterious energy that you can control is controlled by the killer and your efforts are hijacked by distractions or avoidance behaviors. The distraction may be as simple as an item out of place. As you pick it up to put it away, a second object catches your eye and you become engaged with it.

At your desk or workstation, you engage in paper shuffling as you organize and clear your space. Time passes while you are engaged in trivial and non-essential activities. The killers that control your command center are twofold. One—there are conflicting programs in your subconscious mind and the completion of one project will jeopardize another. Two—your thoughts are not focused on the reward that the completion of the project will provide. Your thoughts repeat statements of inaction until it is time for a scheduled activity and you no longer have time to work on that project.

Excess physical effort and agony to achieve a goal indicate that there is an ongoing battle for control of your command center. Your adversaries are your self-talk, imagination and the programs that reside in your subconscious mind. When combined, these adversaries become a killer force that uses your solar plexus to prompt you to choose the path of least resistance. Killers are the dominant programs that prompt you to consciously agree with what you sense at that moment. When the battle is over, you feel worse because you did not have the determination or inner strength to adhere to your best intentions. You are discouraged and back at the starting line. Your sixth sense (intuition) was used against you.

Overriding the compelling force of killer habits requires clear instructions that influence or alter your self-talk, imagination and the sensations in your solar plexus.

If you are reluctant to call a client, ask:

"How will I *feel* when this is completed?" [*Pause – repeat.*]

If you are reluctant to exercise, ask:

"How will I *feel* <u>after</u> my work out?" [*Pause – repeat.*]

To restrain that impulse to abandon your diet, ask:

"How will I *feel* when I weigh x kg/lbs.?" [*Pause – repeat.*]

To combat the killer phrase—this time won't matter, instantly state:

"This time does matter. Every day I get better and better."

By default, the response to your question or statement autonomically instructs your subconscious mind to generate the appropriate behaviors. Repeating the question commandeers your subconscious mind and self-talk to respond with the results you desire, and therefore, the killer is instantly suppressed. When the solar plexus relaxes with the answer to how you will *feel* as you imagine completing the task, a mysterious energy pushes you forward and effectively eliminates any sense of physical agony or effort. You are effectively using your emotions to power you rather than have them undermine you. Without consciously forcing your willpower, results appear to be effortlessly and enjoyably attained. The instant you repeat the words of a killer, you remain hostage to the old program (habit).

You have the ability to identify what prevents you from succeeding if you carefully listen for that subtle *first response and associated relaxed sensation in your solar plexus* without engaging in the barrage of rationalizations that follow. With practice, you will become consciously aware of what requires modification or development.

As you mentally verbalize a question or prepare a command phrase, you may experience a physical *twinge* in your solar plexus. If the feeling is uncomfortable, a killer is attempting to distract you due to the new thought or question conflicting with the behavior that you are about to modify. Here lies your power. Any momentary lapse in focus will cause you to reinforce an old program and send you back to the starting line.

Another conditioned behavior that often undermines us occurs when we are explaining something and our solar plexus senses that the person does not understand what we are explaining or requesting of them. It is at this moment that we are consciously aware and have the insight to seek confirmation or clarify our instructions, but out of habit, we unconsciously ask the most fatal question of all—*Do you understand?* vs does that make sense?

Instantly, the response received is an emphatic *yes* or a nod confirming that they understand. Although their answer was a resounding *yes*, our solar plexus (radar) fires impulses to our brain as our self-talk screams, "This person doesn't have a clue what I'm talking about!"

> *Never ask the question:*
> *Do you understand?*
> *It destroys the opportunity*
> *to clarify a confusing situation*
> *identified by your radar.*

By initiating that fatal question, we have backed ourselves into a corner. The person said they understood, yet we sense it is necessary to continue explaining. When your solar plexus identifies a lack of understanding, explore with open-ended questions. For example, "I know what I am wanting to say but

I feel I am not explaining it clearly. Can you tell me what you understand and I'll fill in what I left out."

Just as you are able to sense what others feel or their lack of understanding, the vibes that your solar plexus emit can undermine you when interacting with a confident person. To that confident person, your vibes offer hidden secrets about your weaknesses. Your vibes are picked up by their solar plexus, informing them of your lack of knowledge or confidence or that you are a person who can be intimidated or extorted. A professional or caring person will coach and encourage you. A deceitful person will attempt to maliciously intimidate or take advantage of the situation when they sense your lack of confidence. As their aggression increases, your posture will adjust to defensiveness or submissiveness.

The moment your solar plexus senses intimidation, conditioned responses stored in your biocomputer are activated. Repetition of self-derogatory programs are killers that beat you up and further destroy your confidence. A vicious and downward spiral ensues. The drawing on page 69 illustrates how the power of our mind is shut down when we are threatened. These scenarios occur when encountering aggressive salespeople, con-artists, dominant personalities at work or socially, and all too frequently, difficult family members.

We want to believe that families are caring and supportive. Sadly, some family dynamics are no different than pack wolves establishing supremacy to be the Alpha wolf that forcefully controls the others. Some are bullied into the lowest position of the Omega wolf and are then treated accordingly by others in the pack or family. This book offers encouragement to those who can relate to these unfortunate circumstances. By developing inner strength and confidence, you can break free of these soul-destroying dynamics.

It is the solar plexus that senses these dynamics. In nature, Omega wolves leave their pack of origin and establish their own pack. Should you make this choice, do not think for a moment that the Alphas in your family of origin will accept your choices and new confidence graciously. In the end, enduring the initial angst of separation will prove to be a bargain price to pay for freedom and peace of mind.

The solar plexus and self-talk are invaluable coaches that are with you throughout the day. Daily tasks occupy your conscious mind but your subconscious mind is constantly engaged. When you are relaxed and on autopilot in the midst of a task, your subconscious mind is able to process a previous inquiry while a subtle thought, unrelated to your current task, enters your mind. The message may not be earth-shattering but will assist in solving an unrelated situation or provide information that you were seeking or will require in the near future. Acknowledging and exploring these subtle impulses will make you stronger by enhancing your awareness and the power of attraction.

Based on your conditioning and programming, your subconscious mind is *all-knowing—for you*. By rapidly processing what is occurring around you, the subconscious mind can recognize and warn you of issues that you do not consciously observe but could threaten your safety. One day I was in my garage repairing a small item when I experienced a euphoric moment of knowing that my subconscious mind constantly watches out for me. The repair required the use of a heating torch. It seemed that each time I attempted to light the torch, I would drop something or be distracted. It just seemed that I couldn't get coordinated to light the flame and complete my task. Frustrated, I said to myself, "Okay, what am I missing?" Instantly my self-talk voiced, "The garbage can."

I was dumbfounded because the day before I had discarded paper towels that contained cleaning solvent residue. These towels were within range of the torch that I was about to ignite. I realized I would have created a small fire if I had lit the torch. As soon as I placed the container outdoors, everything went well, and my original task was completed in minutes. You may say it was a coincidence. All I said was, "Thank you subconscious!" The law of attraction is an unexplainable force that can protect you if you listen and work with it. If the law of attraction is not nurtured (listened to), it will not be there to help you.

Analyzing the feedback created by your intuition (sixth sense and solar plexus) becomes a critical tipping point that advances you on your journey to self-mastery. Chapter 26 and Appendix B provide guidance to manage and subdue conflicts created by the relentless killers of procrastination and avoidance behavior.

As you explore the remaining aspects, an awareness will develop of the multiple sources of programming, thoughts or desires that have established themselves as your guidance system settings. It is through quiet reflection that the incredible power of your sixth sense is first revealed. The block or perceived barrier that appears to be calling out the loudest is likely that of a killer. In times of approaching danger, your best recourse is to request guidance calmly and quietly from within.

Self-talk and solar plexus are the audio and kinesthetic components of mind power. Each of the remaining aspects that will be explored are identified or controlled by self-talk or the solar plexus. The third primary aspect—visualization—will advance you to a higher level. This is the topic of the next chapter.

We are shaped
By our thoughts.
We become
What we think.

Buddha (6th Century BCE)

Chapter 16

WYSIWYG
What You See Is What You Get

A primary component of imagination is the visual aspect or process of being able to create an image of an achievement or behavior in the mind's eye. This powerful concept led to the advancement of computer technologies to develop simulators with sound, motion and 3D display screens. The screens provide a visual experience for the participant to see and sense an activity as if it were real. Simulators and computer modeling are utilized by, among others, scientists, pilots, astronauts, equipment operators, marketers, engineers and even gamers. Achievers of all kinds, including athletes, performers, and therapists practice simulation through the process of *visualization.*

Simulation and visualization are used extensively because they are effective and achieve rapid results. Their efficacy is attributed to the power of images and visual perception. Visualization engages the sense of sight and adds images to a thought. The word *image* is the root word of imagination. The aphorism—a picture is worth a thousand words—can be used to describe the power that images possess for programming your guidance system. An image or visual stimulus provides a quantum leap that engages the self-talk and solar plexus to unify and become a powerful internal energy.

The combination of visualization, self-talk and the solar plexus can instantly code or program your biocomputer or alter your behaviors. These three aspects provide visual, auditory and kinesthetic input. Self-talk provides auditory input. The solar plexus provides the kinesthetic input while visualization and imagination provide visual input.

Each form of input records memories in the biocomputer, like the magnetization process that records data in digital computers. Singularly or in combination, we can input data to develop new guidance system settings. Your efforts are supercharged when the three modes are simultaneously implemented—self-talk, solar plexus and visualization.

The mind operates rapidly and your inputting efforts are constrained without pictures or visual input. In Chapter 14, self-talk was estimated to flow at approximately 1,200 words per minute. Applying the previous aphorism, if we were to replace each word in our self-talk with a picture or image that is equivalent to 1,000 words, (1,200 x 1,000), the rate at which our conscious mind processes information would increase from 1,200 words per minute to 1.2 million bits of data, actions or commands. Using an aphorism and an estimate is a simplistic calculation, but it emphasizes the power of images. Science confirms that the calculating and processing capacity of our mind is greater than we can comprehend.

Images are created instantly and without our approval. We can be programmed contrary to our desires. It is the power of self-talk and the feedback from our solar plexus that enable us to intercept and control how we are programmed. Visualizing creates a mental image that either confirms or conflicts with our guidance system settings and is verified by the sensory impulses of our solar plexus. When stimuli or emotions are added during visualization or autosuggestion, the programming/conditioning effect increases while significantly reducing the time required to establish guidance system settings.

Like self-talk, visualization is a feedback monitor and coding process for programming your guidance system. The images in the conscious mind are displayed from memories and past conditioning. They are simultaneously accompanied by self-talk narratives and sensory impulses emanating from the solar plexus. It is the conscious mind that assesses or judges the content according to the responses from the solar plexus. Visualizing or imagining a new behavior or goal instantly activates a series of internal processes. An uncomfortable or uneasy sensation that occurs when you create a new visual, indicates that you are challenging a killer. Pleasant sensations generated by your new vision indicate that you are advancing in your preferred direction.

Regrettably, the negative effects of violence on television, video games, movies and the news are continuous forms of programming input. As the number of exposures to negative activities increases, our minds become conditioned to accept them as a norm. Sadly, our society is evolving into one that is becoming increasingly desensitized and accepting of violence and disrespect.

Imagination is visualization and your mental simulator. Like self-talk and the solar plexus, the visual component is continuously active, whether you are in a state of autosuggestion or going about your daily activities. Fleeting thoughts continuously flow through your imagination creating a natural battle ground. When you think, focus or imagine yourself achieving a new goal, your old habits and guidance system settings are challenged.

Instantly the killers (habits, programs or past conditioning) sense that your new desire or behavior is contrary to their current settings and autonomically activate a defense program. Their ability to break your focus enables them to commandeer your imagination, self-talk and solar plexus, thereby effectively disrupting your efforts. The image that you are left with in your mind is the program being reinforced. W Y S I W Y G is computer lingo for:

What You See Is What You Get.

As the subconscious mind cannot select or identify right from wrong, any thought imagined or visualized that generates a feeling of fear, intimidation, anger or reluctance will develop and reinforce a program that prevents you from performing actions that are required to achieve your goal. The negative thoughts and images take control of your mind power as your command center receives negative or avoidance instructions. This is your point of power and the critical moment to insert a quantum leap by imagining the action required or the desired outcome with a supporting narrative in your self-talk. Instantly, the negativity in your conscious mind is replaced by positive energy that provides the appropriate commands to your command center autonomically. Repetition creates a new setting and causes your solar plexus to accept the new image as normal as it emits a new sensation of confidence.

The combination of self-talk, visualization and the solar plexus enables you to examine your programming. When you visualize and clearly express your goal or desire, listen closely to your self-talk and the sensory impulses from your solar plexus. The subconscious

mind will clearly identify visual, auditory or kinesthetic conflicts—
that is—if you listen. Explanations, excuses or actions required are
explicitly expressed in your self-talk. You will hear monologues
like—I just can't *see* myself doing, being or having... I don't *feel* I can
do that. There's no way I can *say*... and so forth.

The explanations or excuses are feedback from *your subconscious
mind identifying the new programming that your guidance system
requires.* To create the new program, imagine a vivid picture as you
verbally state or affirm yourself doing, being or having achieved
your goal. Maintain the mental image until you can create a
sensation that it feels real, without any ifs, ands, buts or doubts. This
single action concentrates your mind power to initiate a quantum
leap and establish a new guidance system setting. Without clearly
imagining the successful outcome, the subconscious mind has an
incomplete request, and like any digital computer, it will not
compute.

Programs that the subconscious mind is processing are instantly
verified the moment you become aware of what you are thinking,
saying, imagining, visualizing or sensing. Although it took 10 to 15
seconds to read that last sentence, the verification process
happens in an instant when you become aware of your thoughts
and the impulses from your solar plexus. It is the combination of
these aspects that creates the powerful force that manifests what
you imagine into reality.

The example of drinking from a beverage container and then
deciding to take a second drink demonstrates how a single thought
or imagined desire initiates the biomechanical processes to acquire
that second drink. The force works for or against you and is
controlled by your self-talk and the images held in your imagination.
If negative images of upcoming situations are not intercepted, they
reinforce or become new programs or guidance system settings. An
executable biocomputer program can be identified by the image in
your imagination—what you see is what you get. (W Y S I W Y G).

There is a false assumption that mind power removes the
necessity of physical action or exertion. This is an illusion and a
turning point to reveal the magic. The three aspects—self-talk, solar
plexus and visualization instantly identify what is required to

advance. Effort becomes a moot point if your desire and dedication to achieve your goal are genuine. The agony of making an effort transitions into an invigorating desire (Chapter 5).

As your goal becomes a visual possibility and your solar plexus conveys an excitement of its impending manifestation, a desire to exert effort mysteriously becomes motivating and exciting. Should there be blocks or barriers, your inner coach will identify the obstacles if you challenge yourself with the question, "Can I *see* myself doing what is required to achieve and maintain (*my goal*)?" Your solar plexus will instantly respond and trigger the subconscious mind to disclose what is preventing your success and the changes required. The answer will be clearly revealed in your self-talk—when you listen.

A goal or success is not a destination or finish line but a new lifestyle. Once your goal is achieved, your success requires protection. It is easy to think and focus on that great job, relationship, improved finances or a desired weight, but can you *see* yourself continuing to perform the activities that brought you to that level of success? Once you achieve a goal, your old habits (killers) lie in ambush waiting to be reactivated and decimate your success. Can you visualize yourself continuing to be successful in the future?

Appendix C contains exploratory questions to assist you in identifying areas of specific concern. Whether you label them as past conditioning, habits, killers or guidance system settings, they have become a master program that dictates how you perform and what you will achieve. This is the topic of the next chapter.

We are limited,
not by our abilities,
but by our vision.

Kahil Gibran (1883-1931)

Chapter 17

Your Master Program

It would be wonderful to think that we can simply reformat our biocomputer and begin programming ourselves to be exactly what we desire to be. Unfortunately, it doesn't work that way, but in many cases, you can provide yourself with an update. Your biocomputer is working extremely well. You just need to figure out which programs are defeating you and then add new programs to offset them.

When you experience frustrations and disappointments caused by your behaviors or lack of achievements, your feelings are not the expressions of your ego, but your deep inner being, your soul or true Self. Many of us were not raised in supportive environments that encouraged the development of our true selves. We were programmed by others and evolved into an entity, too often dissimilar to our true or authentic Self. That entity is our ego and at times our Self feels like a captive passenger on a train bound for an unknown destination. As we travel through life, we begin to sense that life could be different and we look for ways to escape or alter our destiny.

When one deeply desires situations to be different, an inner conflict develops. The conflict is the ego battling to suppress the thoughts and desires of your true Self. The ego fights to preserve the current guidance system settings as they are the ego's life force. As the ego develops, it becomes the master program that regulates all your behaviors in every aspect of your life. The image you have of yourself—good, bad, strong, weak, ambitious or lazy is your self-image. The master program is a summation of your guidance system settings that includes your level of confidence, ambitions and self-worth; how you see and what you feel about your educational level, appearance, weight, fitness and body shape; and how well you perform as an employee, manager, presenter, teacher, student, partner, spouse, friend or co-worker. It is everything you do and how you do it, based on the way you see yourself.

Your programming is not based on being good or bad in these roles. It is comprised of learned behaviors and rules that dictate how you live, act or respond to situations. The programs function like a thermostat that adjusts your behaviors and performance to a specific setting. If you perform better than you normally do, then you subconsciously engage in unproductive activities that bring you back to your normal setting. When performance is below your preset normal, the subconscious mind generates behaviors that improve your performance. The performance and behavioral instructions autonomically pass through the command center. Self-mastery is the ability to consciously intercept and inject alternate instructions to override the commands that are being transmitted by the subconscious mind or your guidance system settings.

Your self-talk and solar plexus provide constant feedback about how you see yourself. For example, to assess your level of confidence and self-worth, what does your self-talk reveal and how does your solar plexus respond when you are disappointed in your actions? Do you say, "I'm unlucky, stupid or a loser?" How do you respond to a compliment? Do you feel uncomfortable when you receive praise? Do you dismiss compliments or say, "Oh, it was nothing, I fluked out, or that's not like me." These responses are prompted by your killers, the enemies within. A response that develops confidence and supports your mind power is, "Thank you." Then quietly in your self-talk reinforce your achievement with, "Yea! That's more like me!"

Your guidance system settings are continually revealed and reinforced by what you think, feel or say. Derogatory remarks about yourself, your abilities or how you constantly mess up reinforce negative and self-defeating programs. If you do not recognize positive things about yourself, how can you present yourself as the right person for a position or personal relationship?

As you reflect on and explore the questions provided in the Appendices, you will discover behaviors and conditioning about yourself that you do not like. Congratulations again! Those behaviors are the killers that are holding you back. They are executable (fully functioning) biocomputer programs. The rapid processing capabilities of the brain identify in advance which of your desires and choices are compatible with your master program and autonomically process negative feelings to distract or discourage you from implementing anything that is different.

When you think about, see yourself being or feel nervous, you autonomically signal your command center to connect to programs that cause you to act nervous and project a lack of confidence. You can immediately change those feelings and instructions by overriding them with positive commands. A quicker way to achieve the same result is to first imagine and feel yourself performing that way during an autosuggestion session.

When you think and repeat that you *do not see new opportunities,* *or are unlucky,* you instruct your biocomputer to mask opportunities that are obvious to others, the same as missing a play or move in a card or board game. The opportunity is there, but your subconscious mind filtered it out so you wouldn't notice it. It's near impossible to notice it because you have not instructed the law of attraction to locate it. Friends and family joke about how I locate parking spaces close to entrances, even when the lot is full. Locating parking spaces was a test project that I practiced decades ago to prove that the law of attraction and seeing opportunities can be expanded.

Chapters 6 to 16 described the operating system of your biocomputer. Its functionality is comparable to the operating systems of Windows, iOS or Android based computers. Your conditioning and programs are the applications that achieve your output or performance. Digital computers have regular updates, with new features constantly being added. Similar to a digital device, your self-image or master program requires an *update* to achieve different results. Understanding the programming or updating process is vital. It is through this understanding that the power of attraction and mind power either work or severely sabotage your efforts.

Not only is the programming process vital, but it must not be torpedoed by the killer's words—*this time won't matter.* The old self-image program remains a threat and can silently return. This is observed with people who quit smoking and start again, lose weight and quickly regain it or individuals who successfully attain well-paid employment or a promotion but are dismissed because they fail to perform in that position. Goals are not destinations and require continuous action to support them after they are achieved.

Can you see yourself performing exactly as you desire to be? If your guidance system settings are not updated, your biocomputer will not perform to your expectations. This becomes your insanity App or program.

Mind power is often misunderstood. People believe that by simply imagining and focusing on their goal, it will mysteriously manifest itself. It will—but only when you notice and explore opportunities that your subconscious mind reveals to you. The **omission of a plan of action** causes the euphoric image to become a false memory or a delusional idea. Imagination combined with intense emotion **creates the illusion that you achieved your goal and further effort is not required**. This is a killer program that can be inadvertently created. It subsequently sabotages you as it allows the existing self-image or master program of your current *Self* to continue while falsely believing that you are achieving your goal.

To avoid this oversight, it is essential to evaluate your progress and initiate any required action (Chapter 5). It is also imperative that you coach yourself with specific questions that prompt you to act— *what can I do now to advance me toward my goal? What is the best use of my time? [Pause, listen and repeat]* Failure to do this, places your biocomputer and guidance system back in the control of the ego. If an idea does not present itself, simply state—it will come to me. As stated earlier, the answer may not appear in your self-talk for several days but it will appear when you least expect it.

Goals and achievements that enhance relationships, finances, and health are not destinations, but an enjoyable journey that creates a way of life. New programs that are added to your master program require constant protection and must include activities and plans to maintain them. This will ensure that your success continues. Failure to do this creates opportunities for old programs to sneak back in or for naysayers to discourage you by attributing your good fortune to luck. They can also undermine you by doubting that your success will last. It is vital to defend and reinforce your good fortune (effort) by repeating in your self-talk—*that's their thinking. Every day I get better and better.* As naysayers hound you like jackals, consider—*did I have this 'luck' before I started managing my thoughts and mind power?*

After noticing a few *coincidences,* you will never doubt the law of attraction or your ability to develop your mind to attract opportunities. It is not to your advantage to share your choices or life decisions with anyone who is neither encouraging nor open to exploring new ideas. The act of silently protecting your thoughts, plans and goals generates a feeling of confidence and energizes that irresistible force within.

When we analyze the lives of successful people, we realize that their good fortune did not magically come to them. They were proactive and made their success happen. If your desire is strong, the agony of your actions and efforts fades and you become excited as you enthusiastically engage in activities that promote the achievement of your goal and a new reality. You will manage each challenge and setback, not as failure, but as an opportunity to improve and make yourself better and better. The once perceived agony of effort simply evaporates.

Identifying additional programs (killers) that control you is achieved by evaluating your strengths and weaknesses. This is not from the perspective of others, but from the perceptions you have of yourself (Self-Image). To provide focus, a short exercise is provided below. Record your instant responses. Listen closely for the subtle reply that immediately follows your prompt. You may express your answers confidently, but your solar plexus will identify whether you are truthful or if your fraudulent ego is jerking you around. Do not attempt to prioritize each item. Let each identified strength or weakness be a point or topic of its own.

You can expand your exploration later. To begin, identify 3 strengths that you feel you possess and 3 weaknesses that you believe prevent you from achieving your goals. The more you identify the quicker you will advance.

I see and believe my *strengths* are:

1. _____

2. _____

3. _____

I see and believe my *weaknesses* are:

1. _____

2. _____

3. _____

Finding the Killers

Three characteristics or behaviors that I *like* about myself are:

1. _____
2. _____
3. _____

Three characteristics or behaviors that I *dislike* about myself are:

1. _____
2. _____
3. _____

If your assessment indicates that you have few weaknesses, it may be valuable to seriously question whether you are a superior being or whether you are deluding yourself. If you identify excessive weaknesses or dislikes, it is likely that you are conditioned to beat yourself up rather than appreciate and benefit from the skills you possess. Honesty and awareness are valuable tools.

If you have reflected on your situations and behaviors over the course of a few weeks and are still unaware of behaviors that are limiting you, there may be value in seeking the advice of a *trusted* person. (*Caution is advised as you will identify in a later chapter that individuals whom you think are 'trusted' friends may not be objective, experienced coaches or have your best interests at heart. A casual opinion is not what you are seeking. Discovering that a friend is not whom you thought they were, is devastating. However, it is better to find out sooner than to continue through life thinking someone is a true friend when they are not.*)

Your ego can be meek or arrogant and can mislead you or suppress skills you possess that would naturally develop. An example of the ego not being truthful is when you think you are a talented singer, a great football player or an indispensable employee. You may think you are good, but others have a different perception than what you hold as your self-image. It can be discouraging and humiliating to think that you are doing extremely well, but later be told your performance requires improvement. Some friends may be less discreet and outright tell you that *you suck!* Before consulting others, it is less embarrassing to conduct self-assessments and identify your strengths and weaknesses in private.

Review what you have identified and realize that these are some of the guidance system settings that form your self-image. When you recite a strength or weakness, evaluate the sensation in your solar plexus and the words that you hear in your self-talk. This is a powerful moment. Listen carefully to your mental processing as it provides critical advice. If you ignore the feedback, you undermine an integral aspect of mind power. Each time you ignore a sensory impulse, you autonomically reinforce the habit to ignore the signals in the future.

Except in situations where one is delusional, we are often overly critical when assessing ourselves. We tend to overlook our positive qualities and focus on our negative, inaccurate or nonexistent weaknesses. As you proceed through the remaining chapters, you will identify how your master program (self-image) was programmed.

As you evaluate your strengths and weaknesses, consider whether some of your strengths may be undermining you. Also consider whether your weaknesses may be undeveloped talents. A perceived weakness, when explored, often becomes an asset. Reality may reveal that your confidence is viewed by others as arrogance and your knowledge on some topics may be mediocre. You may not know as much as you think. Honesty is often a humbling experience.

If you are overly confident, you may wonder why you are not liked, accepted or chosen for particular projects, events or social activities. This is not necessarily a disadvantage. Your behaviors may be annoying to others but by reflecting on who you are, you may identify that you have qualities and values that differ from or exceed the group you desire to join. Recognizing and accepting who you are saves you from social situations that would be painfully disappointing and could never meet your expectations.

An example of a perceived weakness that is a strength is in the field of sales. There are those who think that they would not excel in sales because they are not comfortable socializing. They feel that they are not smooth or fast talkers nor do they have the gift of gab. Nothing could be further from the truth. The magic is in the power of the question. Success in sales is based on the skill of asking questions and being a better listener than a talker.

When you introduce open-ended questions to explore what a customer requires, you only need to listen. The customer does all the talking. Your job is to explain and demonstrate that you can fill their order. Similarly, tension and nervous silence in social settings can be quickly eliminated by asking simple and unprovocative questions. The old proverb of having one mouth and two ears counsels us to listen more and talk less.

Appendix D includes questions to explore the constructs of your self-image, master program and guidance system settings. The settings of your master program are constantly being modified. As we grow and evolve through various stages of our lives, our wants and desires change our master program and guidance system settings. The remaining chapters will lead you to many surprising discoveries. But first, let's explore how rapidly these program settings solidify and retain unrelenting control and power over you. It is the point of transformation and the topic of the next chapter.

Chapter 18

The Transformation Point

Mind power is multi-faceted but intangible, like thoughts, gravity and magnetism. Each is invisible, yet its energy and existence are undeniable. The lack of tangible or physical matter to grasp adds to the mystique of mind power. One of the unique aspects of mind power is the act of *believing*. The example of the goose in the bottle demonstrated that a process within your psyche caused a mental block. You believed that a goose was in the bottle and it could not be removed.

Believing is a transformation point that creates power as well as complications. Its impact is rapid. The act of believing instantly solidifies a program and makes it stronger. At times, what you believe may appear irrefutable. You proved that a belief could be formed in a nanosecond when you believed a goose was in a bottle.

It does not matter how proficient you are with your self-talk and visualization if you do not *believe* or have *faith* in what you imagine. For a program to become effective, it must be compatible with and have the support of other programs and desires that are stored in your subconscious mind. Conflicts between old programs and new ideas are caused by killers fighting to retain control of your behaviors. A conflict is any negative sensation in your solar plexus that disagrees with what you say in your self-talk or what is being stated aloud by you or others. The sensory impulses between your solar plexus and your self-talk unveil the mystery of believing. A dominant program is one that you or your ego believes to be true. For centuries, the masses have been intimidated and controlled by clerics who fervently drum the words—Do you believe?

The act of *believing* is the ultimate bonding agent that transforms a new idea into a dominant program. In Chapters 14 and 15, you identified the link between the solar plexus and self-talk. When you expressed a statement, the solar plexus responded with an approving or contradictory sensation or angst that indicated that it was or was not true—to you. The sensation confirmed the self-talk message as true or prompted your self-talk to match the feelings of your solar plexus. Conflicts occur when an existing program within your subconscious mind is not compatible with what you state and believe to be true. Old garbage programs are killers that continually sabotage your success. As emphasized earlier, a new command or statement becomes the dominant program only when the stimulus of emotion is added and repeated until you *believe* it to be true. The slightest doubt ensures the killers win.

There are common expressions like—*If I keep telling myself this, I will believe it;* or *I'll believe it when I see it.* The first expression confirms the power of self-talk. The second expression conflicts with the order of visualization and the law of attraction, placing the power of believing on hold. ***Without visualizing the outcome in the mind's eye before it actually manifests***, the law of attraction is compromised. The subconscious mind is unable to issue the required autonomic instructions to inform you of opportunities, even when they appear directly in front of you. The intensity of your desire determines whether you believe you will achieve your goal.

In explaining the intricate configurations and dynamics of how your subconscious mind responds, the words *have faith* were first introduced as *action* words in the third paragraph of this chapter. Faith was described in previous chapters as an emotion that we experience. The keepers of the secrets and religious leaders added the words *have faith as* a compounding tactic to influence the masses because they understood how our minds function.

Archeological discoveries have revealed that the activities of many civilizations were based on what they believed. They believed in superstitions, barbaric rituals of human sacrifices or waging wars on those who did not believe in the same gods as them. In the 21st century, it is sad to admit that we humans have not evolved. Wars continue to be fought over values that each side believes to be valid and true.

Successfully developing a new habit or program depends on the strength of your belief and faith in achieving your new goal. There is no trying. You either believe or you do not believe. Believing has the impact of a quantum leap. It is or it is not. A *maybe* can be classified as a doubt. Visualizing and imagining enable you to see the outcome making it easier to believe in the achievement of a new goal. Therefore, the phrase—*I'll believe it when I see it*—is valid when you visualize the outcome first in your imagination. For the law of attraction to deliver, you must *first see (visualize) or imagine* the successful outcome in your mind's eye.

When you encounter obstacles, your solar plexus is your most trusted ally. The solar plexus informs you of conflicts between what you are choosing to do and what you believe. Overcoming this conflict becomes easier when autosuggestion and simulation are applied and supported by unambiguous narratives describing what you desire the outcome to be. As you imagine an outcome, you can supercharge the programming process by applying emotion to sense that it is being achieved. Eventually you will believe it will occur.

The powerful act of believing in your goal and your ability to achieve it, will supersede the dominant programs that are suppressing your success. When you believe in a realistic and achievable goal, you are empowered to overcome anything that holds you back.

The power of believing has been used for centuries by the unscrupulous to dominate and control others. Historically, the act of believing has been used to coerce and trick the uneducated masses into following the explicit orders of opportunists or those in power, be they politicians, members of religious orders, gangs, associations or charlatans. Chapter 23 will explain how the masses, including yourself, are coerced, guided and influenced to *believe* in concepts that are self-serving only to those who promote them.

The power of believing has been written about in multiple forms, from coded inferences in metaphysical texts to ancient verbal teachings passed from master to student. In modernity, it is a foundational construct for self-development and training.

The power of faith and believing has been known for centuries. It was a major tenet of the teachings of Confucius around 500 BCE, of the Bhagavad Gita around 200 BCE and of biblical writings in the first century of our common era. When we compare the message of Napoleon Hill's (Hill, 1937) famous quote from the mid-1930's— *whatever the mind of man can conceive and believe, he can achieve,* to the biblical verses of Matthew 21:22—*whatever one asks in prayer, he will*

Finding the Killers

receive, if one has faith; and Mark 11:24—*whatever a person asks in prayer, believe it has been received and it will be yours*—the message is the same. This is remarkable when you consider that their writings were composed nearly 2,000 years apart.

The act of believing is an autonomic process. It is instantaneous, as you proved by believing that there was a goose in the bottle. Each of us has at times fallen victim to a prank, been talked into a questionable purchase by a salesperson or friend or believed a comment to be true until we found out later that facts proved it wrong. For a time, *we believed*, proving that what we believe affects our behaviors but also that our beliefs can be reversed or changed.

Within human nature lurks a dark force that can instantly kill friendships and opportunities. Regardless of how you label it, gossip, rumor, hearsay or false information, it is a lethal and ruthless killer. We often receive negative input in advance about a new acquaintance, product or situation. When this occurs, our first encounter causes us to be tentative. We remain cautious and hesitant to engage because we believe the negative information to be true. We are prejudiced because the advance information became a program preventing us from remaining open minded and forming our own impressions and opinions.

During the course of pursuing a goal, you may receive negative feedback that generates an uneasy sensation. It is important to evaluate whether this is your subconscious mind protecting you from an impractical goal (that you blindly believe in) or whether it is a killer preventing your success. Killers protect themselves by causing you to talk yourself out of implementing your actions. When you recite a new action (command) to achieve a goal, your self-talk and solar plexus will verify if you believe in your choice or action. If your solar plexus is comfortable with what you express as you repeat a phrase that overrides the objections of the killers within, you will begin to advance the achievement of your goal. Conversely, *if your solar plexus is agitated by your declaration, assertion or affirmation,* and if your goal and plan is practical and realistic, it means a killer (old habit) is coercing you to *retract* your command. A retracted command is an act of surrendering your intent and you will not follow through on the action required to advance you to your goal.

You return to the way you were. This is a *fatal trap* that causes you *not* to believe in your plan and you quit.

As creatures of habit, we tend to fall for the all too comfortable words that killers use to create doubt rather than holding steadfast to what we desire. While this causes us to believe our goal is unattainable, this is also a point of power. Your transition to accessing the mysterious energy and developing internal strength occurs the moment you believe you will succeed. Remaining steadfast when confronted with doubt provides the repetition that calms your solar plexus as you create a new guidance system setting for what you want to achieve. An autosuggestion session is not always necessary as you can silently intercept your self-talk at any time or place during the day.

The solar plexus constantly and instantly confirms whether your subconscious mind is programmed to support your efforts or is a traitor and saboteur. Each time your thoughts focus on acting on a goal or desire, the physical uneasiness generated by your solar plexus divulges a critical message in your self-talk. The conditioning that holds you back could be that you do not *believe* that the goal is achievable, you are not worthy of it or you carry a plethora of garbage programs from past decades.

These beliefs have become part of your master program and self-image settings. By regularly exploring your thoughts and memories, you will discover multiple beliefs that you held to be true but upon further evaluation proved them wrong.

As you reflect on the questions in Appendix E, carefully assess the sensory responses in your solar plexus and the simultaneous first responses in your self-talk. To effectively direct your mind power requires a clear understanding that the physical sensation in your solar plexus either conflicts with or confirms what you believe.

The power of believing solidifies programs that are executed autonomically by your biocomputer. Identifying the beliefs that formed programs that remain active today is the topic of the next chapter.

⚸ Believe nothing just
because someone else
believes it. Believe only
what you yourself test
and judge to be true.

Buddha (6th Century BCE)

Chapter 19

Active Programs & Killers

In the last chapter you learned that the power of believing creates beliefs that are executable computer programs. Whether they are true or not, they influence your choices and behaviors. In this chapter you will explore the origins of your beliefs. Your discoveries will confirm how a significant amount of your master program formed without your conscious choice or awareness.

A *belief* is an active program that is verified by the feeling in your solar plexus when the explanation in your self-talk feels true *to you*. A belief ranges from an unrealistic fear to a verifiable fact. Beliefs form the building blocks of your self-image and guidance system settings and you perform according to those settings. As proven by how quickly the goose entered the bottle in your imagination, a program or belief can form in nanoseconds and have an immediate effect on your behavior, whether it is in your career, relationships or social life. Clarifying beliefs is a lifelong process. As children, we believed that mystical or magical characters like Santa Claus, Befana, Krampus, Père Fouettard or the Tooth Fairy brought us gifts. We believed teachers, religious leaders, politicians and others were upstanding citizens and were disappointed when we later became aware of any less than stellar behaviors. Some of us believe in a God, many Gods or no God while others believe in a Universal Energy.

We believe in a broad range of ideas, concepts, theories or philosophies. Our beliefs began to form at a young age when we were not aware of what was occurring. We learned by exposure, observation and repetition rather than choice.

Once a belief is established, we rarely re-assess it, explore its validity or consider what the circumstances were that caused us to develop that belief. The choices you consciously or subconsciously made have merged to create the perfect *You*. Not that you are perfect, but your beliefs and programs, good and bad, have created an ego—*you*. Your ego causes you to behave as you do and suppresses the real you that you think and sense you are. It may be kind, mean or a total mess, but a perfect mess created exactly to the constructs of your beliefs. An awareness of your ability to develop new programs and beliefs is a threat to your ego. Consequently, the ego causes you to feel uneasy about having the power to create a new reality.

Self-awareness, developed by analyzing your beliefs and their effect on you, is often disturbing. You *do not have to change*, but you may never feel at ease or achieve your goals until you do. As you continue to explore the mind, you will eventually recognize that beliefs, once identified as false or unreasonable, cannot reclaim their original power over you. The impact of believing, or not, must be acknowledged as a foundational element for programs to work. The behaviors of naysayers and hypochondriacs continually prove this. When you ask yourself if you believe you can achieve what you desire, the sensations and self-talk triggered by your solar plexus identify the exact issues or blocks that are preventing your success.

Believing and breathing have several factors in common. You might ask—why think about breathing if it is natural? Breathing is an intrinsic process of our autonomic nervous system and will continue without conscious interception. However, while you are breathing, do you question—what am I breathing? Only when your attention is distracted by a pleasant fragrance or a foul odor do you evaluate the situation. It's common for residents living near industrial operations to become immune to offensive odors and accept them as normal. Believing is an innate process that enables us to easily *get used to* and accept unpleasant situations as normal.

As time passes, you become unconsciously unaware yet unconsciously competent at acting on what you believe and accepting the impact it has on you. If you never evaluate what you believe, you will never determine whether you are just drifting through life as an automaton following what others believe or experiencing the excitement and grandeur of all life has to offer.

Self-reflection has been encouraged for centuries. As mentioned earlier, it was Socrates who stated over 2,500 years ago, *an unexamined life is not worth living;* and 17th century Descartes wrote, *at least once in your life, doubt, as far as possible, all things.* The wisdom of these quotes provides an awareness of the importance of knowing how and by what you were programmed and that you can freely choose to remove barriers that you were not aware of previously. When a new idea or process reveals that you have a limiting program or habit, you have two choices—develop a new habit or continue with your limitations and frustrations. Freeing yourself from debilitating habits and beliefs requires exploring why you allow the program protection of killer programs to dismiss or resist ideas that could improve the quality of your life based on what you desire.

Our disappointments and lack of success are, in many instances, attributable to our beliefs. When you realize that your biocomputer is processing garbage programs, you will also discover that these programs were founded on garbage beliefs.

If you do not consciously explore what you think about and the effect that your beliefs have on your life, nothing can change. The beliefs that prevent you from succeeding are killers executing their autonomic program protection as freely as a Monopoly *get out of jail free* card. (Pg. 59). If you are not consciously and continuously fine tuning yourself, you are regressing.

Killers are not just habits that control your physical behaviors. Killer programs also respond autonomically and attack your conscious choice to explore and evaluate your guidance system settings. Their program protection creates illusions, fears and distractions that generate a feeling that an unknown outcome will occur should you explore further. Old beliefs remain active, the same as an undesirable melody in your head that surfaces at random. Beliefs are killers that lurk in the depths of your mind, waiting to resurface like zombies to destroy any intentions to change your current situation.

As you become more aware of your self-talk, you will be intrigued by the broad range of never-ending topics that your mind processes as you go about your daily routines of commuting, walking or performing mundane chores. Self-talk reveals beliefs and active programs that determine the quality of your life (conscious reality). Unresolved issues can continue to create internal arguments with individuals who themselves have long forgotten the incident. When you repeatedly dwell on an issue, it remains an active program. Life is a mind game that has no time-outs or pauses and requires constant awareness to control the plays of the game. The sooner you take control, the sooner negative intrusions will be suppressed and the law of attraction will align to fulfill your desires.

The beginning of an evaluation or change process causes killers to attack every effort, thought or idea that conflicts with your guidance system settings. The greater the intensity with which an idea was imprinted into your subconscious memory, the greater the discomfort sensed in your solar plexus will be when exploring options that are contrary to that deep-seated belief. Whether the belief was promoted by your family of origin, religion, friends, a cult or slick marketers, it has become a program that maintains power over your thought processes and your choices.

Regardless of the rationale, whether it is the fear of punishment or loss or the promise of some form of achievement or happiness, your programming is based on what you believe and accept as true. Freeing yourself from beliefs that were instilled at a young age may require years, especially if the indoctrination was emotionally intense.

Conflicts are not restricted to internal explorations but are also experienced externally when others attempt to control you. They may disapprove of you reading this book because it encourages you to be independent. Your new choices may pose a threat to their power over you. Should you encounter these situations, remember Descartes' encouraging words—at least once, question everything. Your explorations do not require you to be a fanatic, argumentative or unbalanced. With practice, silent and calmly stated questions, assertions or commands will ensure that killers are suppressed and you remain in control.

Music has become a social norm during everyday activities. If you enjoy music and constantly wear earbuds, have a radio or TV on or are easily distracted by external activities, it will be difficult to monitor and explore the activity of your mind during the early stages of developing your mind power. The compulsion to have music constantly playing is a habit. When the conscious mind is overrun by auditory, visual or sensory input, it drowns the subtle responses from the subconscious mind. Balancing your enjoyment of music and other external activities can be a challenge while developing mind power.

Another belief that has developed into a social norm in the era of the smartphone is the expectation that one should be constantly connected to social media and immediately respond to any posting. For many, it has become an addiction. Medical practitioners are reporting that people are suffering from sleep disorders and additional stress created by a self-imposed addiction to social media and electronic devices. The notification that a new post or text is available utilizes the power of the quantum leap and conditions people to *immediately* check their messages. Although the message may be frivolous, not checking it creates an irresistible urge, an agony no different than the draw of an addiction to sweets, substances or activities one attempts to avoid. The belief and expectation to instantly respond to the buzz, ping, call or a text kills your independence and the ability to enjoy a relaxing moment.

Beliefs are programs that control your behaviors and thoughts. If an undesirable idea, thought or old comment emerges from your memory, its existence cannot be denied. The fact that a thought or memory appears indicates it is *alive and lurking in your subconscious mind*. A quick assertion or command instantly defuses its power. Declaring your command once, or even a few times, may not be sufficient to completely suppress it. Regardless of the number of times the thought surfaces, your efforts must be consistently repeated until your new response occurs unconsciously and continues to suppress the killer. If you do not assert control, the killer remains a threat. An awareness of your progress is critical as a program protection tactic may cause you to think you have succeeded when you have not. Killers cannot reason and may appear as tricksters by surfacing later.

Thoughts and comments that surface from years ago are beliefs and programs that still influence your current behaviors. You may think you dismissed them with comments like—Oh, that's when I was a kid. That's so-and-so's ideas and he or she is a jerk. I've ditched those ideas. Those statements did not neutralize the memories with a new guidance system setting. As explained on pages 116-117, the words you applied were not *action* words. The words merely described the situation. It is impossible to break free of their control unless action words that clearly describe what you desire to do, be or have are audibly or mentally expressed and confirmed by a positive sensory assurance from your solar plexus. Original thoughts may fade away but can unexpectedly reappear like zombies. Your vigilance in dismissing negative thoughts through positive assertions is another turning point for self-mastery and success.

As your awareness of the subtle messages and comments in your self-talk increases, you can evaluate them by asking yourself—why do I think that way or where or from whom did that idea or concept originate? The subtle first response will provide the answers. If personal change is important to you, this exploration technique will be easy to perform as you go about your daily routines.

The deepest, strongest and most destructive beliefs and programs are often those that you have never contemplated. They are comprised of ideas and beliefs created subconsciously when you were growing up in your family of origin. You were exposed to a perspective of how people are; a religion or no religion; a political viewpoint; a culture of politeness, manners, generosity and kindness; or one of selfishness or abruptness—everything that makes you who you are today. These experiences formed into your reality or *your* world. Destructive and debilitating beliefs that you carry may be the prejudices and intolerances of your primary caregivers—parents, siblings, relatives or family friends. Their beliefs were implanted into your subconscious mind without your approval or evaluation and you retained them as true. Your subconscious mind absorbed each concept as quickly as you accepted the thought of a grey elephant, a goose in the bottle or your favorite expletive.

Long before you could exercise your power to reason and make choices, situations that you encountered established beliefs at a subliminal level. Herein lies an opportunity to challenge your ego and identify how your past conditioning influences your current behaviors. Additional questions are provided in Appendix F to enable you to explore the influence of race, religion and culture to evaluate whether you are tolerant and accepting or driven by deep-seated beliefs that instruct your command center to execute behaviors that do not portray the real you.

If you could instantly form a belief that you could not remove the goose from the bottle, what other beliefs do you have that might not be true and hinder your achievements? The explanations, excuses and justifications disclosed in your self-talk provide a plethora of ongoing feedback—if you listen. It may be discouraging to realize the amount of garbage your memory banks contain but the awareness gained is empowering.

Digital technology provides rapid distribution of information and misinformation in politics, scientific reports, research studies, corporate disclaimers and product descriptions. Recognizing how hype or emotional intensity can facilitate ideas being implanted into your memory, it is critical to verify if the data is true before purchasing or taking action that could later have a negative effect on your life.

Objectivity and open-mindedness create new opportunities. Indiscriminate dismissals kill opportunities that could improve situations. For example, an immediate response like—this isn't going to work—is based on a belief from *your* past conditioning. Your words confirm what your subconscious mind holds as fact and does not instruct your command center to further the exploration process. No action is taken and the situation remains the same. The idea is proven not to work, but only for you.

It is the same when you say—I don't have time. There are occasions when this may be true, but when planning ahead, the words are feedback from your subconscious mind informing you what you believe and why your subconscious mind does not execute effective actions. It is a distraction serving as program protection to dissuade you from introducing new action that would advance you toward a desired goal. If you do not act, no one will act on your behalf. This is your life, and only as a child or in a positive relationship will a parent or partner assist, encourage or support you. Otherwise, you are on your own.

Unhealthy relationships destroy one's confidence and self-esteem when one partner berates the other with destructive or demeaning words. With repetition, one begins to believe the hurtful words and the emotional intensity solidifies a negative subliminal program that becomes a guidance system setting for their self-image. They begin to believe they are as described by others and it causes them to feel worse. Research studies have shown that people respond according to how they think others see them and expect them to be. It is imperative that you replace destructive beliefs with those of self-confidence, ability and beauty to counter any negative influences from others.

We are exposed to negative input everywhere. Each bit of input becomes an active program. Being prepared with a silent defense neutralizes cruel attacks. When an attack occurs, mentally recite a command similar to—those are his or her thoughts. I get better and better every day. During your exploration, when old memories generate negative self-talk expressed by others, you can neutralize the pain by using the same phrase. In time, the negative effects of the old beliefs are blocked by stronger beliefs that you created through repetition.

The nastiest killers of happiness and success are the ones created by worry. Worry is an active program that instantly takes over your conscious capacity, self-talk, solar plexus, visualization and imagination. It turns the power of your mind against you and destroys any chance of enjoying the current moment. Worry is an unjustified belief or program that an unknown or unpleasant situation is about to occur. It is a killer that tortures you slowly through mental anguish and agony. When a negative situation is encountered, your ability to focus on options is undermined by not recognizing that the negative thoughts that cause you to feel badly can be eliminated.

Killer beliefs successfully protect themselves by creating a worried and non-confident you. The situations you imagine that could go wrong are not just one goose, but an entire flock of geese crammed into your imagination and flying erratically.

From Seneca in Roman times to Mark Twain in the 19th century, quotations abound about people who worry and stress over negative expectations, troubles and problems that never occur. A focus on negative outcomes ensures that killer thoughts will diminish the quality of your life by activating negative emotions in present time. It begs the question: Why would one choose to feel badly when there is insufficient proof or data to expect a negative outcome?

A damaging program is like a song that you do not enjoy. You cannot change the lyrics or melody of the song playing but you can replace it by choosing a new song. You can encourage yourself to take action by repeating—if it is to be, it is up to me. I will act now." Depending on your situation, repeat the phrase until you are moved to act or you feel relaxed and calm. Visualize your new approach as you apply Coué's phrase—every day and in every way, I get better and better. When you focus on a new activity, you strengthen that activity or image of yourself. In time, the new idea becomes the dominant belief and guidance system setting. Your positive responses will become autonomic.

What we attract into our lives is determined by our thoughts and what we emotionally energize. An examination of the negative situations that occur in our lives will reveal that they are eerily similar to the negative thoughts we harbor. The outcomes are often classified as self-fulfilling prophesies.

Negative and unsupported ideas equate to us accepting that we cannot remove the goose from the bottle. We carry with us multiple ideas and beliefs that we bought into consciously or unconsciously and believe to be true. Only a small amount of exploration is required to develop an awareness that a belief may be untrue or unsupported. Appendix F provides questions to assist you in your explorations.

The mechanics of mind power and how your biocomputer executes programs or habits have been explained in detail. To complement the process, there are several aspects that significantly influence and alter your choices as you go about your daily activities. One aspect that influences you is values, or what you have been conditioned to view as important. In the next chapter we will explore how our values affect the power of our mind and can reduce our independence.

One believes things
because one has been
conditioned
to believe them.

Aldous Huxley (1894-1963)

Chapter 20

What's Important — To You

We are programmed from birth, either consciously or subconsciously, to *believe* that certain ideas, objects or status have exceptional *value* or are worthless and despicable. Their significance can be measured not only by what we like or dislike, but also by the degree we desire to possess or protect them.

Each person has a unique and personal value system. The slightest challenge to their values can trigger negative and sometimes violent emotional responses that can escalate and incite wars or riots. Whatever we consider important contributes to our value system.

Values include tangible items like material objects, places or buildings and intangibles such as beliefs, concepts, activities, friendships, marriage, education, status, spirituality and religion. Values also include the character traits of personal conduct, degree of integrity, achievements, fashion, and anything that one has observed, imagined and chosen to be of value.

Values dictate what we purchase, where we go, what we do, who we associate with and what we strive for to enhance our social, family and career status. Living with billions of people on this planet requires an acceptance and tolerance of what others value. The fact that many societies and cultures do not respect or accept the values of others provides a simple explanation as to why there are tribal wars, conflicts, riots, terrorism, discrimination, power struggles in the workplace and major family feuds. One would have to be the ultimate recluse to avoid these conflicts.

We are influenced by celebrities, groups or trendy movements that promote an object, concept, place, activity or an achievement as being desirable. Often, the object is not necessarily better but is perceived to be superior because it is associated with an iconic figure. An endorsement by a rock star, athlete, movie star or noted public figure instantly places a higher value on an object or place.

Values have no boundaries. People place value on fashions, possessions, achievements and actions that include being the first to own the newest product (whether gimmicky or recognizable brands), being the first to arrive at an event, ensuring their children attend a specific school, shopping at brand stores, dining at chic restaurants or belonging to clubs that include distinguished members or celebrities. Vacation spots, restaurants, movies, wines, consumables and events are more alluring when endorsed by famous people. The list of items that people consider valuable is limitless. The inner drive to do, be or achieve what one values significantly affects their self-image, success and happiness. Not being able to achieve or possess what one has been led to believe is valuable, often creates a sense of failure, emptiness, unhappiness and even psychological problems.

Values include beliefs and behaviors that develop into a superiority complex rooted in a belief that one is superior to siblings, neighbors or friends. Some believe that gaining an advantage through cheating and dishonesty is the result of their cleverness. Compatible values facilitate successful relationships. Regardless of whom we are, our values affect our behaviors. Our value system dictates how we assess what others have, do, or achieve. We internally form a comparison based on what we value.

Achieving what is important to us determines our happiness. Choices and decisions are constantly required and certain decisions are more difficult than others because of social, family, employment and cultural pressures. Many end up in unhappy situations or relationships because they do not place value on having respect for themselves. They put up with and accept undesirable behaviors from others, including how they are treated or pressured to accept situations. The simple truth is:

⤞ ✠ *What you put up with* *You end up with.*

External pressures challenge our values. A serious challenge to my values occurred when I was in my early twenties and was relocating to another city. The moving company had scheduled the furnishings of four families on the same van. I had not secured a place to live in the new city and had requested that the movers load my furniture first so that when they arrived, they could complete their other deliveries first. This would provide me additional time to secure an apartment. To my surprise, the movers contacted me on arrival advising they had loaded my furniture last and that it required unloading as quickly as possible. The pressure from the movers was strong and rental vacancies in the new city were low. They were adamant that I place my furniture in storage and incur a double charge for handling and storage costs. Reluctantly, they gave me another day to locate an apartment.

At one point, the only affordable apartment I found was an old and poorly maintained unit in a less desirable part of town. The carpet had cigarette burns, an old relic of a refrigerator and a view of abandoned appliances in the alley. The landlord's predatory eagerness for me to lease the property suggested that he saw me as easy prey. With the pressure from the moving company and a low vacancy rate, it seemed that I might have to consider the possibility of this undesirable apartment.

Deep within my solar plexus I felt I could not succumb to living in such a despicable place. Although it seemed like I would not locate a better unit, something within me suggested that I should defer my decision until the next day. The next morning, I checked out a modern high-rise in a pleasant neighborhood. I had been advised that the rates were atrocious for high-rise units. Surprisingly, there was a vacant apartment on the eleventh floor with an amazing city view, and rent that was ten percent less than the despicable apartment. The property managers also agreed to put in new carpets and new appliances if I could wait until the next day to move in. My inner voice shouted, "No brainer!" The movers had to wait one more day. At that time, I was unconsciously unaware of the power of my mind as my solar plexus, self-talk, beliefs, values and law of attraction performed with amazing precision. On reflection, it was an excellent example of what you put up with, you end up with.

Values in our modern society are particularly challenging in the area of family dynamics. Issues arise anywhere from how children and grandchildren should be raised to the liberties and entitlements extended to family pets that are at times revered just as much, if not more than humans. Irresponsible pet owners think nothing of letting their pets jump on others because their values are different than responsible pet owners. Our values determine our behaviors.

Values influence our self-esteem or how we feel about ourselves, including our appearance, dress and level of confidence. This is a double-edged sword as what we strongly desire may be what we already are, but our sense of worth is suppressed by an incompatible self-image we hold of ourselves. In our consciousness, a rational dissonance occurs as we strive to be what we already are but feel frustrated because our biocomputer keeps telling us we are something different. This is a killer created by accepting standards (values) set by others of how we should be or self-induced by imagining a need to change based on a false belief of ourselves. By assessing our values, beliefs, self-image and behaviors we can reconcile this disparity and be free to be ourselves.

The example in Chapter 8, pertaining to overcoming the habit of nail biting, was based on values. The change was easily achieved by an awareness created from an external source that struck at the core of my value system. For some, the habit of nail biting may not be significant, but for me, it was a detractor to my image as a professional in the board room and with those I coached. Once an awareness was created, my behaviors were subconsciously altered by my values. Each time my subconscious mind alerted me that the habit was about to be repeated, I consciously changed my behavior.

A constant battle exists between the values of corporations and commerce and the values of an individual. Business values focus on market share and profit or the bottom line. To achieve this, skillful strategies are engaged to manipulate the lack of awareness and insecurities of the general public. Unfortunately, commerce applies the proverbial—every trick in the book—including every technique presented in this book, to divert your financial resources to their bottom line.

Corporations promote the value of their products or services as being indispensable to daily living and status. Through clever and psychologically designed advertising, marketers, vendors and salespeople constantly target our self-esteem through our values. They attack our value system in a way that if we do not purchase their product, we will miss out and not be part of the *in-crowd*. After all, caveat emptor, let the buyer beware, has been publicized since the 1500s. Businesses have one goal and that is to continually make those kill shots. Corporations are one of the external killers that will be explored in Chapter 23.

There is nothing wrong with enjoying the luxuries that life offers. The danger occurs when we become automatons and fall for the lure of an implied measure of status, success or achievement that drives us to acquire residences with a specific address, expensive autos or fashions that promote a specific body type. Anyone in a position of influence can declare any object or fashion as a status symbol.

Our values are constantly being modified. New values may be compatible with our existing guidance system settings while others, though enticing, can create conflict. When we venture off as young adults to establish our lives and careers, the values of our family of origin tag along with us and remain part of our subliminal guidance system settings. The values that were instilled in us at an early age are either strong motivators or motivation killers. An example would be a person who was raised within a structure of financial limitations and minimal encouragement. They face two opposing possibilities.

One choice focuses on having a career with a lucrative income and purposefully setting out to do whatever is required to attain a comfortable lifestyle. They focus their efforts on establishing financially rewarding careers that provide the conveniences they lacked growing up. They value education and hard work and forfeit various leisure activities to achieve their goals.

The opposite occurs when an individual perceives the situations created by financial limitations as manageable. The effort required to generate financial comfort, or even a small surplus, does not seem worth it, especially if they have to improve their education or change careers. They consciously choose a marginal lifestyle that allows them to exist with the least amount of effort. They hold a value that accepts going without or making do with only the essentials. They exercise their choice and accept a marginal standard of living.

These two examples are based on values. Each may be comfortable and content as they exercise their power of choice.

Finding the Killers

Those with a marginal lifestyle remain unconsciously unaware as they invest incredible amounts of time and energy putting up with the hardships and inconveniences of a marginal life, rather than applying that same energy and effort to creating a better life. Sadly, we often hear them justify their position by pointing the finger at government, lack of opportunities or other restrictions that they *believe* are the cause of their situation, rather than their own choices. In this way they continue to reinforce their beliefs and values.

Regardless of the goals that we set out to achieve, what was valuable at one stage of our life may be inappropriate years later. Achievements and setbacks alter our perspective on what is valuable. Remaining in a state of yearning for an unrealistic or unachievable goal only erodes our happiness. Not only is it unhealthy but it is a waste of time and energy.

Evaluating your goals and values on a regular basis is essential. An assessment provides an opportunity to explore why a particular goal is of value and whether it is compatible with your real interests, means and your future. Assessing your values reveals whether the purpose of a particular goal is to enhance your life or merely impress others. If it is the latter, it may be a subliminal program implanted and validated by others that is completely irrelevant to the lifestyle you now desire.

An example of how values are set at an early age is demonstrated by a rewarding experience I had with my children when they were aged seven and nine. I encouraged reading when they were young and they were attracted to a variety of books. I was enrolled in a course at the local university and had purchased a course textbook. When they came home from school, my daughter immediately saw the new book and began leafing through the pages. When she turned to the back cover and saw the price tag, she uttered in disbelief, *"You paid $95 for a book?"* That was an exorbitant amount of money to a nine-year-old.

A few days later we were returning home late one evening after visiting their grandmother. It was a long drive and after an exciting day their tiredness created the occasional silence. But I was soon to discover that self-talk is just as active in the minds of the young. As we drove along, the silence became longer until suddenly my daughter blurted out in a disbelieving tone, "You paid $95 for one book!" Without any external reference to the book, her young mind flashed back to the event that occurred days earlier. I acknowledged her concern about the high cost of the book and explained that at times information is expensive—but knowledge enables us to learn and avoid costly mistakes in the future. Again, there was silence in the car. A few minutes later, my son piped up with:

I would sooner pay a hundred dollars
for one book than know nothing.

(Chase Anderson – age 7)

Even at the age of seven, values and beliefs establish themselves to become powerful motivators.

It is normal to meet people who value items that are considered weird or obscure—to you—because you are unaware of their story or life experiences. Those who suffered the trauma of war will value peace and a free society that many of us take for granted. Those who experienced food shortages and rationing do not waste food. What we value guides us throughout our lives. A person raised in an abusive environment may choose to develop a kind and caring home. On the other hand, an abusive upbringing has the potential to develop the belief that negative behaviors are acceptable, thus, perpetuating a vicious cycle of family violence. Only through an awareness experienced by the individual can the cycle be changed.

Insisting that one's ideas and values are better often causes irreparable harm. History is filled with warring nations insisting that their religious beliefs and practices should be accepted as the right choice, while ignoring their own religious tenets of acceptance and respect for others. For centuries, countries conquered new lands and territories, imposing their beliefs and values onto the existing peoples who were expected to adopt their conquerors' way of living or face death. Under duress, the majority chose life but at a most undesirable price.

Your values are constantly being attacked through advertising. For non-essential industries to survive, they require new styles or models to be introduced regularly and rely on the masses to purchase these new products. To turn a non-essential item into a got-to-have item, the power of your mind is turned against you through advertising. Advertisers use the power of words, images and emotions to influence customers to believe that the new style or gadget is valuable or necessary to avoid being classified as a loser by fashionistas or status conscious peers.

You may recall a time when you felt obligated or at least under pressure to purchase an item that was stylish or fashionable, even though it was non-essential or you could not afford it. Each of us would benefit greatly if we constantly assessed our situation and asked ourselves—are trends, styles or fashions controlling the quality of my life or placing unreasonable financial expectations on me? Why is the internal pressure to acquire the new style or gadget so strong? Personal power is the ability to exercise choice and resist being unduly influenced.

In personal relationships, compatibility and harmony are increased when both partners share similar values. This includes but is not limited to—domestic life and daily chores, leisure activities, intimacy, spending habits and money management, religion, holiday preferences, child rearing, pets, politics, friends, relatives, work ethics and manners.

Succeeding in sales requires an understanding of what the customer values. To insert your values while ignoring or dismissing the customer's perspective is a fatal sales mistake. Successful salespeople identify their customers' needs and values and then present their product or service to fill those requirements. Features showcasing new technical advances are interesting to observe, promote and discuss, but are often seen by buyers as bells and whistles that increase the price with no practical value.

Case in point—Several years ago, my wife and I moved to a mountainous area where cell phone coverage is nonexistent within a range of several miles. We installed the old-fashioned land line and realized that we no longer required two cell phones. We decided to keep one cell phone for travel and cancel the second cell phone. Anyone who has ever had a dispute with a major Telcom will appreciate what transpired.

I was informed that cancelling a phone could not be authorized by frontline agents and my call was transferred to a supervisor. After several failed attempts to convince me not to cancel, the supervisor transferred my call to an Escalation Team. The same pointless presentation was made until my patience began to run out and I was transferred one more time to the Customer Retention Team.

Sadly, this last agent kept offering me multiple options and upgrades with an intense expectation that he would convince me to keep that second cell phone. There was euphoric jubilance in his voice when he offered me 100 different ring tones for free! I just couldn't resist asking him what the value of 100 ring tones would be in a location without cell service. Deflated, he responded, "I just thought it would be valuable." When I asked him to look up the year that we became clients, he then responded, "Oh, I'm not even that old."

The interaction was obviously frustrating yet humorous. The perspective and position of each participant was determined by values. Telecoms know that it costs more to acquire a new customer than retain an existing one. Agents are often paid or penalized for their retention rate, demonstrating that for this agent there was value (to him) in retaining our account but no value to us.

Whether it is in career, social or personal interactions, you may value and feel enthusiastic and excited about a particular cause, product or process. However, the individual you are interacting with may not share your values. Attempting to convince them may jeopardize your relationship with them.

Workplace complications occur when employees do not share similar values. If leadership is not evident and professional standards are not set, the dynamics become tense. Work ethics, punctuality, quality, accuracy, manners or professionalism are values held in high regard by some, but not everyone.

The average person cannot afford to purchase all the latest fashions, trends and gadgets or attend pricy events. After basic expenses are covered, whether single or a family, most people are financially limited and cannot indulge in the luxuries of entertainment or non-essential purchases. When one is overly desirous of a specific item, be it clothing, an auto or improving one's living conditions and that desire cannot be met, the result leads to disappointment, unhappiness, stress and at times even depression.

We become disappointed when our expectations, based on what we value, are not met. A job or promotion not offered, a partner not found, an event missed because of financial constraints or a life spent in an undesirable situation, all erode our sense of happiness and personal well-being.

Years ago, I learned a simple and most liberating lesson. It was:

> *Success is not having the best,*
> *but doing the best with what you have.*
> *(Author Unknown)*

One does not require the latest fashions, expensive garments, flashy jewelry, luxurious cars or mega million-dollar homes to enjoy life. Unhappiness occurs when desires and values are disproportionately placed on specific items, creating programs of yearning or obsessing. These belief programs are based on values that are bought into and become killers of happiness. Each time one sees or thinks about these objects, their sense of well-being is instantly attacked. The self-talk recites what one yearns for but does not have, reinforcing a program of failure.

Doing the best with what you have requires reflection and insight into your values and beliefs. We've all heard the expression—money isn't everything—but it is required for the basics of healthy living. A balanced lifestyle requires a balanced financial center and the understanding of fundamental concepts that can improve your financial position. Financial gain can only be achieved through three actions. The first is to increase income; the second is to reduce expenses and the third is to create an awareness of your spending habits through accurate record keeping. An accurate account of your expenses allows you to choose where to modify your spending. Assessing your spending habits will instantly cause you to evaluate what is important to you (your values).

You will be amazed where you can save or eliminate unnecessary spending and enjoy new activities. By managing your finances based on your values, you protect yourself from others influencing how you should live your life or what you should do, be or acquire.

The evaluation process is more effective when discussed with a trusted confident who does not encourage you to spend, and you are prepared to receive objective and constructive criticism. Spending practices are habits that develop based on what you value or are enticed to enjoy. Only by evaluating your values, financial or otherwise, can you create an awareness and begin the cycle of change.

Reassessing what you value can be a liberating experience. As your awareness expands, you will notice other behaviors, habits and actions that consume valuable time and resources or impede your achievements. It is impossible to provide an all-encompassing list of questions; however, Appendix G provides a starting point to explore conflicts in values that you have created or that have been subliminally implanted as your guidance system settings.

We have identified several techniques, processes and constructs that influence our behaviors. An awareness that the mind can be controlled or stimulated is a prerequisite for turning on that mysterious energy. Accessing this energy through mind power is the topic of the next chapter.

To be yourself in a world
that is constantly trying to
make you something else
is the greatest
accomplishment.

Ralph Waldo Emerson (1803-1882)

Chapter 21

The Power Booster

Understanding self-talk and managing it with discipline are remarkable skills. Caution is required, as like all skills, self-talk can be countered and undermined by killers. Mind power is an energy that can be instantly boosted or terminated. Both actions are controlled by your *attitude*.

The influence attitude has on the mind has been recognized and discussed for centuries. It takes only a microsecond for attitude to alter a situation for the better or worse. Attitude is a chosen behavior. As it is applied positively or negatively, a corresponding guidance system setting is established. Because attitude has a profound and immediate effect on situations, it is a popular target of humor in talk shows, movies and cartoons. Yet, it is a foundational building block for personal development and controlling the power of your mind.

Over a hundred years ago, William James (1890), an American philosopher, psychologist and the first educator to offer a course in psychology, stated:

The greatest discovery of my generation is that human beings can alter their lives by altering their attitudes. – William James (1842-1910)

We have learned that choosing not to act is a choice and what is expressed in our self-talk directs our command center to activate emotions that instantly affect our reality. Our power lies in our choices or decisions. We can decide to be happy by choosing positive and encouraging thoughts—or we can choose to rehash negative and discouraging events and feel miserable. Some insist that remaining positive is delusional. We return to the question posed in Chapter 19—why would one choose the attitude of a hypochondriac and remain in a state of feeling miserable when that state is easily altered by modifying one's self-talk? Bad things do happen and require time for us to grieve and adjust but *continuing* to remain miserable taints the present and cannot alter the past. The sooner one moves on, the sooner one notices and enjoys more of what life has to offer. The loss of a loved one is painful, but with time one can enjoy the happy memories that were shared.

Our attitude affects those around us, whether it is at work, home or social gatherings. Attitude sets the tone for current and future interactions. We can all relate to a time when we were excited about an upcoming event, trip, or activity but then were totally deflated by a single comment or a facial expression from another person. The comment may have been one of disapproval, caution about what they perceived to be risky or their own lack of interest in participating. Yet their disapproving facial expressions or tone of voice instantly destroyed the excitement for us.

When we encounter these situations, our solar plexus instantly twinges and redirects our self-talk. Our desire to continue is all but extinguished. The person's negative attitude is a killer that creates emotional discomfort for all those involved. This impact often leaves us silently pondering, Now what? The negative result is entirely caused by the attitude of another person.

Bad Attitude = Lost Opportunities

Attitude is simple to evaluate and adjust and a powerful tool to develop. Simply stated—attitude is your enthusiasm or lack of it. Attitude influences your first response and instantly discloses whether you see opportunity or feel threatened. Noticing opportunity instantly stimulates the imagination, whereas feeling threatened diminishes your mind power according to how you have been conditioned. The threat may not be serious. It could be as insignificant as an irritation at having to listen to a boring explanation or an obligation to attend an activity that is of no interest to you. Your attitude can develop a resistance that causes you to remain close-minded to new opportunities.

Based on your beliefs and amplified by emotional stimulus, attitude is an energy booster or a programmed killer. Attitude triggers self-talk to respond either *positively* or *negatively*. When you encounter a situation that is not compatible with your value system, again, the conflict is identified by a discomfort in your solar plexus. Instantaneously, a quantum leap is created by the thought or belief programmed into your guidance system for that type of situation. The words you express autonomically instruct your command center to source the subconscious mind for a program to initiate a destructive behavior. Your power lies in taking control at this precise moment by intercepting and altering your self-talk. Developing the skill to curb your conditioned responses, rather than jumping to conclusions before acquiring as much information as possible, is self-mastery and mind power in action.

By choosing to remain calm, you may sense that an individual who was normally comfortable with you, has become uncomfortable in your presence. This is your radar or solar plexus informing you that the behavior you chose is working. The vibes emitted from the *new you* cause the other person's solar plexus to recognize that something is different. This is an indicator that your choices and new programs are transforming you into that new you.

How we respond to a situation creates or destroys our sense of well-being. If choosing a calm response to suppress a negative thought process is delusional, then the label of being delusional is misplaced. We choose our responses; therefore, we choose our reality. Every choice or action promotes happiness or stress.

When self-talk is allowed to run freely, it bounces randomly from one fleeting thought to another. It instantly takes control of your command center which can produce devastating results. Gaining control and influencing a situation is easier when you are prepared for an attack. Like the grey elephant, your mind can instantly focus on the negative aspects of comments during conversation, causing you to become irritated or discouraged. Silently initiating a previously prepared phrase or command creates a quantum leap that instantly blocks negative thoughts from controlling your command center. Their comments can no longer trigger your negative emotions.

A positive attitude is maintained when you coach yourself with positive commands or words of encouragement. Influencing and changing the attitudes of others is at best a challenge. We often encounter those who have been conditioned by others or have conditioned themselves to be negative. A polite response to shift their topic of conversation by initiating a quantum leap can be effective, but be prepared as they can choose to ignore your tactic and continue with their negativity.

Attacks on our enthusiasm stem from two sources. The first is an internal attack from our conditioning as expressed in our self-talk. The second is from external sources that include those we interact with, advertising and music and our own observations of what others do differently. The input immediately affects our attitude and continues to reinforce or adjust our guidance system settings.

Attitude killers are everywhere. They subtly or aggressively ambush you. Your subconscious mind is under continuous attack by slogans on coffee mugs, plaques and tee-shirts and by negative comments that are intended to be humorous. Subliminally, they encourage or doom your day under the pretense of humor. A slogan can intercept your thought processes and influence you as swiftly and fatally as the phrase—don't think of a grey elephant. Repetitive exposure to these types of influences develops programs the same way that you acquired your favorite expression or expletive. After a while, you are unconsciously unaware of the influences they have on you. Your attitude and outlook project the input you accepted.

External killers strike without warning. When attacked, you can defend yourself by reciting an assertive phrase like—those are their thoughts, every day and in every way I get better and better. Following a quick assessment of the comment or situation, you will undoubtedly conclude that there is no value in discussing your perspective with those less aware, as it will only frustrate you and waste your time. Negative input is seen and heard in abundance, but there is no reason to accept it as your own.

Having an awareness of people who are usually negative to new ideas or are inclined to offer discouraging comments forewarns you to be prepared. An effective defense is to prepare an approach or response that includes a quantum leap to bypass their expected negative responses. This technique is invaluable for coaching and to retain a positive focus.

Managing your attitude and maintaining enthusiasm requires monitoring your self-talk. The moment that any negativity is identified you can insert an assertive quantum leap similar to—I will succeed. This too shall pass. How will I feel when this is finished? Or a variation of—every day and in every way, I get better and better. Investing the time to prepare positive self-coaching phrases not only develops your mind power, but it builds confidence and peace of mind.

There are days when you may feel that you must slog along until the end of the day and defer relaxing until you are at home. One does not have to wait until the end of the day. Recall how you leaped into action when your friends called unexpectedly. Your attitude and state of being can be instantly adjusted at any time by applying a quantum leap to shift your conscious focus and emotions. Mind power has zero value if it is not applied.

Encouragement is derived by managing your self-talk as it dictates a positive or negative outlook. Waiting for others to encourage you places you at the mercy of others. Your confidence increases when you are the source of your own initiatives. Memorizing several phrases to intercept negative thoughts that surface during the day will provide a more relaxed sense of freedom and independence.

Wisdom is realizing that not all your days can be filled with laughter, but they do not have to be downers. Except in the case of severe loss or a disaster, it is not the situation that makes us feel badly, but how we respond to that situation. When you recognize that you are becoming upset, assess the severity of the situation and ask, *"Is this the hill I want to die on?"* Your perspective is your attitude, and your reality is what you program the law of attraction to deliver.

Appendix H offers exploratory questions to evaluate the effects of your attitude and conditioned responses. As masterful as you may like to think you are, there are other aspects of yourself that undermine or destroy your advantage. There are emotional snipers that lie in wait ready to kill your efforts. Identifying the snipers and defending against them become crucial. This is the topic of the next chapter.

A pessimist sees the difficulty in every opportunity.
An optimist sees the opportunity in every difficulty

Winston Churchill (1874-1965)

Chapter 22

The Snipers

Until we develop a habit of awareness and preparedness, we risk being attacked by snipers that instantly undermine our efforts and personal power. Snipers are your *emotions* and strike without warning. The element of surprise is as lethal as a stealth missile. Emotions are accompanied by self-talk and solar plexus impulses. When negative emotions combine with self-talk, they consume your conscious capacity and destroy your personal power and state of happiness.

Small issues sometimes upset us the most. For example, when you hear or notice something you do not like, instantly, the image or words trigger a conditioned response that expresses negative self-talk. The message conveyed by self-talk instructs the command center to intensify the negative emotions. The emotions cause the negative self-talk to increase until you are revved up into an inner rage. Recognizing this vicious cycle is a point of power. You have total control and can instantly intercept your self-talk. How you respond affects your mood, interactions with those around you and your happiness. At this juncture, you have two options.

You can launch yourself into a tirade and become upset, yell, curse and berate the perceived culprit. Rarely does it resolve the situation. It does, however, build anxiety, stress and negative energy that reduces your mental ability to generate positive solutions. While some may say they are venting, this negative response does not display poise or respect in the presence of others.

Option two involves making a quick assessment and asking your subconscious mind for help by silently asking—what are my options? The situation remains the same but your calm demeanor enables your subconscious mind to offer more constructive options to manage the situation. Is it frustrating? Absolutely. But you won't be as revved up or disappointed and precious energy will not be wasted by an emotional reaction.

Happiness is a choice except when you are dealing with an unexpected death or a tragic situation. Bad news of an accident or illness requires acknowledgement and time to reflect on the incident. During challenging times, introducing positive thoughts enables us to remain strong without ignoring or downplaying the situation. Disappointing issues such as poor health, restricted finances, excess weight or relationship issues can extend over longer periods of time. Each has an emotional effect on one's ability to stay focused on their original goal or their survival.

This does not imply that one should dismiss a situation and move on as if nothing is wrong. Each person requires a different amount of time to grieve or prepare themselves to move forward. The danger lies in not recognizing when self-talk prevents them from moving forward. Options to break this cycle include seeking support and coaching from external sources, listening to positive recordings, meditating, enjoying quiet time, reading or engaging in physical activities. This allows the mind to relax, assess situations and explore various options.

We experience a multitude of emotions. The effects of four are presented to demonstrate how they undermine you. An awareness and discipline to manage your emotions are attainable by applying mind power.

The first and one of the most adept snipers we encounter is *fear*. Fear was introduced in Chapter 11 as a stimulus that can instantly program your subconscious mind and establish guidance system settings. We are conditioned to believe that fear is a negative characteristic. But fear can be your guide when you correctly interpret the message vocalized in your self-talk that was triggered by sensory impulses from your solar plexus.

Fear is any idea, thought, concept or suggestion that generates a negative or uneasy feeling about a current or future event. Some fears, like not playing with fire, are justifiable as they were formed during our childhood when we were warned about this specific danger. While some fears may not appear logical to us, they are real to the individual experiencing them. With repetition, they become guidance system settings that the subconscious mind applies to initiate action or inaction. Unsubstantiated fears confirm that false memories are programs that originate in one's imagination.

It is healthy to have a fear of vehicles when crossing streets or a fear of criminals when passing through a less desirable area of a city or country. Unfortunately, fear is a killer of success when it causes one to doubt and not explore opportunities. Fear is the greatest killer of intuition, or the sixth sense. Common fears include negative thoughts of interacting socially, public speaking or feeling intimidated by one who is perceived to be in a position of authority or high status.

Fear can be induced by your self-image settings. It could be that you do not believe in your idea, or without facts or verification, believe that others think your idea is unworkable, silly or ridiculous. Fears can cause you not to act, or when you do act, demonstrate a lack of confidence. When this occurs, you repeat a pattern of loss and you will not feel relaxed until you give up and return to your old setting or comfort zone. Your efforts are destroyed by the program protection of your existing guidance system settings.

If no action is taken, your self-talk and solar plexus continue with their negative tirade, even when there is no evidence that the consequences you fear could or will occur. The imagination runs rampant until it is out of control and creates an anxiety attack. By applying mind power to assert control over your self-talk, calmness is regained. The effect is the same as calming someone who is distressed over a sudden loss or accident.

The first step in analyzing fear is to determine whether the issue creating your angst or apprehension is valid. It may be your sixth sense protecting you. In Chapter 15, the example introduced was that of a one-foot-wide plank that you initially traversed easily on the ground but later cringed when the plank was placed across a chasm or between two tall buildings. Your solar plexus responded with a sense of fear. Everything you thought, feared or experienced with that example occurred in your imagination. Fears that keep you from succeeding are often unsubstantiated. These fears are a product of your imagination, created by you or by external sources.

What you sensed, thought and experienced demonstrates that you can create a sense of fear where no danger exists. In your imagination, there are no restrictions for doing anything you desire. The thoughts that flow through your imagination are guaranteed to influence and affect your performance as they instantly provide instructions to your command center and override your guidance system settings. Without a doubt, the imagination always wins.

Worrying, fretting and longing are forms of fear that originate in your imagination. The negative thoughts activate negative emotions that cause you to feel threatened, lonely or abandoned. With sniper-like accuracy, they quickly overwhelm your self-talk and instantly transform your reality into a state of unhappiness. These thought processes function the same as a computer program that loops or repeats itself. Your biocomputer is locked in a loop controlled by your imagination. Worrying is a killer that wastes emotional resources and the power of your mind. Extreme energy loss is experienced by those who worry excessively, pine over unrequited love, long for unrealistic lifestyles or crave outcomes that cannot be. To control the power of emotion. .

> ⚓ *Do not invest energy or emotion*
> *in anyone or anything*
> *that does not enrich your well-being.*

The settings on your guidance system are laden with fears that prevent you from achieving or creating a dynamic life. When an exciting idea emerges that invites exploration, fear is the sniper that takes you out and paralyzes you from acting. If there is a possibility that harm will occur (financially, physically or emotionally), your subconscious mind will prompt you *to act*. It will steer you to avoid a situation by implementing a reflex action to minimize your loss or extricate yourself from the situation, according to your knowledge or conditioning.

Fears can prevent you from performing simple and basic actions, like making a phone call, speaking in public, initiating a new venture, applying for a job, asking someone to lunch or exploring a new educational option. Your fears are killers that can decimate new opportunities.

Unsubstantiated fears are created when you focus on what others *might* think, do or say. The truth is that you have no proof that they will act the way you imagine. If you feel that they may respond as you imagine, that is your subconscious mind coaching you to prepare yourself to respond to their comments or behaviors. One of the basic mottos of the Scouts and Girl Guides is—Be Prepared.

There is not one fear that is commonly shared as the greatest fear. Our fears are formed by our experiences, culture, imagination and by what we have been taught and believe to be true. In general, our common fears are—public speaking, heights, deep water, financial problems, health issues, flying and in seventh place, death. The irony is that death is rarely the number one fear. Many people fear other situations more than death itself. You may have heard someone say they would rather die than speak in public or confront a particular person. This must not be uttered in jest as the subconscious mind has no sense of humor and cannot identify right from wrong.

Understanding that fears are real places you in a position of power. Mind power provides the ability to intercept and redirect your thoughts by repeating a silent phrase or affirmation. Instantly, the fear dissipates or becomes manageable. Fear is a sniper and a fierce adversary.

The second sniper is Cupid disguised as the emotion of love. When you have love in your heart but lust on your mind, the strongest stimulus is the desire for *sexual expression*. Whether your attraction to a person is physical or a deep and sincere love, your command center is hijacked in that literal heartbeat. When the feeling of romance or desire for sex escalates, the human mind tends to abandon logic and reality. An innate animalistic drive causes us to see only what we want to see. Advertisers have perfected the art of applying sexual inferences to capture our attention as accurately as a sniper's kill shot.

Cupid has no honor or loyalty and can be mean and deceitful. If Cupid is unable to urge you into making new conquests, he becomes bored and restless. Cupid morphs into an evil sniper and threatens relationships by causing one to respond to urges and be attracted to others who exude or radiate sexual energy, commonly known as chemistry.

Personal relationships are weakened when we ignore advice from our best friend and partner, yet at a subconscious level are charmed and intrigued when a stranger presents the same advice. Cupid impishly prompts individuals to notice more than the advice. This risk increases in relationships when familiarity replaces spark and spontaneity. Indifference creeps in and individuals tend to invest less effort romantically than when they first met. Relationships do not grow, thrive or function on their own. They require constant monitoring, energy, respect and regular maintenance—no different than pets, plants or upgrades to your computer. Unlike a digital computer with a virus protection program, our thoughts are not automatically protected and require monitoring, care and protection.

The third deadly sniper is *anger*. Anger attacks from within and instantly dominates your self-talk, solar plexus and command center. It prevents rational thinking by overloading the capacity of the conscious mind with negative statements.

Each person has a different level of tolerance to withstand attacks on their emotions, values and self-esteem. An awareness of being under attack is a warning to apply mind power and control your self-talk, emotions and responses.

We tend to allow strangers some latitude when they utter hurtful or insensitive statements. Many of us have social graces. To remain polite, we suppress how we would like to respond. However, when we interact with friends and loved ones, we tend to speak more freely. Our familiarity causes us to ignore their feelings enabling us to carelessly lash out with anger, rudeness, silence, avoidance or other negative behaviors—these are the same behaviors we suppress when interacting with strangers.

It is equally important to be prepared when loved ones do not interact or respond respectfully. Their harsh or emotional response may have been triggered by our words. Their perceptions and conditioning instantaneously cause their biocomputer to process a defense. Not knowing how they perceived our input places us at a major disadvantage. To compound the situation, we react negatively to their response. As described in Chapters 7 and 9, many conflicts are not created by what we say, but how we say it. An immunity card does not exist. Self-reflection is valuable for identifying if our words and manner of presentation were antagonistic. An impasse may develop, unless one of the parties applies their mind power to introduce a constructive response that diffuses and prevents the situation from escalating.

Mind power is not always used for the good of all. There are those who intentionally choose evil behaviors. Occasionally, we encounter people who thrive on agitating others by uttering inflammatory or inappropriate comments or disrespectfully prying into private affairs. They appear to enjoy expressing or implying disrespectful comments about your person, property or choices as it boosts their sense of superiority. Often, they engage in a passive-aggressive approach and when confronted, reply with an insincere smile that they were only joking. Like bullies, they avoid direct dealing and their offhand comments are often made sarcastically in public, confident that few people would dare to make a scene by challenging their arrogant and rude behavior. They strut with a sense of superiority, unaware that others consider their behavior to be rude and offensive.

Others are simply unenlightened and are unconsciously unaware that they unnecessarily provoke others. Their provocations include subtle insults, condescending comments, sneers and facial expressions that imply disapproval. Whether their attacks are intentional or not, their words and body language instantaneously trigger our emotions, causing our killers and snipers to take over.

Managing these frustrating situations requires two skills. The first is to recognize their behaviors as acts of their evil natures. The second is to have a prepared response to extricate yourself or others from their attacks and presence.

The fourth and last sniper is the emotion of *hate*. Hate ranges from a casual dislike to an intense loathing. Hate is a belief that is nurtured and grows like a malignant tumor. Love, romance or chemistry are naturally intrinsic sensations felt by those who are experiencing them, whereas hate emanates from an unpleasant experience or observation, or is taught or encouraged by others. Individuals must take ownership of this killer once they incorporate it as part of their beliefs and values. If you feel hateful, it is strictly and totally your emotion.

Hate is an internal anger. It surges from the solar plexus and overwhelms the self-talk. The conscious capacity of the mind is consumed and leaves one unable to evaluate a situation objectively. Fortunately, hate can be instantly suppressed by intercepting self-talk with a constructive command or pleasant affirmation.

Snipers attack mentally and emotionally. When fear, anger or hate triggers a negative response, your self-talk erupts and instantly instructs the command center to activate negative emotions. Although love is perceived as a strong and positive emotion, love can also negatively inflame the emotions of fear, hate and anger in the form of jealousy. An internal rage increases until you consciously take control or someone intervenes and calms you down. The moment you become aware of an emotional rage, your self-talk will simultaneously disclose the belief, value or threat that is causing the reaction. Although it is necessary to listen for that subtle response and take control, it is difficult to be rational when you are emotionally upset.

When you return to being calm, it is important to evaluate the dynamics that occurred and prepare a phrase or command that will enable you to control your self-talk in the future. The command may be to simply take a deep breath, listen, respond more slowly or in a lower tone, excuse yourself or suggest that the matter be deferred until you have had more time to think about the situation. Later, it may be beneficial to offer a sincere apology for your previous response.

Your point of power is the awareness of the internal dynamics that are occurring within you or that you detect in others. Control is achieved by quickly applying previously prepared commands to intercept the barrage of negative words and neutralize the intensity of your emotions. This action is the reverse of psyching yourself up for an event. By initiating calm and constructive statements, the net effect is that you are able to psych yourself or others *down*.

Developing an awareness of situations that trigger negative behaviors is a powerful step toward self-mastery. After several attempts and repeated successes, a new habit or guidance system setting forms for dealing with negative issues. Will you ever lose your cool again? Probably. When this occurs, review what transpired to ascertain whether anything was different or added to the dynamics. If not, avoid dwelling on the conflict and focus on ways to respond more constructively next time.

After you take that decisive step to improve your circumstances, expect constant attacks from internal and external snipers. Externally, those who were conditioned to your past behaviors may find your new behaviors threatening and could respond with negative comments. Internally, your self-talk may be attacked by killers protecting old programs and calling upon your emotions (snipers) for reinforcement. Your subconscious mind is likely to remain a traitor and launch attacks if you fail to develop guidance system settings that complement your new desires, goals and behaviors.

You can begin to develop strong countermeasures to prevent snipers and killers from attacking by analyzing your responses to the questions provided in Appendix I.

Undeniably, our emotions are triggered by our thoughts and by external entities and objects. External influences take the form of powerful hackers, hijackers and programmers that employ the techniques described in this book to attack your self-talk, solar plexus and emotions to influence your internal guidance system. In the next chapter you will discover how external entities control you and aggressively position themselves to retain that control.

Close scrutiny will show that most crisis situations are opportunities to either advance, or stay where you are.

Maxwell Maltz (1889-1975)

Chapter 23

External Killers

By now, you should be feeling confident to take control when overwhelming thoughts and feelings rage in your self-talk and solar plexus. But you can never let your guard down until you have developed a habit of being aware of what is occurring around you. When everything appears to be under control, killers appear in disguise, not just in your mind but in the environments through which you pass. The danger is rarely recognized because you have become unconsciously unaware of the killers that hide in plain sight within your environment. They are external killers that instantly hack your biocomputer. The first defense against external killers is awareness.

You came into this world unable to walk, talk, care for yourself or know the rules for living. You required constant guidance and programming until you became an independent adult. Guidance was provided by your parents, caregivers, teachers and friends, and through social interactions and your own observations. Programming input continued until you reached an age of independence, or so you thought. Armed with your conditioning, you ventured into the world to begin an exciting life. The possibilities seemed endless.

One day you realize that your life is not progressing as you thought it would. In addition, you have silent longings, the origins of which you do not understand—you wonder why they remain unfulfilled. Each time these longings emerge, so does the confusion about your past and what awaits you in the future. You begin to realize that many of your conflicts are the result of the ideas you bought into that were instilled by others.

As you strive to be *you*, you discover that choices you made did not originate from the *you* that you feel you are. It is as if you left your biocomputer portal open and hackers entered and sabotaged or manipulated your guidance system. The sad truth is—that is what actually happened.

History confirms that what evolves in cultures, whether good or bad, eventually becomes the accepted norm. The amount of input our subconscious mind continuously receives is staggering. In the fast-paced environment that we live in, the deluge of program input increases daily. The movies, videos, TV shows, blogs and social media that we follow set new constructs that we accept as new norms.

Younger generations are becoming desensitized by constant exposure to violent video games, bullying, crime, gang related movies and hatred on video clips, to name just a few. When platforms breed defiance and disrespect for others, they become a norm—for their viewers. We cannot refute that external programming significantly influences us. The recent banning of President Donald Trump from Facebook and Twitter demonstrates that even the mega networks acknowledge this influence and their responsibility to help control it.

Technical advancements in the 21st century have created a dependency on social media. The sophistication of social media has developed beyond our common awareness and tracks patterns of our communications, behaviors and interests. This advancement places us at the mercy of large tech corporations and advertising sleuths that track our every move and control us by attacking us on a subliminal level. They count on their subscribers falling for the clickbait that they believe to be true. Whether the information is fictitious or exaggerated, we are magnetically drawn by our curiosity to explore, follow, purchase or participate in ways they suggest.

The world of retail and commerce focuses on constantly changing your values and beliefs. It would be naïve to think that marketers and advertisers seriously focus on the pleasures or benefits that their products or services provide you. Through their understanding of human behavior, they can intercept your command center, causing you to act and purchase their products or services. They generate an aura of pleasure and excitement and bombard your senses through advertising. They achieve this by subtle deception and repetition to ensure their messages are received and embedded.

In the 1920's, Edward Bernays (1891-1995), a Master of Public Relations, became an expert in propaganda and manipulation of the human mind. Interestingly, he was a nephew of Sigmund Freud. Bernays realized and presented how the weaknesses in human behavior can be exploited for financial gain. Bernays was the mastermind behind promoting smoking as being stylish for women. He described the general public as having a herd mentality and lacking the mental faculties required to stand alone. Advertising campaigns that influenced millions became his legacy. A hundred years later, it is nearly impossible to escape or avoid advertising.

Advertisers are aware that they are powerless over free thinkers and instead focus on influencing the masses. Self-mastery requires careful reflection on what influences you and the courage and strength to stand alone and make independent choices. The power and the magnetic draw that hold you back from being different can be overwhelming. Your conditioning produces a sensation of angst felt in your solar plexus at the mere thought of doing anything that doesn't conform to the accepted activities that are occurring in your environment.

In our modern-day society, individuality is promoted through fashion, design, products and activities. But when we step back and observe what is actually happening and evaluate the responses of the masses, we recognize that people are not expressing their individuality at all. Instead, they are blindly following the latest and greatest fads and trends as they become copycats and followers, with a herd mentality no different than sheep or lemmings.

It is critical to realize that advertising is the most blatant form of brainwashing or external programming. Advertising is aimed to attack the core of the individual. Advertisers use every stimulus possible to develop programs in our subconscious minds that cause us to purchase a product or service immediately or in the future. The attacks are directed at our self-image, beliefs and values—to look good, fit-in and be accepted. It is common for promoters to apply advertising tactics that subliminally attack your self-worth with messages implying that if you do not aspire to fit-in, you're a loser.

To demonstrate the power of advertising, one has only to consider the NFL's Super Bowl game. It is an annual event that audiences the world over watch, just to see the advertisements. Although the Covid-19 pandemic of 2020-21 affected the event, the cost of advertising has increased from approximately forty thousand dollars for a 30 second commercial in the mid-1960's to more than five million dollars in 2021. Advertising is mega business.

In the same manner that you thought of the grey elephant or a goose in the bottle, advertisers understand that they can influence enough purchasers in fifteen to thirty seconds, through well-chosen words, sounds and images, to justify the cost of advertising. It is a guaranteed investment. They effectively target your emotions and desires. They are predators and you are their prey.

We cannot escape advertising. Advertising is everywhere and attacks all our senses. Wherever we go, whatever we search on the internet, we constantly hear or see advertisements. The messages are positioned strategically to catch our attention and stimulate sensations in the solar plexus, adding emotional reinforcement to a new or existing belief. This is not a random coincidence. They are well-trained assassins whose only mission is to attack and manipulate your value system.

The effectiveness of advertising is frightening. For decades, advertisers have perfected their methods, applying techniques to attack your biocomputer, identical to those described in this book. They continually introduce new approaches to profit from the weaknesses of human behaviors. Few recognize that advertising is a programming/conditioning process to establish or modify our beliefs and values.

The danger is first created by the vulnerability of our biocomputer. We subliminally accept the messages and can only reject them if we perform a conscious action. The audible component of advertising is accepted as background noise and the visual effects are casually observed in passing. Unfortunately, as you learned, our subconscious mind records all that we hear, observe and sense. How or where else could you acquire that annoying commercial tune that you autonomically hum?

To combat the attacks from promoters and advertisers, I respond with the same phrase that I use to combat negative input or unacceptable behaviors—those are their thoughts. I enjoy being me.

No one is aware of what is going on in my head. This phrase provides a defense against peer pressure and blindly following trends or suggestive social expectations. Blind acceptance, without considering the consequences, forfeits your freedom of choice. I am not saying that I do not benefit from advertising that contributes to my values and goals. It is necessary for most businesses to advertise to connect with their customers and for consumers to locate products and services. What I warn against are the subtle subliminal approaches that imply what your goals or values *should be.*

As mentioned earlier, the fashion industry is a formidable mind programmer that skillfully manipulates the masses. It survives by constantly changing trends with skillful and refined techniques to ensure a steady stream of customers. This is achieved by taking advantage of the unsuspecting and less confident and programming them to be followers. By focusing on the compelling desire to be in style, hip and fashionable, advertisers prey on their customers' insecurities and fears of being left out, a loser or not stylish. The irony is that while fashionistas believe they are expressing their uniqueness and their individuality, in the end, they all look the same by wearing the same style of garments. Not only do they look the same, but many express how ugly or uncomfortable the styles are but wear them anyway. If people had confidence and purchased only what they liked and what suited them, the fashion industry would suffer a catastrophic financial loss.

Regrettably, conformity is a major trap. Individuals allow themselves to be conditioned rather than develop their real identity and individuality. It is surprising how few assess the dangers of becoming a follower or even notice when they have become one.

In late 2018, The Payless Experiment demonstrated how people are gullible and easily influenced. The experiment involved a popular discount shoe retailer opening a pop-up store that presented itself as a high-end, high-fashion shoe outlet. They offered discount shoes that normally sold for under fifty dollars for over $500. Within a few hours the pop-up store was overwhelmed by purchasers who believed they were acquiring high-fashion and value at the exorbitantly high prices. Each customer was later informed of the experiment, their money was refunded and they were allowed to keep the shoes. The organizers of the experiment set out to discover whether people could be influenced by the illusions of high-fashion and status. Their conclusion was that people could indeed be easily duped.

The experiment is not presented to discourage or judge your desire to dress fashionably and feel good. The intent is to have you recognize the effect and the power of promotions and advertising. In the Payless Experiment, the lure was the compelling need to stay current with high-fashion. The danger occurs when you are unconsciously led to believe that a product is valuable by someone else's standards and that you need to act or purchase it immediately. It is critical to maintain an awareness of how external sources can cause you to surrender your independence, individuality and free choice.

The examples of not thinking about a grey elephant or removing the goose from the bottle demonstrate the speed and simplicity by which an external source or entity can seed an idea or message in your subconscious mind. Repetitive external input reinforces beliefs and the acceptance of ideas, whether they are beneficial to you or not.

When watching TV or web browsing, we are often bombarded by the same advertisement multiple times. The power of repetition is applied to condition and program you to become a customer or follower. Studies have shown that for a message to be remembered, a person must be exposed to it at least seven times before they remember it or are conditioned to take action. Any repetition becomes an unconscious process of autosuggestion as described in Chapter 12. To guard against becoming a follower, you must protect yourself.

External programming is not restricted to fashion or marketing of products and services. It also includes interactions with family, friends, co-workers, organizations and religious groups as well as exposure to movies, events and activities. All ideas or input become instantly recorded memories that remain in your subconscious mind. With repetition, they evolve into guidance system settings.

Guarding against external programming is the warning provided on page 152. Repeatedly reciting phrases and slogans or pledging a commitment to a work campaign for any group or organization is a conditioning process that places the priorities of the group or cause above your own. In dictator-controlled countries, this is performed at relearning and rethinking camps or facilities where brainwashing and political ideals are repeated until the subject is compliant or subservient to the powers that be.

In fashion, business, cults and religious settings, repetition ranges from the enticements of success, style and glamour to attacks of being unworthy, a sinner, a loser, not with the in-crowd or a loner. Your self-image and beliefs are altered through emotional stimuli and repetition. Sometimes the process is obvious. At other times, it is subtle and carefully presented as you agree and excitedly defend the process of your entrapment.

Each time you attend a gathering, be it for political, environmental, religious, sales or work related reasons, your subconscious mind is subliminally being conditioned. Unethical presenters humorously make comments that are berating or soul-destroying as a form of control to guilt or bully you into accepting their belief system and structure. If you surrender and do not exercise your freedom of choice, decisions are made for you. Caution demands that you question why you are accepting their decision about what you should do or be, and ask yourself—is this what I truly desire?

In addition to advertising and personal interactions, there are multiple forms of passive external input. The subconscious mind absorbs data through stimuli, whether you are at work, home, on the street or in a store. Your senses are stimulated by billboards, music, desk signs, plaques, bumper stickers and as mentioned earlier, even your coffee mug. Wherever you are, an evaluation and awareness of external input should require you to constantly question—how am I being influenced (programmed)?

As you observed in Chapter 8, music is a powerful stimulus. Music is a primary component of commercials, exercise classes and training processes. Historical documentaries reveal that indoctrination of young Nazi recruits was conducted with music. This technique continues to be used for military training around the world. Background music, or music streamed through earbuds, conditions the listener at a subliminal level. The lyrics may be upbeat and positive or may promote violence, limitations, loss of love or a variety of negative life situations. Lyrics that express yearning, loss, loneliness or misery negatively influence and reinforce your belief system, self-image and your law of attraction. Through repetition, the lyrics can program a setting of co-dependency, slowly eroding your confidence and independence. External input and internal repetition bypass our conscious awareness and are fast-tracked through the command center to the subconscious mind.

The effect of slogans can be demonstrated by your morning routine. When a burst of energy is required to begin your day, you reach for your coffee mug. Your subconscious mind instantaneously scans the slogan, and as an external source of programming, it reinforces your conditioning. What is written on the mug? What kind of day are you going to have? The message that is visible is instantly conveyed to your subconscious mind and your mood and outlook are adjusted accordingly. Is the message motivating or is it demeaning or discouraging under the guise of humor? To the subconscious mind, all input is recorded as true.

Quotations meant to be helpful often generate damaging or misleading messages at a subliminal level. If you search the internet for quotes and evaluate what the words imply, you will be appalled by the number of negative quotations that are presented to adjust one's perspective to accepting the misery they are experiencing. Before accepting or adopting a quote, carefully review the wording to determine whether the message motivates you to alter your current situation to make it better or whether it advocates accepting your misery or disappointment as normal. Remember—what you put up with, you end up with. Quotations are powerful affirmations that establish subliminal program settings that can be detrimental to your mental well-being.

To provide an example of how external killers attack, think back to when you were doing your best to cut back on unhealthy foods. As you passed through a mall or grocery store, you noticed flashy displays for ice-cream and junk food, accentuated by colorful packaging depicting slim, svelte, physically fit and sexually attractive models endorsing the product. It required intense effort and focus to maintain your discipline. Advertisers utilize multiple stimuli to attack your command center as it ensures their message is implanted into your subconscious mind to succumb now or later.

Powerful sources of external programming or conditioning are friends and trends on social media. As children become young adults, the influence and power of friends is often stronger than family. Peer pressure among friends is an emotional stimulus that conditions one to accept ideas, concepts, trends and activities, either freely or under duress. A psychological and emotional desire to be accepted coerces one to respond overenthusiastically with flattery or dishonesty to demonstrate one's agreement and commitment.

When accompanied by friends in an emotionally charged setting and stimulated by alcohol or drugs at concerts, dance clubs and parties, one's data banks and subconscious mind are constantly programmed by the stimulation of surrounding sounds, ideas and observable activities. The desire to be accepted or fit-in is a powerful emotional stimulus. When combined with the stimulus of music, a herd mentality is easily established.

The advice we receive from our best friend, strangers and colleagues requires one to consciously evaluate the input to prevent the subconscious mind from accepting everything as true. Gullibility has no limits. From the time of ancient Greece, wisdom included knowing the importance of questioning all things—not to be a cynic, but to clarify, learn and understand.

As you explore and identify the real you, it is common to discover that friends and family are not necessarily the be-all and end-all of your happiness. To know and be content with whom you are not only provides a strong sense of confidence, but is pivotal for influencing the law of attraction. When you discover that you are your own best friend, you will also discover much peace and contentment and look forward to time by yourself, free from external influences.

Friendliness has its traps, especially when you are feeling down or lonely. A new friend may be a user whose friendliness is a ploy to lower your guard. Their only purpose for being friendly may be to extract as much information as possible or have you pick up the tab as they move on and leave you feeling used. These types are skilled at making you feel that they like you when in fact they are disarming you. These killers use you and lose you. They have perfected the skill of schmoozing and can hack into your biocomputer using charm in devious ways. Others are more direct and pry to the point of being rude. These friends seek you out, not for the sincerity of genuine friendship, but for the information or benefits they acquire by interacting with you.

External sources influence and control people by attacking their vulnerabilities. Some of the meanest and cruelest forms of external motivation and influence are often created by family members and those closest to us. Thankfully, not all families function in this manner, but negative environments do exist. The pecking order and control exercised by parents, siblings and relatives are maintained through guilt or judgmental comments that create an illusion that they are superior or know better. The survival of their egos requires them to attack and suppress your positive qualities and achievements to ensure theirs remain superior. They maintain control through personal attacks, put-downs, chastising and sibling rivalry. Cruel and damaging programming is delivered in divorce situations when one parent expresses accusations or innuendoes about the other parent to the children. Their young developing minds are more receptive to input from those in a position of trust, particularly a parent. The facts may never be verified and the children grow up believing the situations are true. These are vicious forms of manipulation and brainwashing.

The tipping point that often destroys family dynamics does not evolve by honest, sincere or insightful discussions but by unexpected conflicts and negative encounters. When the pressure and frustration of family dynamics exceed an individual's tolerance level, an emotional breaking point triggers an explosive or silent termination of the relationship. It can be a liberating feeling and the relationship may never be restored. Assessing your values provides the option to choose if the criticisms received or the expectations to be subservient are worth the price of your happiness and peace of mind. Developing mind power builds confidence and distances you from external killers that destroy your quality of life. It cannot be disputed—*what you put up with, you end up with.*

In a Utopian world, one would be free to express opinions and needs and still be respected by others. Our societies are not Utopian. Many are driven by greed or the arrogance to demand control and employ bullying and intimidation to coerce others into agreement. Occasionally, a defense is required that carries a significant impact to ensure one's position is not dismissed. Encouraging physical violence *is not* the message. However, it is beneficial to develop confidence and presentation skills to address aggressive individuals in a manner that is constructive rather than confrontational. Before initiating action, it is prudent to assess the various outcomes and be prepared for the consequences. In these situations, the loss of their friendship or association may be a benefit in disguise.

When a killer within cannot directly alter your actions, it distracts you by shifting your focus onto objects within your immediate environment. For anyone studying, working from home or operating a home based business, distractions are a constant hazard. Taking a break can lead to disaster as killers wait in ambush. As you enter another room, killers are processing options within your traitor subconscious mind and cause your eye to notice an item or a magazine out of place. As you pick it up you begin to read or you notice a smudge that requires a quick wipe, followed by another. Soon you are reading or into another project but you are no longer performing your work, studies or attending to your home-based business or your original task. Our environment is a minefield of external killers waiting to undermine the achievement of our goals.

I had the good fortune to attend a seminar on productivity. The speaker encouraged us to develop a habit of regularly discarding items that are no longer of value as they tend to distract and interfere with activities. If one wants to maintain a clear and organized mind, free of distractions, one requires a clear and organized physical environment. I decided that to declutter my environment, my New Year's resolution would include recycling, discarding or disposing of one item each day for the first 100 days of the year. The item could be an envelope, a magazine, an article of clothing or a redundant object in my home, garage, office or briefcase. The process became effective and enjoyable, not just at the beginning of the year, but whenever the urge occurred throughout the year.

Sometimes I went on a rampage and threw out multiple items; and yes, I am guilty of discarding items that were around for years only to find that they were required days or weeks after they were discarded. The new habit was easily transferrable to other areas of my life. If a social event or activity was no longer enjoyable or of benefit, I discontinued it from my life and routine and replaced it with an enjoyable activity.

It is difficult to be happy if our conscious and subconscious minds and command center are constantly under attack by pictures, influential words, romantic implications or images that represent a lifestyle that isn't ours. Completing the exercises on pages 39-44 allows you to focus on activities that enhance your happiness and live the life you desire.

Confidence and self-mastery are based on your ability to stand alone and make decisions based on what you desire, regardless of the distractions or rejections from others. Mind power builds internal strength to effortlessly deflect negative influences. The exploratory questions in Appendix J provide a format to identify external distractions that killers use to prevent you from achieving your goals and being your true self.

As time passes, there will be moments when you feel that you are not progressing but repeating old mistakes. This is a result of missing the clues that the subconscious mind provides. These clues are habits or conditioned cycles that are often overlooked. There are additional cycles that we cannot change but are beneficial when we incorporate them into our daily lives. This is the topic of the next chapter.

Chapter 24

Why Is This Happening Again?

There will be times when you believe that you applied every technique in this book, dealt with all the unpleasant tasks and felt you were clearly focused on your goal, but still find that you are repeatedly running into the same obstacles and are not progressing. You are correct. Your biocomputer executed old commands or guidance system settings rather than new commands. This is referred to as looping or cycling in computer lingo. One line of code loops back to the beginning of a sequence and executes the same process. We are computers and function the same way.

Your biocomputer constantly informs you through your self-talk and solar plexus when it is looping or about to repeat a conditioned behavior. Although your biocomputer or subconscious mind is providing feedback, you may have become complacent or immune to the messages.

The universe, with all its components and entities, operates on *cycles* – the weather, seasons, wildlife migrations and life in general. As a subset of the universe, we function and operate on conditioned cycles as well as natural cycles that are intrinsic to the functioning of our minds and bodies. Initiating change requires an awareness of when you function best and how to capitalize on your cycles.

Studies conducted on people identified as achievers have shown that those who succeed are not always the smartest, most ambitious or the cleverest people. Many people who are deemed brilliant or show the highest potential fail to achieve much in life. Those who succeed do so because they are aware of their abilities and repetitive behaviors and use that awareness to guide, coach and manage themselves.

There are three cycles that significantly affect us and are easy to identify. We have an internal biological clock that influences our abilities physically, emotionally and intellectually. Early 6th century BCE Greek philosophers emphasized discipline and were guided by the laws of self-mastery. Inscribed above the entrance of the Temple of Apollo in Delphi were the words—Know Thyself. Although the temple was destroyed by an earthquake in 375 BCE, the truth of the message remains valid. Self-mastery requires knowing oneself.

We have a physical cycle that determines our level of energy. This is the physical energy that provides stamina and powers the biomechanical motions of our body. Regardless of how extensive or short our To-Do list is, or how urgently the tasks must be completed, we may feel like we do not have enough energy and are simply burned out. There are days when we have sufficient sleep but still feel tired or lethargic. And there are days when we are energetic, socialize multiple evenings in a row and function with marginal amounts of sleep. Our high and low energy levels parallel our physical cycle.

Our intellectual cycle influences our cognitive abilities to think logically and imaginatively. When we attempt to perform a task that we've recently learned, it's common to struggle with how to begin and ask for instructions to be repeated. Yet the moment we hear the beginning of the instructions, our biocomputer instantly responds— oh yeah! I know how, and we are back on task. This would indicate one is on the higher side of their intellectual cycle. At other times, a person will provide an explanation and we remain bewildered, with no clue about what to do. They may explain it again and we still don't understand the explanation or the process. If the explanation is not too complex, it indicates that we are at a low point in our intellectual cycle. The fluctuations in our intellectual abilities are similar to the highs and lows that we experience in our physical energy.

The third cycle is our emotional state which influences the degree to which we can become excited or discouraged. Emotional energy is a supporting component of the stimuli described in previous chapters. There are times when we are enthusiastic, times when we could care less and times when we get upset about the most trivial of issues. On occasion, situations that have upset us in the past do not rattle us now and we continue as if they are no longer a concern. Your emotional cycle also influences your behaviors and has a significant impact on how your day progresses.

From a scientific perspective, in the late 1880's, Wilhelm Fliess (1858-1928) devised the theory of biorhythms. His theory was formulated on the belief that from birth, the human body cycles regularly through a 23-day physical cycle, a 28-day emotional cycle and a 33-day intellectual cycle. He described each cycle as oscillating between a high point and a low point. The three cycles—physical, emotional and intellectual—were referred to as biorhythms. This theory has since been validated.

There are individuals in the field of science who dismiss the effects of biorhythms and only acknowledge them as a phenomenon. Regardless of the naysayers, transportation companies, police services and airlines in Switzerland, Japan and North America consider biorhythm cycles significant and use charts to reduce accidents and increase the safety of their operations. As one who has coached hundreds who have been able to relate to these high and low cycles, I have concluded that the supporting evidence outweighs the doubts of the naysayers.

Our biorhythms are real but intangible and can be temporarily altered or influenced by mind power. The example in Chapter 5 of being re-energized when friends unexpectedly called, proves that the power of your words, or influence from an external source, can override the psyche and provide a surge of physical energy. You can enhance your personal skills and performance by understanding the effects of biorhythms, thereby coordinating your planning to best utilize the power of your natural cycles.

The physical cycle refers to physical energy. Beginning at birth, the cycle repeats every 23 days. At the top of your cycle, you feel energetic and at the lower end of the cycle you feel lethargic or less interested in performing physical activities.

The emotional cycle has a range of 28 days. This corresponds to becoming easily excited and emotionally positive at the higher range of the cycle and less so at the lower range of the cycle. Women are generally more in tune with their emotional cycles as they often match their menstrual cycles. Recent studies indicate that men have the same emotional cycles but are less in sync with their emotions.

The intellectual cycle is calculated over 33 days. At the higher range of the cycle, one grasps ideas and processes information quickly and easily. At the lower range of the cycle, problem solving and processing instructions may feel like a challenge.

The mid-point for each cycle is deemed a critical point and your behaviors could fluctuate between high or low, creating unpredictable outcomes. Understanding why you react or respond to situations assists in making better choices.

Developing an awareness of our cycles is invaluable when working with others or in personal relationships. It is likely that at any given time we will be at a different point in our cycle than the person with whom we are interacting. This may explain why people respond more quickly or slowly when assessing situations.

The validity of biorhythms is undermined when newspapers or information outlets include biorhythm or biodex charts along with horoscopes. When a biorhythm is published and linked to the month of birth, simple math identifies a critical error. For example, the physical cycle of 23 days has two highs or lows in the same month. For a person with a birth date on the 10th of the month and another born in the same month and year but on the 21st day, their cycles could not possibly match and the information is inaccurate. For some it could be right on, but as 19th century Austrian writer Baroness Marie von Ebner-Eschenbach wrote, *a broken clock is correct twice a day.* External input requires constant verification and validation.

Numerous computer programs and apps are available that offer biorhythm calculations. A dependable app is often simple to locate and free to download. An app is not only beneficial to you, but it is also helpful when interacting with others—providing that you know the person's exact birth date. When interactions involve several people, it is impractical to identify the cycle of each person. Focusing on your performance and conditioning remains your best option. In your interactions with others, your solar plexus is a valuable assistant for identifying subliminal messages and sensing the vibes of others.

In the world of electronics, software developers are constantly looking to build a better app with jazzy and enticing new features. New to the market are biorhythm apps that, in addition to the physical, emotional and intellectual components, include intuitive and spiritual cycles. As stated earlier, computer geeks seem determined to develop an electronic app for every conceivable aspect of our lives. Although we benefit significantly from the world of electronic conveniences, our spirituality is one aspect of ourselves that cannot be digitized. Spirituality is an internal growth process that leads one to personal freedom and a sense of well-being. If one equates spirituality to their belief in a deity, it is difficult to think that their belief or faith (spirituality) is stronger when at a higher point of the cycle but weaker when they are at a lower point of the cycle. An electronic device that tracks one's spirituality is one gigantic quantum leap that cannot be supported in this presentation.

The physical, emotional and intellectual cycles provide useful foresight. If you are aware that you are feeling physically low or are heading into a physical low cycle, it is better to avoid committing to projects or activities that require high levels of energy. Plan or commit to a time that would be best for you. For activities not in your control, it is advantageous to assess your energy levels in advance and be better prepared. Your personal power and confidence increase when you are prepared and rested.

If it is a long or extended project, a few early nights and sleep will prove to be a good solution. During the activity, self-coaching and occasional power naps can provide short-term energy boosters. These techniques trick the mind into providing a short-term boost of energy, but the physical body still requires sleep for total rejuvenation. When one is deprived of sleep, irrational behaviors, including suicidal thoughts, are common. Sleep deprivation continues to be a form of torture practiced in some countries.

Biorhythms provide critical information for personal relationships. Relationships often fail because of physical incompatibility. Physical compatibility is more likely when the physical cycles of both individuals are similar. Taking the time to explore your cycles early in a relationship can foretell future conflicts and benefits.

Expanding on the earlier newspaper example of two people born in the same year and month, but one on the 10th of the month and the other around the 21st of the month, it is apparent that they have physical cycles that peak eleven days apart. If they were a couple, it would indicate that on the 23-day physical cycle, one partner would be highly physical and energetic while the other is at their lowest. The energy required to be physically compatible in sports or social activities, and especially physical intimacy, would likely become a constant conflict. Short-term physical attractions often generate a chemistry that obscures the lack of compatibility that would make long-term relationships difficult.

Contrary to physical compatibility, differences in emotional and intellectual cycles are often beneficial in personal relationships. A caveat should be added—providing that the two individuals are reasonable and possess a strong desire to work together. When two people have different cycles emotionally and intellectually, their differences can complement each other. When one is on an intellectual low, their partner is in a better position to offer input, solutions, warnings, solve problems or notice opportunities that the other could miss. Conflict and bad decisions can occur when two individuals share high emotional cycles or when both are at a low or volatile point.

There will be days when you feel that you are not keeping pace with others and they are performing better at tasks, solving problems or understanding concepts. An awareness of these situations creates an opportunity to be better prepared or take time off to recharge your system. Effective coaches and managers develop an awareness of when each team member's performance is not optimal and plan accordingly.

Biorhythms are an intrinsic human characteristic but there are other cycles that affect us. They are conditioned behaviors and circumstances that we created through repetition and became programs (habits) or guidance system settings.

These cycles are identified by listening to our self-talk or what others say when we hear phrases like, "every time I...; every time he or she...; it always happens when...". The use of absolutes, like every time, always, never or all, are words that reveal a repeating situation or behavior that creates frustration or conflict for you or the person making the statement. By listening to what you or others say, you can modify your behaviors to effectively accommodate or navigate these situations. Counteracting potential conflict requires awareness and conscious action by you.

Utilizing the techniques presented in this book can prepare you for tasks, challenges and potential confrontations. To maximize your performance, it is imperative that you:

1. Realize that the energy levels and the attitudes of those you are interacting with are different—physically, emotionally and intellectually.

2. Be prepared to compensate for those who may not perform to your expectations. It is efficient to plan, but it is equally important not to over-plan or set unreasonable deadlines.

3. Ensure regular time off to recoup and re-energize yourself. Be mindful of your diet, exercise and rest patterns. It is unrealistic to think that you can continuously operate at peak efficiency without rest and relaxation. During times of low energy or enthusiasm, relax and reflect on what will be required when you return to action.

Developing habits, skills or program settings requires time. A desire to give up or quit is a killer program that creates agony or discomfort. It discourages you and causes you to return to where or what you were. The agony begins gradually and intensifies as you get closer to overpowering the killer. On low cycles, you are more easily discouraged and the desire to give up is more difficult to counteract. An awareness of what you are experiencing is a point of power. It is the time to push on as success is within reach. The power of your words to coach and encourage yourself is your only chance of breaking the old and restrictive cycle.

Often, new diets, exercise or training programs recommend remaining diligent for 21 days, 28 days or 35 days. These numbers may seem arbitrary but they correspond directly to the cycles of your biorhythms. If you identify a conflict between how you feel and what you mentally express, recognize it as a point of power. Any conflict or discomfort is an old program fighting to discourage you from advancing toward a new goal. All barriers or programs are emotionally, physically and/or intellectually connected in the subconscious mind. By maintaining new efforts for a minimum of 33 to 35 days, you will have transcended the highs and lows of each cycle of your biorhythms. After 35 days, your chosen actions will be easier and enjoyable to perform but you cannot ever let your guard down. Old habits are snipers or zombies waiting to regain control.

Appendix K provides additional self-coaching questions to explore your cycles and repetitive behaviors. Identifying your cycles can be simple and straight forward, providing you listen to and evaluate all the feedback that you receive—both internally and externally. What you do with the feedback is your choice, but remember, choosing not to act is a choice.

The previous chapters presented multiple techniques and processes that will enable you to fulfill your desires and overcome challenges by applying mind power. Knowing these skills does not guarantee success unless one understands one common cause of failure. This is the focus of the next chapter.

Chapter 25

The Main Cause of Failure

This chapter encourages you to act. It provides a powerful process to channel your energy and mind power to resolve issues and achieve your goals. It is another point of power. If you do not act, the killers within will hold you hostage. You are the only one who can act and escape their power. You have the power (technique) to overcome your killers.

By applying only one or two of the techniques presented throughout this book, astonishing results can be achieved. All the issues that you identified do not have to be addressed at once. It is the introduction of one small, but well thought out modification, that can alter your life for the better (Page 64).

Many attend motivational seminars, read inspirational self-help books and become overly enthusiastic. They feel they have the knowledge and their lives will change. Sadly, in three to six weeks they are back on their treadmill of life. Knowledge is of no value if it is not put into action. The world is filled with people who possess great knowledge but never leave the starting gate or launch their projects because they do not understand the *power of planning* and thereby, fail to begin. Benjamin Franklin and Winston Churchill are credited with introducing this simple but powerful quote:

Failing to plan is planning to fail.

We often become excited about an idea but if action is not implemented, the excitement wears off and we quickly return to our conditioned routines. Without a plan, your best intentions to diet, exercise, attract a relationship or begin a financial venture fade within days.

Achieving success requires the identification of specific goals; otherwise, a plan cannot be created. Beginning a diet is different than aiming for a specific weight or establishing diet and exercise programs that complement each other. The idea of attracting more money requires a plan to increase income by promoting a product or service, acquiring a better paying position, developing an awareness of opportunities, reducing expenses or purchasing more economically. When you completed the exercises on pages 39-40, you identified goals that are meaningful to you. They can be modified at any time.

During the Covid-19 pandemic in 2020 and 2021, almost everyone in the world was required to self-isolate for weeks or months. For some, it was agony and felt like an eternity. Self-isolation created a significant increase in the number of people who experienced anxiety, frustration, mental illness and depression. Vast numbers of people didn't know what to do with themselves. The constant external stimuli that were major influences in their lives were instantly removed, forcing them to rely on their own resources. Others excelled because they acted on the opportunity and engaged in activities that took second place to their employment and hectic schedules. They set out to enjoy those activities.

When desires are not set as goals, the subconscious mind (your autopilot) does not have a target (destination or focus) and your guidance system causes you to meander through life. Without a new goal that is supported by a commitment and determination to make it happen, life remains the same (Page 56). The search for the meaning of life has sparked philosophical debates for centuries. Over two thousand years ago, Aristotle (350 BC), provided sage advice regarding the power of goals:

> *[People] are goal-seeking creatures.*
> *Their lives only have meaning when [they]*
> *are striving for goals.*

Individuals who have activities and plans in progress have more energy and are more enthusiastic than those without them. We often hear of seniors in their 60s, 70s and 80s who climb mountains, complete university degrees or begin a variety of hobbies or interests. Their achievements are not for employment purposes but for their own personal enjoyment and satisfaction.

Retirement can be a time to take advantage of opportunities, yet many retired individuals feel at a loss. They did not plan or prepare for retirement. Plans, goals and activities are more likely to develop into a lifestyle when established years before one retires. One can look forward with excitement and anticipation to doing more of these activities in retirement. It is never too late to plan for the next chapter of life or make the most of tomorrow or next week.

Too often a belief is formed that one requires money, education, opportunities or better health before they can enjoy themselves. As stated in Chapter 20, achieving happiness and success involves a process of discovering what is meaningful to you and doing the best with what you have. Again, no one can do it for you. Achievement begins by making a choice to explore new activities and overcome the killers that are preventing your success.

Compare how you feel when you have nothing planned versus when you plan to meet someone for dinner, attend an event or purchase a gift for someone you really love or admire (Page 53). Whether your goal is short term or long term, having an activity to look forward to creates enthusiasm. The surprise phone call from friends was a perfect example. Suddenly, you were motivated not to be observed with a messy place, and with the energy of a whirling dervish, you tidied up in record time. By setting goals that are compatible with your desires, you can tap into that mysterious energy. The challenges become exciting and invigorating.

Society places excessive hype and expectations on living the dream, yet rarely is guidance provided to maintain the momentum required to ensure that success continues. Many increase their incomes, locate better positions, attract a compatible partner or attain a desired weight, degree or other goal, only to realize that the achievement was short-lived. They gradually gravitate back to their old lives. Planning should not be a map to a single destination, but a process to achieve and keep dreams alive. Success and happiness are the result of a well-planned journey that adjusts for disruptions and enables modifications along the way.

Planning and scheduling small events, purchases or meetings are achievable by simply setting a date. Larger events, projects or acquisitions require written plans to ensure activities are coordinated to occur in the proper order. A desire that continues to elude you requires addressing avoidance behaviors that are preventing you from setting a plan in motion. Whether your goal is large or small, this is your opportunity to put the concepts and techniques presented in this book into action.

Finding the Killers

Goals are personal and easily destroyed. Discussing or sharing them is risky until you are clear and committed to achieving them. It is not unusual to become discouraged and abandon a goal that you genuinely desired after sharing it with someone who holds different values or beliefs. When it comes to changing your life, be assured that killers, zombies and demons are determined to quash your plans. Your power lies in a weapon that is not a secret. That weapon is placing your plan in writing.

Shortly after I left high school, I learned the value of planning on paper through a brief, but friendly difference of opinion with my older brother. We were looking to make a financial profit on a particular venture. As the elder, he assumed the lead and quickly laid out his idea on a piece of paper and said, "This is what we should do." Direct, no argument, and as in past family dynamics, I was expected to agree and follow his lead.

How was he to know that my ego and pride were tired of having my ideas and suggestions take second place or be dismissed? I decided to challenge his plan with my idea. After all, I was 18, had reached the age of majority, and knew a lot—didn't I? I barely finished my proposal when he slowly slid the paper toward me, handed me the pen and quietly said, "Show me how that works."

As he called out numbers for revenues and expenses and other variables, it was becoming apparent that my idea was going up in smoke. To add insult to injury [my ego], he took the paper, added additional expenses and then slid the paper back saying, "If it doesn't work on paper, it won't work in reality." Hmpfr. @#$!#. He was right. To this day, regardless of the project, I have found that writing a few notes, numbers or sketches on whatever is at hand—scraps of paper or a napkin while having lunch—records the idea until I can develop a more detailed written plan. Thanks, Bro!

A workable plan on paper, on your computer or on your phone is a great beginning but not a guarantee of success. For a plan to work, it requires action. As identified in Chapter 5, action is the fourth element of motivation. Action is initiated by mind power. The negative words, beliefs and solar plexus resistance that you had to overcome to create your plan are going to return. Plans and actions are a declaration of war on your killers. Their defenses will be instantaneous.

Killers are automatons or programs that are not capable of reasoning or thinking. They are programmed to terminate any efforts and actions that do not conform to your previous settings. Killers ambush your self-talk with a plethora of ideas and doubts that discourage or distract you, like names of people to call and trivial activities that require checking. Their program settings cause your solar plexus to become agitated by the mere thought of changing the way you do things. The subconscious mind returns to traitor status as multiple beliefs conflict with your plans (intentions). If you follow the tirade of garbage in your head, it is nearly impossible to begin.

If you were not successful in achieving a previous goal, the instructions and constructs in this book will provide you with a new perspective. You may experience several "Aha" moments as you identify where your past efforts have fallen victim to killers. When your biocomputer detects that a new approach is another attempt to replace that existing killer (habit or belief), it will immediately summon snipers and assassins to attack with distractions or discouragements. Their defense is to force you to stop or quit striving to achieve your goal.

You may become irritated by a recurring explanation or concept in this book. Realize that this irritation is an internal sensation and is your subconscious mind saying—this is where you need to act. The annoying sensation is a killer attempting to distract you from examining or implementing that concept. The rapid processing of your biocomputer detects that your intentions are on a collision course with your old habit and any change will usurp it. Overpowering the killer requires perseverance and continued action.

The killer's survival depends on you quitting. Have some fun here. If you feel irritated by a repetitious phrase, silently counter with—too bad Killer. I'm learning this, putting it into action and you're going down! Counter each attack and motivate yourself by repeating Coué's words—every day and in every way, I get better and better.

A written plan is a powerful external coach that assists in the development of mind power and keeps you on task. It is important to *Keep It Simple*! When it is in writing, you do not have to recreate it or start at the beginning each time a life situation, external force or old habit tosses you off course. You can glance at your progress and proceed from where the last interruption occurred.

Here lies another critical tipping point. If habits and programs are developed with and without your choice or consent, will you not be more determined to develop a new habit that ensures the achievement of a goal you desire? In 1940, Albert Gray revealed the behavior that constitutes a common denominator for success. He stated that the secret of success of every [person] who has ever been successful—lies in the fact that [they] formed the habit of doing things that failures don't like to do.

This simple statement describes a basic procedure, process, concept or principle that can be applied by anyone. Throughout this book, the terms habits and programs have been used interchangeably. This is to demonstrate that a biocomputer generates your behaviors by instructing your command center to channel all the biomechanical and mental functions required to execute that action. You are the computer programmer who can hack into and stop any program by intercepting your command center. Setting a goal and creating a plan are the acts of developing an external program. A program (plan) that is introduced and consciously reviewed (repetition), becomes a primary or dominant program that your biocomputer will execute on your behalf. By following your plan, you coax and pace your biocomputer toward a particular goal. As you do this, a program innately develops that will begin to guide you autonomically, like the random melody you often hum.

As you completed the various exercises, you unconsciously began developing building blocks and identified components that your new plan requires to be effective. If you did not complete the exercises, it is because your killers subtly duped you. If it felt like too much of a bother or you didn't feel like doing the exercise, it was because a killer generated those feelings.

Planning is a habit that people who fail don't like to do. To form a habit that failures don't like to do is the same as developing a program to be successful. Your actions to explore this book identify you as one who seriously desires to learn new concepts. Part of the process is to identify what you do not like to do and establish a plan to do the things you are not currently doing. It shouldn't take long to realize that the things failures do not like to do are the same things that most people do not like to do, including you.

It is at this point that the concepts presented in this book either work for or against you. How the mind works, the power of the question, your self-talk, solar plexus, visualization, fears, beliefs, values, attitudes and external interferences control your actions or inactions.

Failures do not like to lead or stand alone and effortlessly gravitate to the path of least resistance or their past conditioning. You too will gravitate toward this fatal path and relinquish your power if you do not develop an awareness that taking charge and action are required. For example, how do you feel and what does your self-talk reveal when you silently verbalize the following?

➢ I will develop confidence and communication skills to deal with situations that are uncomfortable or confrontational.

➢ I will assess situations and identify what is specifically required to improve my life.

➢ I will develop power phrases and assertive statements that enable me to remain focused and avoid distractions.

➢ I will invest my energy into making a better life rather than waste my energy by putting up with situations I dislike.

➢ I will develop plans and schedules that establish an effective and enjoyable routine that enables me to monitor my efforts.

➢ I will do whatever it takes to modify my behaviors to achieve my goals.

➢ I will act because my actions will develop a more enjoyable lifestyle.

The statements are carefully worded so that when you read them, your solar plexus will react with a sensation of excitement *or* angst. The negative sensations are killers attempting to dissuade you and cause you to quit.

To confirm that this is the case, reread each statement slowly and visualize yourself making these statements to a group of friends. Your solar plexus and your self-talk will clearly reveal your conditioning. This exercise instantly identifies killer programs that prevent you from initiating new ideas and formulating plans. Be especially mindful when you hear yourself say, "I'll do it later, or I read that," or any comment that prevents you from rereading a statement. It is a defining moment to act and break the cycle of failure.

If you do not act and overpower the killer that these feelings are protecting, nothing will change and the killer wins. These are the efforts and actions that failures do not like to do.

When you realize that you can eliminate discouraging feelings by applying the techniques described, you will understand that changing your life is more than possible. To be successful, you will have to commit to making changes. Otherwise, procrastination sets in and you invite failure the moment you say, "I need to think about it."

You do not have to be at a specific place to develop a plan. If you are at your favorite café and an idea pops into your head, write it on a napkin, enter it into your phone, email yourself a note—just record it somewhere to explore later. The ideas are your intuition in action but are fleeting thoughts that silently fade into the ethers if you do not capture them. Your choices are simple—use them or lose them. The limitations of the conscious mind cannot retain all your brilliant ideas. They vanish like apparitions.

Whether you are a student, career person, retired or on vacation, planning is a requirement for maximizing the enjoyment of each day. Your life goals should be as important to plan as a vacation. Think back to the amount of time you spent planning or organizing surprise parties, weekend events, get-a-ways and vacations. You created notes, lists, arrangements or reservations to ensure events and connections occurred on time. By comparison, how much time have you invested in planning to achieve the things you desire (hobbies, relationships, finances, new ventures) over the next 2, 5, 10, or 15 years?

Students often begin their careers based on the guidance and structure of their education system. When students graduate from high school, most have applications and plans for university, college, technical school, the armed forces or they are off to see the world with a passport, prearranged visas and detailed itineraries. Unfortunately, planning for how you want your life to evolve is seldom considered after that initial entrance into the adult world.

Failures do not plan. They are the proverbial ships without rudders. Without plans, they leave school and gravitate toward a routine of finding a job, going to work and taking days off. The pattern will be repeated in every aspect of their life unless they desire to change their circumstances.

As enthusiastic as we may be, life throws us curve balls. Goals that we set out to achieve may become undesirable during the process of achieving them. Studies conducted in late 2018 indicated that one-third of university and college students changed their majors in the first year and 75%–80% changed their majors before graduating. Planning is a continuous activity, not only for education but because changes in life demand it.

Whatever venture is chosen, one requires a specific plan for the next few weeks, months or years, yet that plan must have the flexibility to be modified or adjusted as circumstances change. Projecting long-term is a challenge. What you desired when you were 20 years old is rarely the same when you are 30, 40, 50 or retired. As our relationships and careers change, so do our desires. Goal compatibility with changing lifestyles is a critical factor that many do not foresee. Every so often, goals need to be modified.

Effective planning is not time consuming, but it does require some dedicated time to develop a workable plan. A goal or plan can be tangible, like attracting a compatible partner, property or a specific item. Or a goal can be intangible, like developing inner strength, discipline or mind power. To achieve any goal, a plan first requires a clearly defined starting point that includes an honest assessment of one's current skills and available resources.

Secondly, a plan requires a specific or clearly defined goal, destination or achievement. Thirdly, the specific steps required to attain the goal must be identified. If a step or process appears too large, break it into several steps. And lastly, each time you review your plan, your solar plexus and self-talk will subtly and specifically identify where a killer is attempting to stop or discourage you. That is—if you listen. If required, add the steps necessary to eliminate the killer.

After a plan is drafted, the review process is simple. Depending on the complexity of your goal, reviewing it daily, weekly or monthly only requires a few minutes. If additions or alterations are required, they can be quickly inserted. To maintain motivation, continue applying a powerful self-coaching question like—what is one specific activity that I can perform or complete (now) that will advance me toward my goal?

Refer often to Appendix O on self-coaching. Call it a secret, a treasure map or your battle plan. No matter how you classify or label the information in this book, it can become your private coach that empowers you to remain motivated and in control.

Distractions and interruptions are guaranteed. The power of a written plan eliminates the need to return to the starting line after each interruption. It may be days before you realize that you have diverted from your plan. When the disruption ceases, take a deep breath, review your plan to identify where you are and continue. If your plan is set for ten days and ends up taking ten weeks, don't be discouraged. If your desire is strong, in ten weeks you will be better off than when you began, or if you had quit. When a plan is developed, it becomes a compass for identifying your next move. Placing your plan on your phone, tablet or computer makes it simple to add steps and continually evaluate where modifications are required.

There could be times when we drift into a void of inactivity and are not motivated to begin or continue with a project. This is the time to review your plans and apply mind power. Motivation and energy are generated by initiating power questions similar to—what is the best use of my time? What have I been putting off that I would enjoy completing? What one task or action can I immediately perform to improve this situation? These types of questions cause the subconscious mind to generate ideas that release the energy that causes you to act. As you develop the habit of coaching yourself with the power of questions, you will become aware of how much more you can do and achieve.

You may begin to feel excited, but remember, zombies and killer programs have not gone away. The enemies are within. They will continue to surface and attack your plans and best intentions. Your choices determine your future—do you want to attract and enjoy new opportunities or join the rank of failures that Albert Gray describes? The Viking Runes counsel us that we are not *Doers* but *Deciders*. Once we decide, the doing flows naturally.

People avoid planning for one of two reasons. They lack motivation because the goal is nothing more than an idle wish. Or two, they do not understand or recognize that they need to redirect their thoughts and energies. Motivation mysteriously appears when one evaluates the inconvenience, expense, frustration and effort required to put up with an undesirable situation versus creating an enjoyable outcome by investing the same energy and resources.

For example, the energy required to physically carry excess weight has physical and emotional ramifications. Health risks increase, including hypertension, heart failure, type 2 diabetes and osteoarthritis. Excess weight reduces enthusiasm, mobility and physical energy. Not feeling good about oneself extends to losing interest in physical activities and one's physical appearance. The negativity can spiral into depression. The energy required and the price paid to compensate for excess weight is far greater than the efforts required to change one's lifestyle.

Benefits increase exponentially when you choose physical activities that you enjoy. As a by-product of your activity, you soon recognize how great you look and how much better you feel. The activity becomes a catalyst as it generates increased physical energy and enthusiasm. When your goal is achieved, managing your weight will not be such a challenge. Every day you will sense the rewarding feeling of being an achiever. The same comparison can be made for changing careers, learning new skills, managing finances or attracting a compatible partner.

Some believe that goals are only for long-term projects. If you believe that, you will miss out on enjoying many minor day-to-day activities that bring excitement and add value to life. Inserting an activity into your planner, calendar or phone reminder provides you with an enjoyable experience that would have been missed had you not planned for it.

The goal can be an activity during your lunch break or on your way home. You could help someone with a project or visit a friend or relative confined to their home. The goal does not require a specified length of time to validate its importance. A goal or an event could last half an hour, a weekend, a month or be a lifestyle choice. The casual intent exchanged with acquaintances that we must do lunch sometime, will never happen until someone takes the initiative and schedules it.

Occasionally, it is rewarding to enjoy some spontaneity, like ambling along a street with no goal or specific destination or taking off on a short get-a-way on the spur of the moment. Where the roads or sidewalks lead you for those few days or hours becomes an adventure. Being in the moment of that place and time is rejuvenating. Ironically, this is a spontaneous choice that becomes a goal when you specifically choose to do nothing in particular. The spontaneous moment may be your subconscious mind prompting you to explore an unknown opportunity. If you do not go down that road, by default, your guidance system settings guide you to repeat your previous behaviors and you miss out on another opportunity.

The power of a goal is activated when it is personal to you and has a meaningful purpose (second element of motivation Page 53). If the goal is a mundane task, like tidying your home or workspace, the purpose may be in the mere satisfaction of getting it done. Motivation is that mysterious energy that is triggered when you repeat one powerful phrase—how will I feel when this is completed? When you discover the power that this phrase generates and how it causes you to act, there will be no stopping you. Remaining determined and pushing forward are actions that failures do not like to do.

Choosing and setting goals create focus and energy through the power of anticipation (imagination). People who claim to be bored have only one person to blame—themselves. They obviously have not explored or scheduled activities that they enjoy. The irony is that their declaration of boredom implies they have idle time that they are choosing not to use. This example proves that not choosing is a decision and a choice. If this paragraph creates any discomfort in your solar plexus or conjures up thoughts to discontinue reading, your conditioning is a vicious killer discouraging you from acting.

A common excuse for not planning is the perceived lack of finances. Numerous activities are offered free or at minimal cost in every community. A simple check of upcoming events in your area or a walk in a park does not require money. If tickets for your favorite performer are cost-prohibitive or unavailable, this does not prevent you from enjoying your hobbies, attending a community event, visiting friends or participating in other activities. The undeniable truth is—regardless of the activity, it requires planning and exploration—actions that failures don't like to do.

Planning is important but excessive planning becomes another killer. The act of needlessly revising a plan is an avoidance behavior that prevents one from beginning or taking action. Other distractions occur when a killer prompts your self-talk with—I need to check on this or that. I'll just do this first. This is too complicated. I do not have time for it. It's too expensive. You can't do that. I'll do it later. Even with a specific plan, if you do not control the rambling words in your self-talk, killers will overwhelm your conscious mind and stop you dead. The killer is your existing self-image (Ego) fighting your new conscious choices and making every effort feel like agony or an inconvenience. It is for this reason that it is critical to have a reasonable plan and focus on the benefits you will enjoy when you achieve your goal. That which you imagine will always take precedence and win.

Control your imagination and
you control your happiness.

If you are not already in the habit of setting goals, do not attempt a massive makeover. Begin by creating a short To-Do list that maximizes your weekend or a few evenings a week or explores a new project. With repetition, you develop a habit of making plans or To-Do lists that become external prompts to accomplish multiple tasks or projects. Again, these are things that failures do not like to do.

Your mind is active every second of every day. If a task is not significant or you think it is easy to remember, you might omit it from your list, but be aware that the limited conscious capacity of your mind will undermine you. Occasionally, when I return from running a few errands, my wife will inquire if I picked up an item and my reply is, "Nope, I didn't write it down." If you are intent on accomplishing several tasks on a given day, an effective coach is the simplicity of a written list. If you are prone to worrying about completing an important task, this self-coaching technique allows you to relax. Its placement on a list removes the requirement of having to remember it in your conscious capacity, allowing you to enjoy the moment wherever you are.

Having a plan does not guarantee success. When a plan is not reviewed or monitored, it is the same as not having a plan. Regardless of your plans, goals, enthusiasm and faith that it will happen, without taking action to perform the next step that brings you closer to your goal, nothing will be accomplished. The old proverb—*Faith without works is dead*—is valuable advice. But Nike's slogan sums it up best—*Just Do It!*

It is interesting and motivating to observe others and fantasize about a career other than your own. The bottom line is that reality is dictated by aptitude. After a goal has been identified, it is advisable to perform a *Reality Check*. A reality check creates an awareness of your aptitude and what is required to achieve a chosen goal. It is critical to acknowledge that if you cannot master a particular skill, it does not indicate that you are dumb or stupid, only that you are not suited for that particular activity. Without exploration you will never identify the activities that you can excel at or simply enjoy.

One of the keys to happiness is following your curiosity to explore new activities. The critical element of success and happiness is that you must enjoy the activity. For example, you may want to be a professional singer but if you do not have the voice range or cannot accept constructive criticism and coaching, it may not be a wise investment. Planning a career as a singer is likely an unrealistic goal, but not a reason to quit singing in the shower or while walking in the woods. Revel in the sheer pleasure and the personal enjoyment it provides. The same applies to studies in a particular field or the desire to be an athlete. You can still learn to play a musical instrument, participate in a sport for fun or explore a field of interest for the pure enjoyment of learning. As Aristotle stated—our lives only have meaning when we are striving for goals.

Appendix L provides worksheets to explore and assess your goals and desires. As you proceed, reflect often on your values, beliefs, external influences and fears. It is an excellent time to challenge yourself and verify *if what you think and believe* are the real barriers that are blocking you. These are not the only questions to consider. Create additional questions to explore your unique situations. When you seriously evaluate your answers as to how you would like your life to be, transformation is assured. When in doubt, consider the following:

What you put up with, you end up with.
Is your current situation your chosen goal?
Are you applying your power of choice?
Do you have an action plan?

With a written plan, you are on the road to success. During this journey, you will encounter every killer, assassin and zombie from your past. They are programmed to thwart your every move. Shoring up your defenses is required. Specific instructions for applying mind power techniques to defend yourself are provided in the next chapter.

Mastering others is strength. Mastering yourself is true power.
Lao Tzu
(Unknown 6th – 4th BCE)

Chapter 26

Assassins, Killers & Zombies

You are constantly under attack. But you cannot anticipate every scenario that you will encounter. Whether your new initiatives survive and thrive depends on your awareness and preparedness to apply defensive mental maneuvers to defend yourself when conflicts arise. Using the techniques presented throughout this book, this chapter expands on the exploration processes to identify guidance system settings that prevent or restrict the completion of a goal or project.

Each of us has projects, issues or tasks that remain unfinished and are set aside to avoid dealing with them. Unless extreme effort is exerted to complete the task, we keep evading their completion. The delay is caused by three persistent killers that prevent us from achieving our goals.

The previous chapter offered guidelines for planning and creating action. Beginning is easy. Staying the course for your best laid plans is when you are at risk of being attacked by assassins, zombies and an army of other killers. The most deadly assassins are procrastination, distractions and fear. These ingenious killers can be quickly disarmed when you become aware of *the moment* your efforts and intentions are under attack. As identified in the Cycle of Change (Chapter 8), awareness is a prerequisite for change.

After you have prepared a plan and are excited about your goal, you become a target for internal and external killers and assassins. At first, their attacks are subtle hacks that intercept your self-talk and regain control of your command center. Their success is guaranteed when you engage in avoidance behaviors that consume your time and energies but ignore the activities that could achieve your goals and change your life. *The best laid plans that were never acted upon* and *the road to hell is paved with good intentions* are two great sayings that have become programs and a way of life for many.

The dilemmas presented in the *Introduction* described how you miss opportunities or within days or weeks of beginning a new endeavor you noticed that you were no longer on task. It did not matter how committed you thought you were, you remained unaware that you were quitting your routine until several days later after you realized that you had stopped.

Now, with your new awareness of how the conscious and subconscious minds control your command center, you are in a tactical position to detect killer attacks. The dynamics are straight forward. As you push forward with your willpower to begin or complete a task, your previous conditioning triggers your solar plexus and self-talk to resist. An internal conflict ensues. You anguish over the effort required to continue and your self-talk expresses that you don't feel like doing it. As your negative self-talk rants on, discouragement sets in and you quit. You may minimize your guilt by saying you'll do it later. Whether you justify your actions or not, you engage in alternate activities instead of investing the same, or even less effort, into performing the actions that your new goal requires.

The moment that you are aware of an attack, you are in a powerful position. The killers that control your command center and your behaviors are the narratives expressed in your self-talk. If you truly desire to succeed, now is the time to apply mind power. Mind power is a process of taking back control of your self-talk when you are required to act. As you experienced, self-talk cannot be stopped, only altered. Therefore, not acting is a program protection command by a killer that ensures the negative situation remains the same if you do not proceed. The required action appears simple but can be surprisingly frustrating to maintain until your awareness increases and it becomes a habit. Determination and perseverance are required.

Mind power can be applied two ways. First, by stating a power phrase, direct command or assertion that instantly instructs the command center to respond accordingly. Alternately, asking a question creates a quantum leap that causes the subconscious mind to answer with the appropriate instructions for the command center to follow. The biomechanics are processed subconsciously without your awareness. When this thought process becomes a habit, you will no longer think about the initial physical effort required to perform or begin a task. At times, it will feel as if a mysterious energy is gently pushing you into action.

The dynamics are explainable. When the thought to exercise or complete a task occurs, the thought is in your imagination. The physical effort required to move forward is your willpower that is controlled by your imagination. The two unify and generate the irresistible force described by Coué (Page 121). For the killer, it is life or death. To survive, the killer attacks your efforts to achieve your new goal by triggering a conflict in your self-talk (imagination). The killer wins the conflict and instructs your command center to quit advancing toward the pursuit of your goal the moment you think or utter words similar to:

> ➢ I am too tired.
> ➢ I don't feel like it.
> ➢ It will not be destructive to my plans.
> ➢ This time won't matter.
> ➢ I'll do it tomorrow.

The moment you think (in your imagination) that it is time to exercise, avoid a certain food or perform a task, your past conditioning triggers a discomfort in your solar plexus that prompts your self-talk to say, "I don't feel like it." These words appear in your imagination via a quantum leap. The two statements, *it is time to exercise* and *I don't feel like it*, are not compatible. They **do *not equal each other*** and only one can be voiced at a time in your self-talk (conscious capacity). In computer lingo, ***it does not compute.***

The conflict requires you to consciously intervene. As you process or rationalize your intent (in your self-talk) that *it's time to exercise*, that self-talk is instantaneously altered by the sensations in your solar plexus causing your self-talk to repeat commands like—*I am too tired. I don't feel like it. It will not be destructive to my plans. This time won't matter. I'll do it tomorrow.* The last statement is processed instantaneously and becomes the instruction forwarded to your command center. Those last words are your ***killers.***

Finding the Killers

When a killer program generates a negative message in your self-talk, *__the moment you repeat that negative statement__*, your imagination and your willpower *__become equal__*. Your imagination has overpowered your conscious desire and you lose focus. As Coué stated, the imagination always wins.

The negative and disabling statements overpower your efforts or willpower and become your current conscious thoughts. Your self-talk (willpower) equals imagination (subconscious mind) and both agree that—*I don't feel like it*. Therefore, knowing how one word prevents or creates action, it is impossible for you to act, do or perform what is required to achieve your new goal. By default, you repeat the old behavior. Mind power is applying action that is first initiated by you *consciously* in your self-talk.

Some readers will have experienced this when I insisted that an exercise be completed. They kept on reading because they *did not feel like doing it* (the exercise). Their non-action was a program protection maneuver by an existing program. Their biocomputer processed that the new exercise would threaten the existence of the old program. Ironically, it is the primary reason that one would choose to read this book. The program in their subconscious mind relayed a sensory impulse to initiate a discomfort in their solar plexus that triggered their self-talk to state that they *don't feel like doing it*. Without a doubt, they acted according to their self-talk (imagination) and did not complete the exercise. I am sure you were not one of those readers. ☺

The words in your self-talk prevent your command center from acting. If these words are not replaced, your best intentions are dead. Regaining control of your command center requires a new command that will change your behaviors to what you desire. If you are unprepared when an attack occurs, you can use the power of the question to trick your subconscious mind. The response from your subconscious instantly alters your negative self-talk with a favorable command. Your conviction and repetition of the question counteract the negative influence and you win. Failure to provide a new command allows the old program to remain active *by default*. The slightest lapse in focus allows the killer to return in a nanosecond. Be prepared to repeat your defense phrase or question multiple times (without chanting), as the killer is a program operating by design and retains zombie characteristics that allow it to surface and continue attacking.

This becomes a continuous battle. You would not go into battle ill prepared, without a plan and appropriate weapons to combat seasoned warriors. The warriors you will battle are your old programs and negative thoughts. Your army is mind power and your techniques are its soldiers. The only weapons you need are your plans and memorized commands. When your traitor subconscious mind attacks and you immediately respond with a confident counter-command, a quantum leap is created that replaces the negative self-talk. Instead of forcing your will, it is easier to trick your subconscious mind with a question. Examples of questions to redirect the power of your subconscious mind are:

➢ How will I feel when this is completed? [pause]

➢ How will I feel after I exercise? [pause]

➢ How will I feel when I learn to control my mind? [pause]

➢ How will I feel when I learn these techniques? [pause]

➢ How will I feel after I make this phone call? [pause]

➢ How will I feel when/after...? [Fill in your desired goal or action.]

If you did not recognize how the power of a question alters your self-talk, a review of Chapter 9 would be beneficial. The subconscious mind cannot resist responding to a question. Do not stop asking your question until you realize you are into performing your task. The technique cannot work if you ask the question and then allow your imagination to express doubt or a desire to avoid the task. The negative response from your imagination is the program protection battling you. You must continue with your question(s) until you receive the appropriate response from your subconscious mind (imagination). Your response to the question must emulate the feeling that you will have when you complete the task— otherwise your command center will respond to the last words inputted and you will quit.

The time that passes between repeating the question and the realization that you are performing the task, will feel like a time warp, amazing or almost magical. You will not be aware of what was holding you back or that you are beginning your task. You will only realize in a few minutes that you are into the task. Your understanding and ability to apply this technique is crucial for overcoming procrastination.

This technique is applicable to any goal, task or challenge. Once a plan of action is created, prepare for a major ambush. Applying mind power requires precise and specific words that describe the results you desire. A guideline of words for improving your employment and finances or attracting a relationship can be reviewed on page 139. The following explanations further demonstrate how you invite assassins and zombies to attack.

The subconscious mind may appear to be the devil or a traitor but it is just doing what it has been programmed to do. There is a significant difference between focusing on a *desired weight* and using expressions like *weight loss* or *overweight*. The latter expressions act exactly like the words grey elephant. These words must be eliminated. Once the desired weight is attained, the focus must remain on the desired weight or your self-talk and subconscious mind will cause you to gain weight so that you have weight to lose. We often hear, "I lose weight, but I put it right back on." This is a self-fulfilling prophesy that causes your subconscious mind, command center and the law of attraction to work perfectly, but against you.

Success is attained through the law of attraction. It requires establishing a self-image or a magnetic setting to attract what you desire. The easiest approach is by applying autosuggestion (Chapter 12) and creating a new image of yourself with words that direct your subconscious mind to solidify or reinforce an image of what you desire.

To attain and maintain a desired weight requires a carefully designed plan. It becomes a guide for approaching each meal confidently by selecting healthy foods and portioned servings. Your healthy eating choices begin to establish new guidance system settings. As you finish your meals, the new program is further reinforced by feeling good (emotion) about your successes.

Suddenly, you are struck by a **ZOMBIE ATTACK.** Your total focus is on a cookie, a candy, a potato chip or some form of junk food. Old killer programs operating in your subconscious mind begin to stream through your conscious mind (Page 56). This is your battlefield and point of power. If you do not immediately use a quantum leap to replace the subject of your thoughts with a constructive phrase to support your plans, your self-talk will coax you by saying, *"It will not be destructive to my plans. This time won't matter. It's only one."* Should you pause, like magic, the bag of chips is empty, the cookies are gone and you feel badly because you let yourself down. If you recite a negative statement inferring that you *cannot stay on a diet or exercise program*, not only has the killer (sniper, assassin, zombie) taken you out but your *negative* comments *reinforce the old program that you specifically don't want and need to suppress!* Recognizing the monologue in your self-talk offers a second chance to win. Use it as a learning experience and control your self-talk with statements like—okay, I messed up [or I *#!@-UP!!] I made it this far and realize how I was attacked. This time did matter, and knowing this, every day and in every way, I am getting better and better. I am winning.

Mind power works against you when your self-talk is not monitored and controlled and you allow your words to flow randomly. The words—desired weight—activate the law of attraction to notice healthy foods and physical activities. Rather than focus on the agony of discipline, restraint and drudgery, ask yourself how you will feel when you achieve your desired weight or after you complete your exercise routine. Asking yourself these types of questions creates positive energy and motivation. Your self-talk is a constant monitoring device that verifies whether your mind power is working in your favor or not.

Throughout the day, and as you prepare to act on your plan or new goal, silently manage your self-talk with encouraging words like—each and every day my routine becomes easier and easier. The killer words that can surface and distract you will be crowded out. By mentally focusing on a successful outcome, the threat of being bombarded by negative thoughts is reduced. With repetition, your guidance system remains on the new setting. The new setting becomes a program (habit) and the positive reinforcing words begin to naturally appear in your self-talk, like that phantom melody you autonomically hum.

If you followed these instructions or recited a variation of positive command phrases that eliminated negative words, you will have discovered mind power. The more you practice and develop it, the more you can depend on it. It is *always* there for you. If you don't act—your killers and assassins will. Think back to the example of friends calling and coming over on short notice. That unexplainable energy or power is always available and at your command.

You can never let your guard down until your new mode of thinking becomes naturally positive, without being fanatical. It is paramount that after a goal is achieved, you incorporate plans that *continue* the activities that propelled you to your achievements. If they are not in place, killer programs are guaranteed to return, and the results can be devastating. When you become proficient at overcoming procrastination, yet one particular task or goal continues to elude you, your efficient biocomputer may have identified a critical conflict. The subconscious mind may be protecting you from a future disappointment or nudging you to notice an opportunity that is not consciously obvious. As stated in Chapter 15 on intuition, your self-mastery and the law of attraction combine and form a law of protection.

The delay may be the only method your subconscious mind can employ to prompt you to explore other hidden programs or evaluate what you may be missing. The next chapter focuses on hidden programs or past wishes and old desires that may return to haunt you

Chapter 27

Sleepers and The Law of Attraction

The concept that we use less than 10% of our brain is a myth. Scientists have mapped the complete human brain and have identified the function of each area that controls our physical and mental activities. By employing functional resonance imaging (fMRI), they have identified that all aspects of our brain are accessed throughout the day, even while resting, but not necessarily at 100% capacity. As advanced as science is, many processes and capabilities of the mind remain unknown. New discoveries continue to be revealed. When you performed the various exercises as you explored each chapter, you proved that you are not required to have specialized skills or be a scientist to identify and activate intricate and unexplainable powers of the mind that control your actions.

As a significant portion of the brain is not well understood, we can only speculate where the subconscious mind stashes all our memories and experiences. In an unknown part of our mind, programs are formed without our awareness, including false memories. Many memories (programs) do not require a conscious prompt. They emerge spontaneously, like those that cause us to hum that phantom melody, hear conversations from past experiences and initiate behaviors that we may later regret.

The instructions to channel the powers of your mind may appear overly simplistic. It may appear so, but it requires a diligent and concerted focus to master them. After applying the techniques to set goals, overcome procrastination and manage distractions, you may still sense that something is holding you back.

The blocks and barriers that you sense are the ones that you created or were created subliminally by others. They include past desires that are no longer of interest to you and unjustified beliefs or fears that have never been explored as your life evolved. What you intensely valued, believed or desired as a teenager or young adult, established programs that could be potential killers to your current plans and dreams. The autonomic subliminal processes that caused you to adopt slang expressions, expletives or humorous lingo also developed these programs of old beliefs and fears. As you have come to realize how susceptible the mind is to words and suggestions, it should cause you to question what else may be sabotaging you. There are hidden or sleeper programs that impact your success, similar to how a computer virus interferes with the performance of a digital computer.

Your desires change over time. Reviewing what you desired and thought about years ago will reveal goals and beliefs that conflict with your current desires. If these previous goals contained an element of emotional intensity, they are more likely to be in conflict with a current goal. The subconscious mind contains incorrect interpretations of past situations, ideas and comments from others that established false memories. These memories do not dissolve over time. They remain viable programs waiting for an opportunity to be activated.

Identifying hidden programs provides an insight into current behaviors and an understanding of why we sometimes cannot achieve the goals that we so desperately desire. A hidden program is easily verified. If you can recall the slightest detail about a past idea, comment, incident or desire, then program settings matching these memories exist. They are guidance system settings that severely impact or prevent the achievement of your current goals.

Hidden programs can save your life, while at the same time cause you endless amounts of frustration. It is impossible to identify every one of them. Identifying a few and removing their negative effect on you will have an enormous impact on your life. You cannot alter history but you can renounce past desires, beliefs and fears and prevent them from interfering with and jeopardizing the law of attraction.

Hidden programs are part of your belief system and include superstitions or jokes you heard when you were too young to decipher their meaning. The subconscious mind recorded the misinterpreted messages as truths. Years later, if you still believe the message to be true, it could influence your perspective in a real life situation. As you get older, you can verify whether specific sayings or explanations are true or not.

Without assessing and questioning your beliefs, you will continue to respond according to what you originally believed. The same holds true for religious and belief-based activities that one chooses to follow. By evaluating what is or is not true, one can make better choices. Ideas that were implanted at an early age through fear and guilt remain in your memory banks for years, even when conscious choices to pursue a different direction are made. Some religions implant beliefs that severe retribution will follow if the tenets of their faith are challenged. The key is to identify and evaluate those unwanted thoughts and memories and each time they surface, negate them with a replacement phrase. Instantly, they will be unable to control or influence your new choices, unless you carelessly repeat them.

Programs and beliefs acquired years ago can have negative influences, even when they were positive experiences. During my research of the power of the mind, I made a shocking personal discovery. I realized that the law of attraction, emotional intensity, beliefs, values and external input created a positive experience, yet a decade later became a sleeper or hidden program that manifested itself to become a lethal assassin in my career.

At the age of 20, I had an incredible opportunity to join a dynamic organization as a project accountant. Shortly after my arrival at the company's head office, I was befriended by several junior engineers who were in their early twenties. At the time, I had less experience and listened intently to the issues they discussed.

They were an enthusiastic and ambitious group, intent on achieving success. Coffee and lunch breaks centered on debates about what they believed constituted success. During the early 1970s, salaries for junior engineers were in the range of $15,000 to $22,000 per annum. Their consensus on the meaning of success was that by the age of thirty, one should be earning their age in thousands—i.e., Age 30 = $30,000. With this identifier agreed upon by all, debate ensued daily about how one was to achieve this success. The suggestions were limitless and hilarious but everyone agreed that dedication and hard work were required.

After a few years, I moved on to new opportunities with other companies. Several years passed as I continued my studies through night classes and became a corporate accountant. One day I realized that my annual earnings exceeded $26,000 and I had just turned 26. When I realized this, an echo from six years earlier of the young engineers' equation for success reverberated in my mind, age = salary. According to their formula, by the age of 30 financial success was definitely achievable.

A few months later I attended a seminar promoting success through real estate and how *I too* could be successful and earn in excess of $100,000 a year! The seminar was exciting, intriguing and definitely motivating. Seeking greater success, I changed my career from accounting to real estate and set a new goal of earning $100,000 per year. Over the next few years, my earnings rose to $45,000, then $69,000 and as I turned 29, my income was slightly over $89,000. The future and goals promoted by the real estate seminar were proving to be prophetic.

As my income had increased rapidly, I decided not to focus on a finite dollar amount but simply to aspire to be successful—let there be no limit! During my 29th year, an unexplainable series of events unfolded that included several buyers reneging on offers due to fraud or misrepresentation. I felt that every scallywag that was around had sought me out. It was devastating and discouraging as I had never experienced a setback in my career.

The year ended in chaos. It was not until I completed my income tax that I had an astonishing realization. When my net income was totaled, my solar plexus exploded and an eruption of echoes in my self-talk overwhelmed me. My net income was $29,980. I instantly realized that I had become successful—not in sync with my new goal of real estate success, but precisely to the young engineers' definition of success that echoed in my mind—to be successful, at the age of 30, earning $30,000. I was flabbergasted and unable to believe what had occurred. With an awareness of the law of attraction and how the mind functions, I simply could not accept this situation as mere coincidence.

The power of the mind continued to fascinate and intrigue me. As I examined situations, issues, conflicts and successes in my life, I realized that what I thought about seriously and energized emotionally seemed to materialize or manifest itself in the future.

James Allen was correct in his book—*As a Man Thinketh* (Page 121). Conflicting thoughts or goals left to emerge randomly are lethal killers. While the subconscious mind appears to be operating in ways that are contrary to our current plans, it is merely fulfilling wishes and desires implanted years ago.

In the ten years following my encounter with the young engineers, my subconscious mind followed the belief that success equaled a specific income at a specific age. Later, a new definition of success was defined by income only, without an age qualifier. The two programs could process simultaneously in the short term; but a major conflict occurred at a specific point in time when a predetermined age was reached. It was impossible for my biocomputer to process the equation to guide me to my current goal when a previously dominant program existed. The original program and belief were:

$$Success = Age\ 30 = \$30,000$$

When the financial goal was adjusted to $100,000+, it created a second and conflicting program in my subconscious mind. The goal was later changed to *success only* with no age or financial qualifier.

$$Success = No\ Limit\ \$100,000+$$

Like songs in a music library, my subconscious mind retained the belief that at age 30, success equaled $30,000. Therefore,

$$Age\ 30 = Success = \$30,000 = No\ Limit\ \$100,000+$$

My biocomputer processed it as, *Does not compute!* Our biocomputers cannot stop or pause and are constantly in the *On* mode. Mine autonomically defaulted to the stronger belief program of success, one that was emotionally charged over many years. In my case, *Age 30* and *Success equals $30K*, was an emotionally charged belief program. *Be careful what you ask for* is sage and foretelling advice.

This story demonstrates how deep-seated programs are developed as we go through life. Ideas, beliefs or programs established from long ago reside in the subconscious mind and can be activated without any conscious awareness. Subliminal instructions are forwarded to the command center, and combined with the law of attraction, prompt you to notice and act.

The subconscious mind can be compared to online purchasing. After placing an order online, computer programs process the details and coordinate the delivery to your door. If you decide to change your mind, it may be too late to cancel the first order, but you can reorder and receive exactly what you desire. Since the first order could not be cancelled, it too, will arrive—but in the physical realm of online commerce, you can return it.

The subconscious mind is significantly more complex and requires a different *cancel order* request. You are now aware of the fact that when you energize a new desire, it does not suddenly erase or discard what you previously desired. The subconscious mind continues to process all ideas and beliefs as guidance system settings. When a conflict occurs, only one program can prevail—the one that is most dominant or emotionally charged. Obviously, in my real estate career, the subconscious mind coordinated my behaviors to execute the goal for success in my 30th year as I had quit focusing on a financial number. The identifier for success was defined ten years earlier as a specific age and dollar value. With a new focus on an open-ended dollar value for success, a complacency was created as my earnings trended upwards. Into an abyss I fell as the old success program was executed exactly as formulated.

The law of attraction and the subconscious mind work in ways that are difficult to comprehend or explain, except in hindsight. Hidden programs are not quickly revealed when we enthusiastically engage in new ventures.

In Chapter One, I referred to a time when my hypnotist encouraged me to locate a particular book that happened to be out of print. He said, "Don't worry. You'll find it." At the time, the internet did not exist and I had to search extensively and diligently. For weeks I phoned local bookstores and book dealers and visited secondhand bookstores, all to no avail.

A few weeks later, a friend and I were discussing the powers of the mind when I made reference to the book and how difficult it was to locate. She inquired where I had finally found it and a moment of confusion overcame me. I had found the book but to this day, I cannot recall how or where I found that book. I am sure it didn't mysteriously materialize via a Star Trek transporter. For me, it confirmed that the *law of attraction* is indisputable.

The concept of coincidence was introduced in Chapter 3. Ironically, the term coincidence cannot be applied unless a thought or idea preceded an action or event, regardless of when it was conceived. For example, you say to yourself that you need to contact someone. A day or two later you run into that someone at a coffee shop you never visited before. Scientists can define the laws of magnetism and gravitational forces. Yet by contrast, the law of attraction provides more than scientists are able to explain.

The power and mystery of hidden programs, silent desires and the law of attraction were clearly revealed during a coaching consultation I once conducted. The incident involved a mother and her fourteen-year-old daughter. The mother was insistent that the daughter continue pursuing a professional figure skating career. From an early age the daughter was relentlessly pushed to excel. The mother sought my counsel to coach her daughter to regain her enthusiasm, as she was becoming disinterested in figure skating. She had already won several major competitions and was in position to win a prestigious regional championship. I cautioned the mother that the goal and desire had to be her daughter's dream as undue pressure would induce negative ramifications for her daughter.

In private, the daughter expressed how she dreaded the competitions, the pressure, the long days and the lack of a social life. She confided that at night she secretly wished that she would break her leg. About six weeks later, I received an unexpected late-night call from the hospital. The daughter was ecstatically shouting on the phone, "I broke my leg! It's over!"

I could include multiple chapters recounting stories of results that mysteriously occurred due to unexpected and unusual events. Occasionally, outcomes that at first appear unpleasant may later yield benefits that aid in the acquisition or achievement of other goals. Self-assessments often reveal that the events are uncannily similar to long forgotten or deeply held desires and thoughts we once possessed.

An example of how a hidden program affects our behavior involves recalling a time when we needed to purchase a gift for a child. While searching for the perfect gift, we were surprised to notice an item that we wished we had possessed or could have afforded when we were the age of the child. Instantly, our excitement ran high and the anticipated reaction from the child made this the perfect gift. But when the gift was presented, the child at best displayed a lack luster reaction to the gift. The difference between our over-the-top enthusiasm and the child's indifference was that our choice was not based on what the child desired, but a deep-seated desire for an item we craved, coveted and valued when we were a child. Our childhood desire was never fulfilled and remained as a hidden program until it was activated when an opportunity arose.

The law of attraction continues to fulfill our desires, regardless of when they were established. The mysterious realm of attraction, magnetism and psychic experiences is greater than we can imagine. Numerous accounts exist of people who missed a connection, had their vehicle break down or abruptly changed plans only to meet a key person, avoid a tragedy or be in a position to act on an opportunity they long desired. Their presence at that place and time would not have occurred except for the unplanned diversion. There are countless stories of people missing deadlines for job postings, only to notice a better position later, or receiving subsequent news that would have made choosing the first posting a career disaster. We often hear people say—things happen for a reason.

Philosophical and metaphysical debates continue as to whether these occurrences have connections to a greater energy grid or are merely coincidences. When an event, long lost acquaintance or an object or opportunity is suddenly in front of you, you may catch yourself saying—I was just thinking about that the other day. That thought activated your subconscious mind to be on the lookout for you. Although science cannot explain this phenomenon, you can simply call it a coincidence or appreciate it as the law of attraction.

When a situation turns out badly, there is a tendency to focus on the disappointment. Sometimes, it isn't until a new opportunity presents itself later that you realize you would not have been in a position to act had the unpleasant incident not occurred. The negative event may not have been enjoyable but was necessary to achieve a specific outcome that you desired. The negative situation may have provided an important lesson, contact or an awareness of what was required to protect you or achieve a goal that you *once* or *still* desire.

As you strive for a goal, you may feel that there are barriers holding you back. There may be a conflicting hidden program that is undermining your efforts to achieve your goal. It could be that your subconscious mind is protecting you by ensuring that you do not achieve that goal. The achievement of your goal may induce a negative outcome for those close to you or place you in a position that compromises your relationship, finances, values, safety or other opportunities.

A simple approach to identifying a memory or setting that is impeding your performance, is to question your subconscious mind. The subtle feedback or answer will identify a specific incident stored in memory. Often, you will remember the event in detail. The original thought may not have been yours but a comment from a close friend, relative, stranger, person of authority, someone you despise or even an old radio or TV program. The comment from memory may not hold one iota of truth, but it was recorded in your subconscious mind as if it were true. When an opportunity presents itself, the subconscious mind instructs your command center to perform to the exact constructs of that belief or program setting. When a memory is revealed through this process, be assured that it is a sleeper or hidden program inhibiting your achievements.

Answers to your questions can be revealed in the form of intuition. Intuitive feedback cannot be forced. Intuition flows naturally but answers may not be immediately revealed. The answer may unexpectedly surface days later. You may be on public transit, driving a car, in a meeting, waiting for an appointment, on vacation or walking when a picture, thought or word suddenly sparks the answer to pop into your conscious mind. At times, the impact is so enlightening that you may issue a deep sigh of relief or feel an unusually calm sensation in your solar plexus. An alternate reaction is to doubt, wonder and question whether the answer or blockage could be that trivial or straightforward.

By continually exploring your subconscious mind through questioning, additional and meaningful information will be revealed, often when you least expect it. The process will solidify into a habit as you become unconsciously competent at exploring the extent of your mind power.

Neutralizing the energy of an old desire or idea can be effectively achieved during an autosuggestion session or by consciously acknowledging and neutralizing the thought when it surfaces. It is important to take control of your self-talk and declare that the old belief has expired and describe or assert what you currently desire. If the memory was an insult, put-down or attack on your character, instantly dismiss the person and the comment and confidently affirm who you have become or desire to be.

Developing this technique transforms your subconscious mind from a traitor into an invaluable coach and friend. A hidden program can be your sixth sense prompting you to do or go somewhere, a heads-up that the person you are talking with may be the best person to ask about an idea, resource or project or a warning to guard yourself against that person.

Developing your mind power requires exploring subtle ideas, hunches, sensations and intuitions that are revealed when you least expect them. The sensing or prompting to engage in a get-rich-quick scheme and gambling are not solutions for enhancing your financial situation. They become program settings that guarantee failure. Acting on ideas that prompt you to explore part-time jobs, a career move or a business opportunity are solid steps for success. Successful people follow up and explore ideas or hunches that become profitable or beneficial. Failures watch them and insist they are lucky or they get all the breaks. Acting on intuition or hunches requires effort, another action that failures avoid and don't like to do.

As you explore your memories, remember, they are not necessarily true or reasonable. The events may have never occurred. Many memories are not your words but recollections of what others stated or what you imagined. The thoughts could have occurred when you were a child, in school or at an event. It may have been a passing comment that your subconscious recorded as fact but remained an influential guidance system setting. The memory could have been an insult that implanted itself with intense emotion and became a belief that your self-image setting executes as the way you see and portray yourself.

Some of the memories and explanations might have been stated in humor or were malicious attacks by a friend, co-worker, stranger or relative. When you were young, a parent, friend or sibling may have made cruel comments about your appearance. Or you may have felt embarrassed when friends dismissed your ideas and aspirations. When you identify the source or recognize the voice of a particular person, you can terminate the effect that memory has on you and create an overriding positive belief.

A situation that generates multiple sensory impulses is criticism. No one enjoys criticism. However harsh or painful, feedback is valuable when we evaluate our behaviors or the vibes we conveyed to cause the person to say what they did. We often reject the criticism by quickly applying a quantum leap. We conclude that they are rude or stupid to diffuse the sting of the feedback and protect our ego. There is value in reflecting on the situation later by asking—what vibes, expressions, body language or subliminal messages or behaviors did I exhibit for them to perceive me that way? Honesty can be brutal; fortunately, your thoughts are private.

It could be days before a thought flashes through your mind about the behavior you exhibited that caused them to drop the stinger. It may be that you are too insensitive or indiscrete and offended them. It may be jealousy on their part or they may have felt slighted. There may or may not be a logical explanation for the feedback you received as their response was based on their conditioning and beliefs. Your solar plexus will confirm its validity by the level of assurance sensed when you assess the explanation from your subconscious mind. Caution is advised. The level of discomfort can be a trap that offers an opportunity to dismiss the issue and protect the ego. By applying the exploratory techniques offered in this book, you can validate whether your conclusion is true or whether it is a killer distracting you from the real issue. Without a resolution, the conflict is likely to occur again.

Hidden programs develop when excuses or feigned illnesses are created to avoid a situation. When someone pretends to be sick or unavailable each time they wish to avoid a situation, a habit forms to repeat the practice. Someone else might discover that their weight gain was a subconscious diversion to avoid participating in physical activities. The subconscious mind is supremely capable of causing injuries and weight gain or creating excuses to avoid issues or activities. Individuals who seek partners through new ventures and clubs that are radically different from their normal lives, develop incompatible relationships and rarely do they pursue the new activity once the relationship is secured. The new activities are not compatible with their true Self. Subliminally, they introduce tactics to discontinue the new activities and return to being who they really are. The conditioning of their authentic Self remains a hidden program and undermines the new relationship.

A hidden program or belief was a direct link to the origin of my migraine headaches. It manifested at a young age from repeatedly hearing conversations about an accident that I had when I was two years old. Visitors would inquire about a scar on my forehead with questions like—how did that happen? Is he okay now? Does he get headaches? Over time and with repetition, an idea was implanted that I should have headaches. Ironically, the accident occurred during an enjoyable and pleasurable event. Later, my migraines never occurred during high stress or times of difficulties, only when events were exceptionally enjoyable. It was as if my guidance system activated a migraine as a protection program to terminate further participation. The feelings of comfort and happiness were forewarnings of danger or an unpleasant event that was about to occur.

After I identified these conversations, I was able to dismiss them through autosuggestion. My hypnotist directed me to isolate the accident, visualize it in my imagination and burn the picture as I repeated, "I am free of this accident." I was instructed to repeat the process involving the memories of the visitors who discussed my accident. During an autosuggestion session, I created a picture of the room and the people in it and burned that picture. Although simple to perform, the process seemed weird and rather silly at first.

Within three weeks of implementing this technique, I sensed an internal *knowing* that these issues would never return. The power of the mind is not to be underestimated. By identifying and overriding these memories and conversations through autosuggestion, except for the occasional minor occurrence, the headaches have mysteriously disappeared for over forty years. The memories are still there but they no longer have any power over me.

This process can be applied to multiple situations, including issues that involve people, beliefs and ridiculous comments. Imagining old goals, previous desires, phrases or beliefs as plaques or pictures and neutralizing them as you express being free of their power is extremely effective. You may also imagine other actions to effectively defuse the power of a concept, belief or event. Drop it in the ocean, launch it into space, crush it with a wrecking ball, vaporize it with a ray gun or toss it into a burn barrel or fire. Whatever means you choose, imagine the scenario dissolving or disappearing and be free of these menacing killers. The old program remains a retrievable memory but it no longer has any energy to control you. After performing this exercise a few times during an autosuggestion process, you will be able to neutralize old thoughts and desires as you go about your daily activities. Imagination is powerful.

No one, other than you, can interpret the subliminal messages. Only through trial and error and a dedicated approach will you decipher what the feedback means. Neutralizing past and hidden programs can take time, but the results are invaluable. Although the process of identifying them provides favorable results, it is easier to train your imagination and develop new dominant programs. Hidden programs cannot surface if you maintain an intense focus on a specific goal. It is the lack of focus, inattention or passivity that allows hidden programs to return and sabotage you.

You can create an overall protection plan to neutralize or prevent hidden programs from surfacing. When practicing self-coaching, autosuggestion or developing power phrases and assertions, preface each command by stating, *"With the free will and for the good of all concerned, I now attract..."*. These words program your guidance system to remain in harmony with those around you. Your energy will attract outcomes that are compatible with your current goals and relationships. When you remain focused on a specific goal, any conflict that would have been created by an old and detrimental goal is rejected by your biocomputer as it *does not compute to achieve the good of all concerned*. You are then harmoniously guided to opportunities that are compatible with your current desires. The moment an old idea, desire or thought surfaces that is contrary to your current goal, neutralize it with your favorite mental weapon.

The worksheet on page 305 will assist you in identifying hidden programs that generate personal and internal conflicts. In the first column, present a question that addresses a barrier, challenge or blockage that you are encountering. It could be the fact that you cannot locate the job or position you want, attain your desired weight, get into an exercise routine or whatever you feel you are working hard to achieve but appears to be eluding you. Ensure the question addresses only one issue or topic.

If you cannot identify a thought or belief that is preventing your goal from being fulfilled, let it go. Let some time pass. It may be several days, but when you are relaxed, the answer will be revealed providing you listen to your thoughts. You can then complete the exercise.

The third column is to record the origin of that comment that is blocking or protecting you from fulfilling your goal. As your memory reveals the words, you will identify the voice of the person who initially stated it. These are the words of the killer that are blocking your success. Additional exploratory questions are provided in Appendix M.

Your subconscious mind holds a myriad of secrets. Some are helpful while others are killers. If you want to enjoy more of what life has to offer, it is absolutely crucial that you identify and suppress your killers. Many killers are revealed during your daily activities. As you continue to apply the concepts throughout this book, it should become obvious that words are powerful and have a significant effect on your success and achievements. Words and sensory impulses are the main forms of communication between your subconscious mind and your command center. We are easily influenced and sabotaged by our words and the words of others. Understanding the power of words is the topic of the next chapter.

Locating Hidden Programs

(Exploratory questions are provided in Appendix M)

Exploratory Question or Event:	Subtle Answer or First Response	Origin of Thought or Feeling
Why do I repeat or attract...?		
What beliefs prevent me from achieving...?		
What prevents me from...?		
What is the benefit of not...?		
What would happen if I did achieve...?		
What previous desire is interfering with...?		
What would I be required to change if I achieved...?		
What did I gain by experiencing or attracting...?		
Why do I...?		
Other?		

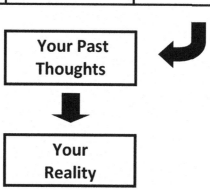

Your Past Thoughts

Your Reality

We are more often frightened than hurt— and we suffer more from imagination than from reality.

Seneca (4 BCE-65 CE)

Chapter 28

The Communication Saboteurs

Effective communication with others and our subconscious mind is a major factor that determines success. It has become common to classify communication as verbal, visual and written. Yet every day, we rarely notice a powerful form of communication—energy. We frequently refer to this energy as vibes or getting on the same wavelength as others.

Interpersonal communication involves various forms of verbal and nonverbal communication. To control mind power and succeed in our careers, social lives and relationships, we must clearly express our ideas, requests and instructions in ways that are meaningful to others. Our effectiveness increases exponentially when we are able to influence the subconscious minds and command centers of others by actively engaging their conscious minds.

The dynamics of interpersonal communications are complex but there are many obvious clues to provide guidance. The development of your sixth sense (intuition) depends on your awareness of the cause and effect of words, tone of voice and body language. In addition, it is important to accurately interpret the feedback from your self-talk and your solar plexus. Ignoring any of these, is a serious mistake. Feeling rushed or impatient during personal interactions causes us to ignore the subtle messages from our solar plexus. We miss the vibes that convey what others are saying, implying or omitting. When mind power is not exercised effectively, not only do we place ourselves at a disadvantage but misunderstandings increase and opportunities are often ignored.

It is easy to recall interactions that did not go as planned. They escalated into disagreements or heated debates. Negative situations can be significantly reduced when we watch and listen to the one who is communicating and follow up on the signals we intuitively perceive.

The continuous monologue of our self-talk distracts our conscious attention from the one talking. Instead of listening attentively, the rapid processing capabilities of our self-talk cause us to focus on a response. We also miss the constant warnings our solar plexus and self-talk provide, generally with the exact words or questions required to clarify what we are subliminally detecting. When this occurs, our conscious capacity is unable to process what we hear or sense and we miss vital clues that affect what is being conveyed.

There are basic words that identify valuable feedback but they are generally overlooked. We transmit and receive information through three specific modes that influence and control our biocomputers. The three modes of communication are—auditory, visual and kinesthetic (spelled *"kinaesthetic"* in the UK). Undeniably, the aspects of hearing, seeing and feeling correspond directly to the aspects of self-talk, visualization and the solar plexus.

When we communicate, we utilize at least one, and at times all three modes, in the same sentence or interaction. The modes indicate how our biocomputers receive, process and convey messages. Each mode is identified by specific words. We've heard others say—Oh, she's so sensitive. She's a visual person. He's always so serious or deep in thought. There is a danger of characterizing a person in one of these modes, thinking that they are always in that mode. You will soon observe how you can be in one mode and instantly switch to another.

We can identify the modes by listening carefully to the words expressed in conversation. Words associated with auditory or thinking are—Hear, Listen, Sounds, Tell, Mention, Inquire, Tune, Vocal, Remark, Say, Report, Rings A Bell, Silence, Heard, Outspoken, Talk, Speak, State, Loud, Articulate, Ask, Describe, Audible, Noisy, Mention, Forgot, Speak and Utter. These words are auditory and are processed by our sense of hearing and thinking—self-talk.

The communication of a visual message is conveyed with words that accentuate images and simulations in the mind. Words that identify that one is in a visual mode include—Show, See, Look, Imagine, Picture this, Watch, Notice, Observe, Focus, Appear, Envision, Dawn, Snapshot, Vivid, Crystal Clear, Reveal, View, Foresee, Illustrate and Scene.

Words that initiate a sense of feeling or activate the solar plexus and emotions are kinesthetic. Keywords that identify a person is in a kinesthetic mode include—Feel, Sense, Uneasy, Not comfortable, Not sure, Bother, Emotional, Assume, Touch, Grasp, Catch on, Unfeeling, Suffer, Smooth, Relaxed, Loose, Heavy, Cool, Whipped, Unsettled, Tense, Stress, Sensitive, Panicky, Intuition, Hunch and Hassle.

Each mode is not affected by the tense of the words. For example, the word hear includes heard and hearing; see includes saw and seeing; and feel and sense would include the words feeling, felt, sensed and sensing.

It is important to assess what others are saying and identify the mode in which they are communicating. If a person is communicating in an auditory mode, you will hear words of an auditory nature. Communication fails when one communicates in an auditory mode and the other responds with visual or kinesthetic words. Both parties can become confused. One party may think that the other did not hear what they said, or feel they are disagreeing with them. Applying mind power requires maintaining a constant awareness of how our minds are influenced by words.

The value of this awareness became apparent to me during a meeting with a client. We were customizing a training manual for his employees. After much discussion, I prepared a new section for him. When I placed the documents on his desk I said, "Take a look at these and see if this is what you had in mind." Without looking at the documents, he leaned back in his chair and said, "How I thought we would approach this is...". He continued to verbally describe his idea and what he preferred to include. Instantly, I was aware that no matter how much time I invested in those documents, he was not interested in *looking* at them while he was in an auditory mode.

Our conversation continued along his auditory mode. I waited for an opportunity to switch his thinking into a visual mode, but the opportunity did not occur for several minutes. Finally, I recapped his issues and concerns and as I pointed to my documents again, I casually inquired, "Taking the concerns that you just *verbalized* into consideration, is this how it would *look* in document form for your employees?"

The moment I was able to steer the conversation by again inserting the word *look* into our discussion, it was almost comical to notice how quickly he leaned forward and dove into the documents. Within seconds, he expressed, "This looks great. I hadn't thought about it that way." He began in a visual mode to review the documents but responded in a visual and auditory mode by stating the words "looks" and "thought."

Incompatible communication modes are the same as one person communicating on an Android based operating system and the other on a macOS or Windows based system. If the parties involved do not communicate on the same platform (mode), miscommunication is guaranteed.

Once you have identified that a person is in a particular mode, e.g., auditory, do not think for a moment that they are an auditory person and are always in that mode. It is common to present a question in one mode, only to have the individual bounce through each mode as they respond. For example, "Jamie, what do you think we should do with that display case?" Jamie could reply with, "Well, when I look at that display, I feel it has no vibes or resonance and I think it would be better to have…".

This example demonstrates that a response in any or all modes is effective. If a person responds using only one of the following—it doesn't look right, or I think it could use more…, or I feel it should…, then the keyword that identifies the appropriate mode in which to respond is look, think or feel. When a suggestion is met with a hesitation or no response, quickly assess not only what you said but which mode was used. An obvious pause indicates that they are struggling with your input and it is likely incongruent with the mode they are using to assess the situation—at that moment.

Regardless of the mode you are in, to respond in a mode contrary to that of the other person, generates conflict and confusion. Should you make a statement and a person does not engage, following up with a few exploratory questions in each mode prompts them to participate. Adjusting your presentation to ensure the other person receives your message in a way that is meaningful to them, eliminates the time required later to clarify misunderstandings.

When I sense that the other person is silent or is confused as to how to reply, I will introduce a blanket question similar to—based on what we're discussing, can you tell me what you see or how you feel about the situation? This enables me to focus on the issue rather than speculate how they are processing information. The solar plexus is a marvelous coach that informs us when something is amiss and prompts us to modify our presentation immediately.

Communication saboteurs are quickly identified. The solar plexus is continuously on the alert and senses the vibes of others. You are instantly informed when your solar plexus and self-talk interpret a sensory impulse as—uh-oh! What's wrong? What are they implying? This becomes another moment of power. If you react rather than respond (Page 69), you are more likely to escalate any conversation into a volatile situation. A reflex action that is instigated by a tone of voice is referred to as mirroring. If you are unsure why a person responded in the manner they did, or with the tone of voice they chose, they were mirroring you. At a subconscious level, our response is based on what we subliminally believe that person is implying. Messages are conveyed by tone of voice, facial expression and body language. The signals have infinite interpretations that can range from patronizing to accusatory or indifference.

Should someone speak to you with a loud voice, your conditioning generates an autonomic reaction to respond in a louder voice. However, the dynamics instantly shift when you respond in a calm, relaxed voice or in a lower tone. Within seconds, the other person adjusts their response to mirror your mode. Customer service representatives who reply in a monotone voice make customers feel that they are an inconvenience to them. A platform for a volatile exchange is quickly created. Although each situation is different, we can choose how we respond.

If you are curious as to why a person responded as they did, it is to your benefit to assess how you approached them. Their response was based on your body language, the words you used and the tone of your voice. Sensory impulses identified by their solar plexus and processed by their biocomputer subliminally calculated their response. It is unlikely that you were aware of what they were thinking, worrying about or what was happening in their life. They could have been dealing with a serious and sensitive issue or were late for an appointment.

At times, we may appear pushy, dismissive, arrogant or patronizing or we may demonstrate behaviors that cause others to be defensive. Without taking the time to reflect on the dynamics, we only have ourselves to blame when interactions go wrong. If you notice that people are tense or their responses are less pleasant, it may be time to reflect on how you communicate with others. A lower and quieter tone of voice is not always the magic solution, as it may appear patronizing. A confident and direct response can clarify nebulous or unjustified beliefs for others. When one responds in a reserved or cautious tone, or lacks confidence, the solar plexus of both parties can trigger their self-talk into a tirade of constructive or destructive possibilities.

One line of code can significantly alter the output of a computer program as you observed on pages 62 and 64. Likewise, it was one word that enabled you to command your hand to drop an object. Our effectiveness can be altered by one word. This includes both communicating with others and what we are processing in our self-talk. For example, a speed sign that reads "60" provides information; but traffic signs that read—Slow Down or Resume Speed—prompt action. Whether we provide information or request action, the message can be severely compromised by the words we use.

As stated earlier, the primary goal of advertisers is to create action. They ensure every mode and means of communication are employed to attack our subconscious minds and command centers with words, sounds and pictures that stimulate our emotions. They effectively infuse a chain reaction into our conscious and subconscious minds by engaging our command center, self-talk, visualization (imagination) and solar plexus. We are instantly or gradually programmed to respond favorably to their messages.

As a communicator, parent, manager, leader or sales consultant, it is your responsibility to ensure that your instructions or messages are received and understood. This is accomplished by introducing questions to clarify what the recipient understood and to confirm that they will respond as requested. When your solar plexus signals your consciousness that the person you are conversing with is not on the same wavelength, one or a series of casual questions can easily clarify the situation.

It is critical that you avoid the most fatal question when communicating—*do you understand?* (Page 184). The moment that you notice your solar plexus is sensing that the person you are talking to is confused or not receiving your message, take responsibility and assist them to relax. Casually, and in a relaxed tone, ask, "I feel I am not explaining myself clearly. Can you tell me what your understanding is to this point and I'll fill in what I left out?" This allows them to save face, relax and freely participate if they were no longer listening. Their response may provide valuable feedback that identifies where your presentation was confusing.

Another saboteur surfaces when one presents a question and continues to talk. The person they are talking to will look at them and wonder—why ask a question if you do not wait for my answer? Immediately after asking a question, it is imperative that you stop talking. Keep Quiet! Avoid making any additional vocal sounds or ending your statements with a higher tone of voice indicating that you might have more to say. Do not say another word or make a sound. In a negotiating or sales situation, the first person to speak after a question or ultimatum often loses.

Silence or a pause after a question, is the decisive action required at that critical moment during self-exploration when you question to seek answers from your subconscious mind. Your sixth sense (intuition) will be drowned out if you keep talking or focusing on distracting input, regardless of the source. To assist in your development of mind power, you may have noticed that the word [pause] is placed after many of the self-exploratory questions.

Various questions and assertions are provided in Appendices N and O to address situations that you may encounter. Your effectiveness will depend on whether you practice vocalizing the phrases aloud—not silently in your mind. No different than public speaking, practicing ensures that your message appears natural and unscripted. Otherwise, you will sound like a bad actor in a second-rate movie who never practiced their script.

To enhance your sixth sense (intuition) while communicating with others, observe their body language and the sensory impulses detected by your solar plexus. Questions and ideas that are generated in your self-talk are prompts from your subconscious mind to act upon at that moment. When observing others, your visual focus should be on their eyes and the area around them. When a controversial or displeasing statement is made, the recipient's pupils will change, as well as the skin below and to the side of their eyes. The texture of the skin will tighten if they are in disagreement or relax when in agreement. Other reflex actions to observe are posture, nervousness, fake or insincere smiles or variations in tone of voice. With practice, you will begin to notice that your solar plexus regularly activates your self-talk with clues as to what to do, say or clarify.

Clarifying the position of another person is quickly achieved by asking open-ended questions. Leading questions alter the true response a person would have provided. Information received that was influenced by this type of questioning does not generate accurate or honest feedback.

Communication saboteurs can be ego driven. The ego is conditioned to focus on statements that require defending itself rather than promoting constructive outcomes. When you are in a controversial situation and position of authority, as a parent, supervisor, manager or advisor, avoid the accusatory word *you* wherever possible. The word *you* will inflame their solar plexus and self-talk, instantaneously detonating an autonomic defense. The recipient often perceives the word *you* as blame, a challenge or a judgment. The situation escalates to a threat (Page 69) and the recipient diverts their limited conscious capacity to their defense. The recipient is subliminally provoked to focus on survival rather than initiating constructive solutions to resolve the issue.

In business, personal or social interactions, it is more effective to approach a sensitive situation with an opening statement that is non-threatening. For example, "Blake, I understand there is a concern about [topic]," or "James, I'm not sure if you're aware of what transpired when so-and-so heard [describe the words expressed without stating 'you said'], but it has created some concerns." A relaxed tone of voice and body language enable this approach to remain non-confrontational. Any sarcastic, intense or leading tone of voice is guaranteed to inflame the situation and undermine your efforts.

Conversely, in a sales situation, applying the word *you* will engage the customer to share their values and requirements. Avoid the word *"I"*. Customers are the ones paying and they need to feel that they are the center of attention—not you. For example—It appears you are selective in your choices. What is your preference as to...? Is this what you had in mind? Between the two, which do you (think, feel, see) is more desirable? A salesperson who arrogantly commandeers the buying process by saying, "I would buy this, or I would do that," often sabotages a potential sale, particularly when they did not make a positive first impression.

As a customer, attention to the words a salesperson uses can be a warning. When you hear your name mentioned too often, take note and assess—is this salesperson genuinely friendly or are they engaging techniques to cause me to drop my guard and part with my money? Schmoozing is an engaging tactic and can take advantage of your insecurities and cause your solar plexus to feel that this person is really nice or cares about you. Schmoozing is a weapon of choice for con-artists as it lures many to fall victim to their insincere charm.

Improving communication requires preparation. Rather than worrying about upcoming meetings and social or family encounters, identify the situations that cause you to feel uneasy or that you want to change. Then prepare a script for each scenario and practice your response, either consciously as you go about your day or in a state of autosuggestion.

A conflict often presents itself at an inopportune time and catches you off guard. If you have practiced your responses during several autosuggestion sessions, they will be easier to recall. Your response may not be stated as eloquently as you imagined, causing you to appear nervous and unsure. The decision to make a stand will cause your solar plexus and your self-talk to explode, but once you act, and as your heartbeat slows to normal, your confidence will begin to soar. You will have taken that first step to breaking the pattern of not speaking up and will have established a subliminal program to be assertive and confident. With practice, your responses will become more natural and effective and create a dominant program.

Direct dealing is a requirement for defending yourself against those whose intent is to bully or intimidate you. Each situation is different and practicing various scenarios (scripts) in advance is essential. When you act, the intimidator's first reaction will be one of surprise as bullies are not used to being confronted. Once you launch a challenge, it is unlikely that it will have to be repeated, as a bully will know that you are not easily intimidated.

Enhancing communication skills and achieving goals require the successful implementation and management of mind power. Like learning to ride a bike, there will be bumps, falls, scrapes and bruises. When we fall, we pick ourselves up and regain control. When we persevere and develop our mind power skills, a whole new world opens up. The next chapter outlines how to get back on task when things go wrong.

Chapter 29

Where It Goes WRONG!!!

Knowing is one thing. Doing is another. You now understand how killers (mental responses and physical habits) are executable programs that can usurp your best efforts. Keeping yourself on the straight and narrow path to success can be a challenge. Killers will continue to attack fiercely or subtly until you are unconsciously competent in defending yourself. Achieving success requires constant vigilance. You must recognize when you are hesitating or have stopped progressing. This is the crucial moment to direct your mind power to engage that unexplainable energy to place you back on track as quickly as possible.

Achieving success also requires a personal commitment and determination to do the things that failures don't like to do. Your power and effectiveness are determined by your ability to override and program your subconscious mind and control your self-talk. Your only weapons are your imagination, words you think or say and knowing how and when to apply these weapons. The power phrases provided in Self-coaching Appendix O will enable you to direct that unexplainable power to control situations and surge forward.

In games where you cannot escape a trap, you are penalized or forced to return to your starting point. If you are determined to achieve a goal, the number of times you are required to begin again is irrelevant. Disruptions are plentiful but the killer only wins when you quit. Regardless of the setback, the time to begin again is the moment you know you are off course. It may play like a game, but this game is more serious—it's *your* life.

Being prepared is your best defense. Yet, as prepared as you may be, there are 10 common traps that you will encounter. Each trap is no different than being held hostage or caught in quicksand where you are drawn deeper into situations you dislike. If you do not extricate yourself from them, killers (habits or programs) will terminate your efforts, keep you hostage and punt you back to the starting line—every single time. A 16th century Latin proverb advises us—*forewarned is forearmed.*

As stated earlier, we are not doers. We are deciders. Without deciding and setting a course for what you desire, you will remain a ship without a rudder as you aimlessly drift along, distracted by the next internal or external killer that hacks your biocomputer. As you wish and dream about new opportunities or acquisitions, that enjoyable feeling is quickly terminated the moment you mentally reinforce limitations or disappointments. This is the first trap. Only by applying your mind power can you escape.

Trap #1: Energizing the Killer Instead of Your Goal

When you dwell on your current negative situation, the conscious capacity of your mind is consumed and you cannot focus on your desired outcome. Negative words are programs that the subconscious mind executes to direct your actions (behaviors) toward repeating the activities that led you to your current and undesirable circumstances. If you are not thinking about the negative situation but not initiating a new action either, you create a VOID that has no goal, outcome or destination. Your subconscious mind and the law of attraction do not have new settings, and because your subconscious mind must have a program to execute, by default, your biocomputer processes old programs to repeat your current situation. A decision to do, be or have, complete with a specific goal or destination, is required to escape trap # 1 and avoid trap # 2.

Trap #2: Lack of New Ideas

You cannot progress without seeing your goal or destination in your mind's eye (imagination) or setting a course of action (plan). Your biocomputer requires a setting that is created when you repeatedly focus on new ideas or activities to replace those that you do not like. Failing to do this will, by default, punt you back to the starting line. Even though you develop new ideas and plans, killers will attempt to force you into trap # 3.

Trap #3: Not Evaluating Your Progress

To be forewarned and forearmed requires regularly reviewing your plans to identify how far you have advanced and what can possibly go wrong. Double check your plan to decipher whether any angst is due to your subconscious mind prompting you to notice a glaring omission or a killer attempting to create a distraction.

Evaluating your plans is also a time for self-reflection. Do you enjoy short periods of total silence to reflect on what is occurring and what you need to do? Until you have developed the habit of applying and controlling your mind power in busy environments, it is easier to train your imagination by turning off all electronic devices and disconnecting from social media. Enjoy your own company for half an hour or more. If you cannot reclaim control of your mind, you will remain as Nikola Tesla described himself in 1919 in My Inventions—*You will have become an automaton devoid of free will in thought and action and merely responsible to the forces of the environment.* You will remain on your treadmill of life and sink into the quicksand of disappointment and unhappiness, all the while yearning for something better.

Trap #4: Doubt and Anxiety

If you doubt that you can achieve your goal, your anxiety and negative thoughts will continue to kill your best intentions and punt you back to the starting line. Listen to what your self-talk says. To escape this trap, a memory or guidance system setting is required. This is best performed through autosuggestion by training your imagination to see yourself achieving your goal.

Only by removing doubts and anxiety and working within the constraints of your time, money and resources will you be able to escape this trap and avoid trap # 5.

Trap #5: Not Believing in Yourself

Do you *Believe* and have confidence that you can and will achieve your goal if you work at it? If not, you cannot escape your current situation. A non-confident answer is an immediate plunge into this trap and Trap #4, and you are punted back to the starting line. You can only escape these five traps by applying a quantum leap and seeing (imagining) yourself doing, being and enjoying your desired activity. When you add emotions and feel that you are living your new goal without any Ifs, Ands, Buts or Doubts—you have achieved a major milestone of success. Believing in yourself is everything. There are no alternatives. Without confidence, the law of attraction cannot guide you to achieve your desires. Now you can prepare yourself for the seasoned killers that are sure to attack.

Trap #6: Unprepared for Killer Attacks

Your road to success is threatened by killers and zombies waiting to ambush you at a moment's notice. They are easily repelled when you express the simplest and shortest mind commands, affirmations or assertions. This is mind power. Use it or lose it. It is imperative that you prepare defense statements that can be instantly recited to deflect the verbal assaults in your self-talk that distract and discourage your progress. If you are not prepared, your best intentions are quickly neutralized.

Having a plan enhances your personal power and enables you to identify and prepare for distractions and attacks, not only from killers within, but from external sources in the form of negativity from friends, co-workers, family, advertisers or social media. Constructive input by others is valuable but it is only you who can identify where, when, how and by whom you may be ambushed. You may be unaware of a killer or zombie, but rest assured, it is lurking, and when you least expect it, an ambush is guaranteed.

Should a killer strike when you are unprepared, you may have no choice but to take the hit. Respond as best you can. Learn from it, but get back on task and script a mental defense so you are prepared to suppress that type of killer the next time it attacks—and it definitely will. You only fail when you quit.

Trap #7: Careless Talk with The Enemy

Loose lips sink ships is a war time warning. Its intent is to caution you about what you say in public. You never know who is listening or intentionally prying into your affairs. The same applies to your ideas, goals and plans. Falling for the bait of carelessly answering questions about your goals and plans, places you at risk of losing the energy that is generated by your inner private thoughts. Talking indiscreetly or openly enables others to sneer, mock or discourage you. Enemies are everywhere and include co-workers, family and friends. An awareness of who is in your immediate environment enables you to protect yourself.

Seeking input from others increases the opportunity for them to question, spoof, doubt or ridicule your goals, plans and wishes. Your thoughts and goals need to be kept private, the same as guarding your passwords on your phone, computer and financial accounts from cyber thieves and computer hackers. You create a huge risk by indiscreetly speaking about your goals during their developmental stage.

When you are bursting with enthusiasm and want to tell someone what you are doing, seriously consider if they will encourage or mock your efforts. You are taunting a killer when you share your goals with those who do not share your passion, will not benefit from your achievement or lack the knowledge of the intricacies required to achieve your goal. Often, advice is worth only what you pay for it. Rather than increasing the risk of being discouraged, either remain silent or consult only those who are experienced in your endeavors, even if it involves a cost.

Trap #8: Avoidance Behaviors Disguised as Important

When you finish reading this book, you will probably be excited, motivated and enthusiastic about achieving a new goal or finishing a project. Your killers will act immediately and set the most enticing traps to destroy that feeling. Avoiding this fatal trap requires an awareness of yourself saying—first I'm going to do X; or I'm going to check on N; or I will start that this weekend. If that action is part of an established plan, that's great. However, if that step is not necessary to get you started, it is possible that you are being duped by an existing killer (habit) distracting you from acting decisively. Even performing a small task that is goal related sends a positive message to your subconscious mind that this goal is important and you are determined to continue until you succeed.

Procrastination appears in multiple forms. Enemies and killers are masters of distraction and avoidance behaviors. They distract you by diverting your attention to menial tasks and relentlessly tempt you to complete them rather than activities that will advance the achievement of your goal. Your self-talk succumbs to the distractions, and by default, instantaneously instructs your command center to follow the distraction. You are immediately punted back to the starting line.

Trap #9: Setbacks

By now you will have identified that there are numerous killers, zombies and assassins that can nullify your efforts, arrest your progress or frustrate you beyond reason. This is normal and happens to everyone. Each of us has been knocked down or experienced setbacks, delays and losses. Success requires getting up that one more time and continuing after each setback. Winston Churchill provided the best advice—if you're going through hell, keep going. You have the option to set your plans aside to die or pick yourself up and say, "This will only make me stronger. Each and every day, in every way, I get better and better. What is one thing that I can do now to continue my plan?"

Trap #10: Chasing Unrealistic Goals

After evaluating these traps, you may still feel that there is a force that is holding you back and your efforts drag on without any advancement or enjoyment. Despite the fact that you may feel and believe that your goal is important, it may be that there are deep-seated programs that are protesting as your self-talk reveals, "*I don't feel like it.*" If so, your subconscious mind and true Self may be directing you to change course and seek a goal that is more inspiring and uplifting—to you. Your honest evaluation of these questions will provide valuable assistance:

➤ How badly do I want to achieve this goal?

➤ Why do I think I should achieve this goal?

➤ Am I doing this for me or to impress someone?

➤ Where or from whom did the idea of this goal originate?

➤ What is the benefit to me if I achieve this goal?

➤ What is the benefit of *not* achieving this goal?

➤ If this goal were achieved, how would my life change?

➤ By focusing on this goal, what am I depriving myself of?

➤ Is this a goal that is compatible with my core values and who I truly am?

➤ Will the achievement of my goal create conflicts with other goals that I'm striving for or the lives of those close to me?

➤ Is my reluctance valid or is a killer attempting to stop my success?

➤ Am I prepared to pay the physical and emotional price required to achieve this goal?

➤ Why don't I want to do this anymore? [pause and repeat]

Failure to continue may have nothing to do with old or hidden programs. It may simply be a lack of desire to achieve the goal you chose. It may be time to consider a new goal. Without terminating your efforts to achieve this goal and choosing another goal, you will continue to be frustrated and inconvenienced. You will waste valuable energy spinning your wheels.

Be prepared to miss a move or two on the board game of life. When this occurs, review this chapter and coach yourself by applying the power of words to get back on task. You will succeed.

Now that you have insight into where your goals and plans can go wrong, it's time to apply some winning strategies. This is the topic of the last chapter.

**Success is a
cause and effect
mind game.
You only win
when you follow
the rules.**

Chapter 30

It's Time to Win

Since we are deciders first and doers second, the next decision should be a no brainer. We can continue to expend valuable energy repeating and attracting situations that we don't enjoy or we can redirect that same energy to attract what we do desire.

A quick review of the things you like, or want to change, (Pages 39-40) will identify your wishes, dreams and desires. You know what you want. Success is for the making, not for the taking. Moving forward requires choosing one goal and outlining a simple plan. Then identify what to do next and apply mind power to motivate you to take action. It doesn't get easier than that.

Every performer requires a game plan and a winning coach. You may not realize the need for a coach, yet you are no different than an athlete, singer, dancer, performer, CEO or student. We all benefit from coaching. Unfortunately, good coaches are expensive, difficult to locate and not around when a crisis erupts. This means that you must be your own coach.

Throughout this book, powerful concepts have been introduced to show you how to direct and control the power of your mind. The bottom line is that your success and achievements are in your control. You must be the coach who keeps you focused and motivated and who deflects all distractions. The Introduction of this book opened with—*This book is written for you and is all about you.* When the chips are down, it is all about you and what you are prepared to do. Standing firmly on your own, you can rely on your self-talk (internal coach) to guide you. Mind power is the controller of that mysterious energy and your source of protection, and motivation. It is there for you—if you command it.

An awareness of the words in your self-talk is the unquestionable link to managing mind power. It won't be long before you notice the negative banter and killers that continue to badger you and destroy your efforts. Mind power is taking control of your self-talk and retaining control of your command center.

If you remain unsure, Chapters 10 and 14 explain how self-talk instantly alters your state of mind and eliminates psychological resistance. A command or coaching directive provides the perfect quantum leap for maintaining focus or generating that amazing internal power. Your thoughts are private. Whether it is during a time of pleasure or conflict, no one hears you or is aware of what you are thinking or saying to yourself.

As you completed the exercises in the preceding chapters, and followed the explanation of what mind power is and how it functions, several realizations should have occurred. The first is that your subconscious mind is a programmable computer that is easily attacked by negative thoughts, either from memory, your conscious self-talk or from a broad range of external sources. Also, the programs that the subconscious mind processes or executes are habits that can't be changed or removed, but can be overpowered. You can temporarily counter each distraction or attack by immediately applying mind power. However, each conflict, or one similar to it, will continue to recur unless you establish and reinforce new programs (habits) to overpower your past conditioning.

The second realization is that success is not a destination. After your goal is reached, it is imperative that the efforts you applied to achieve your success continue in order to maintain your success. Only by confidently applying positive commands or assertions in your self-talk will you be able to prevent these relentless killers from regaining power. Should you become passive or inattentive, the previously undesirable situations will return by default. You will not be aware of the transition until you are back at the starting line.

The third realization is that while multiple behaviors and subliminal instructions are in process, the conscious mind (self-talk) is limited to processing only one action at a time. While you consciously focus on one task, it is your subconscious mind and autonomic conditioning that enable you to multi-task. Your self-talk reveals exactly where you are going, habits you are programming and actions you are about to perform. It is up to you to verify if that is what you want to do. It is up to you to accept or modify these words. Only one command can be executed—your old behavior or a new command that is introduced through your self-talk.

The fourth realization is that the command center is a hub that completes your subliminal and autonomic programs (behaviors) but can be instantly intercepted by your self-talk or an external source. A quick recall of what was required to drop an object, release the grip of your hand or attempt to stand up, confirms that all physical actions are first activated through a mental process of thoughts and words (Pages 112-114). This is the crux of mind power.

With these four realizations, your mind power is activated when an unambiguous command is spoken silently or aloud. Being consciously aware of the cause and effect created by your words is mind power in action. As circumstances evolve, it is up to you to choose how you will respond to them. If you do not introduce new instructions consciously, your avoidance and passivity will enable killers or external sources to manipulate you.

In times of adversity, people often utter affirmations and power phrases, thinking they are magical lifelines or instantaneous powers that can save them. Some anxiously call out to deities, saints or other protectors based on their belief programs. Your only resources are what you have practiced or been conditioned to do. If you are in a serious situation, whether it is physical danger, emotional disruption or a financial dilemma, panic and anxiety are your worst enemies. Applying mind power is a conscious effort that ensures calmness, focus, options and the confidence to act.

As demonstrated, negative emotions instantly overload your self-talk (conscious mind) with worry, fear or loss. You are rendered incapable of action because your conscious mind is unable to receive guidance and creative solutions from your subconscious mind. Negative or self-denigrating thoughts are killers that annihilate your efforts. It is your choice whether you allow the enemy within to control you or whether you engage the assistance of a friendly coach to support you—your self-talk and imagination.

It is paramount that you script and edit commands that focus on what you desire and that they are free of ambiguity. Comments that refer to hardship, lack, debt or negative terms that are not desired must be avoided. Applying the power of a quantum leap instantly immobilizes a killer. Clearly express what you want—not what you don't want.

If your new command sounds weird, feels silly or causes discomfort, realize that these feelings are killers fighting to discourage you from succeeding. The weird and silly feelings are your solar plexus confirming that you are doing and saying the right things to counteract the effects of killer programs. Your positive thoughts are overriding the guidance system settings that are preventing your success. Enjoy that sensation as it guarantees change and future success.

When unprepared for a situation, ask your all-knowing subconscious mind what to do next. Stay calm and listen carefully for that subtle answer and a reassuring sensation from your solar plexus. If a clear response or suggestion is not identified, calmly repeat the question.

Questioning the importance of your goals, wishes and desires on a regular basis ensures that you do not have desires that conflict with other goals or people who are important to you. The law of attraction works best when your all-powerful subconscious mind is instructed to exert its full powers. To ensure conflicting desires are not reinforced, preface each desire by saying:

With the free will and for the good
of all concerned, I now attract...

These words are all-encompassing and function as an insurance clause that protects you from fulfilling old programs or requests that would be destructive if the law of attraction were to manifest them now. As a blanket statement, it captures the power of your subconscious mind to materialize only the things that would be *for the good of all concerned*. This command, repeated often, ensures that your conscious mind, subconscious mind, command center and the law of attraction unite as one powerful force.

Memorizing every response presented is not required. As you become comfortable with these concepts, three to five phrases are sufficient to manage most situations, attacks or challenges. Choose the ones that you feel are appropriate or customize them to suit you. At the onset, they will feel uncomfortable. Remember, a point of power is recognizing that the sensation of discomfort confirms that you are overpowering a killer. Repetition of the commands ensures that you remain in control. When you realize you have taken control of your thoughts, your confidence will soar.

An early feeling of satisfaction and achievement may tempt you to stop your commands. It is critical that you continue your power commands after you have reached a degree of success or achievement. The urge to refrain from repeating a command is an unrelenting killer attempting one last time to regain control. The killers will never go away. They can only be crowded out and suppressed. Repetition of your commands will become a new habit, exactly like that phantom melody that you autonomically hum. In time, the new habits are autonomically processed (without conscious prompting) and will be there to defend you when killers attack.

The new you requires guidance, the same as controlling the steering mechanism of a craft, vehicle or bicycle. You are the vehicle and if you let control slip away, you will crash and burn and return to your old ways. This is indisputable.

Snipers, killers, zombies and assassins are guaranteed to disrupt your life. Nothing will change until you choose to act. Managing disruptions and being able to go with the flow are acquired skills. Regardless of your situations, you have developed the habit of ending up with what you put up with.

Until you initiate decisive steps to take control of your mind power, retrain your imagination, clarify what you want—nothing will change. You are the kubernan or steersman of your life. Steering or controlling your words and thoughts enables you to apply the power of a quantum leap, take control of your conscious mind and direct your command center to release the powers of your subconscious mind.

Mind power is the power of your words. Words activate that unexplainable and mysterious energy that causes you to do, be and have. Challenge yourself to do what failures don't like to do. There you will find your happiness.

**By your words
you are judged,
And by your words
you are condemned.**

**You have the power.
How will you direct it?**

Epilogue

The opening quote in this book was Nikola Tesla's realization that by studying non-physical phenomena, science will make more progress in one decade than was ever thought possible. By engaging in the exercises provided, you have experienced several non-physical phenomena that will influence your destiny. You have been presented with knowledge and instructions to make rapid and concrete changes. It is not the earth-shattering actions that make the greatest differences in life, but the subtle ones. The thoughts and programs you find within you are the influencing factors that Tesla described a century ago:

> *As I review the events of my past life, I realize how subtle are the influences that shape our destinies.*
> *My Inventions, Nikola Tesla (1919)*

My motivation in publishing this book is simple. I want to encourage readers, like you, to be free thinkers and become inspired and motivated to apply the powers of your mind and enjoy more of what life has to offer.

As you discovered, mind power is not a secret. Your awareness has shifted and you no longer need to wonder what to do or wait for others to encourage or direct you. Regardless of your age, this is an opportunity to take that next step and make things happen, or quietly begin a new project just for its enjoyment. Keep asking yourself—what can I do right now?

Here's wishing you much health, happiness and prosperity.

A W Anderson

Bibliography

Cited:

Allen, J. (1903). *As a Man Thinketh*. Mount Vernon, New York: The Peter Pauper Press.

Coué, E. (1922). *Self Mastery Through Conscious Autosuggestion*. Retrieved January 15, 2019, from The Gutenberg Project: http://www.gutenberg.org/cache/epub/27203/pg27203.txt

Descartes, R. (1641). *Meditations on First Philosophy*. (n.d.). Retrieved 2019, from Wikipedia: https://en.wikipedia.org/wiki/Meditations_on_First_Philosophy

Gutenberg Project. (n.d.). Retrieved January 2019, from http://www.gutenberg.org/ebooks/27203

Harris, L.; Taylor, B. (1984). *Escape to Honour*. Toronto: Macmillan of Canada.

Hill, N. (1937). *Think And Grow Rich*. Meriden, CT: The Ralston Society.

James, W. (1890). *The Principles of Psychology*. New York: Henry Holt and Company.

Maltz, M. (1960). *Psycho-Cybernetics*. New York: Pocket Books.

Murphy, J. (1981). *The Power of Your Subconscious Mind*. nglewood cliffs, NJ: Prentice-Hall, Inc.

Petrie, S.; Stone, R. B. (1973). *Hypno-Cybernetics*. New York: Parker Publishing Company, Inc. (Out of Print)

Socrates. (n.d.). Retrieved from Goodreads: https://www.goodreads.com/quotes/117003

Tesla, N. (1919). My Inventions. New York: Experimenter Publishing.

Thomas, P. (1979). *Psycho-feedback*. Englewood Cliffs, NJ: Prentice-Hall, Inc.

Tufekci, Z. (2019). Quantified Self. *Scientific American*, 85.

Additional Readings to Explore:

Andersen, U. (1975). *The Secret of Secrets.* No. Hollywood: Wishire Book Company.

Bach, R. (1977). *Illusions.* New York: Dell Publishing.

Blum, R. (1982). *The Book Of Runes.* Agincourt: Methuen Publications.

Cole-Whittaker, T. (1988). *What You Think Of Me Is None Of My Business.* New York: Jove Books - The Berkley Publishing Group.

Ferguson, M. (1980). *The Aquarian Conspiracy.* Los Angeles: J. P. Tarcher, Inc.

Foundation for Inner Peace. (1985). *A Course in Miracles.* Tiburon: Foundation for Inner Peace.

Hoffman, E. (1981). *HUNA: A Beginner's Guide.* Rockport: Para Research.

Keyes, K. (1982). *Handbook to Higher Consciousness.* Marina del Rey: Living Love Publications.

Long, M. F. (1958). *Self-Suggestion.* Marina del Rey: De Vorss & Co.

Peale, N. V. (1959). *The Amazing Results of Positive Thinking.* Greenwich, Conn: Fawcett Crest Books.

Ponder, C. (1962). *The Dynamic Laws of Prosperity.* Marina del Rey: DeVorss & Company.

Preston, E.; Humphreys, C. (1978). *An Abridgement of the Secret Doctrine.* Wheaton, Ill.: The Theosophical Publishing House.

Schneider, Christine. (1945). *The Power of the Spoken Word. Teachings of Florence Scovel Shinn.* Marina del Rey: De Vorss & Company.

Waitley, D. (1978) *The Psychology Of Winning.* Audiocassette Series. Chicago: Nightingale-Conant Corporation.

Appendices
A-O

Exploratory Questions
For
The Development
Of
Personal Awareness
And
Mind Power

To resolve issues that you discovered by answering
any of the questions, return to the chapter listed
under the Appendix title. Review the instructions in
the referenced chapter and prepare a plan or
commands to practice and resolve the situation.

Appendix "A"

Controlling My Self-talk

(Supplemental Questions to Chapter 14)

As you read the questions, listen carefully to the words or phrases that agitate your solar plexus. Are the words that prevent you from advancing yours or statements from others?

Do my thoughts reveal my perspective or are they beliefs that I accepted from others? (Social media, teacher, parent, boss, friend, society, TV, fashion.)

What do I hear myself say that I *can't* do?

What do I hear myself say that I *can* do?

How often do I hear myself using the word *Try* as a response to a request or when I am about to begin a task?

When I hear a new idea, do I explore the possibilities or do I dismiss it?

When a task requires completing, do I tend to look for excuses to avoid taking action?

What do I say to myself—

> ➤ when someone comments or criticizes my work or preferences?
>
> ➤ when I need to respond in a meeting?
>
> ➤ about my friends or the groups that I belong to?
>
> ➤ when confronted with a challenging situation?
>
> ➤ when I receive a compliment?
>
> ➤ when I do something wrong?
>
> ➤ when I expect an event will turn out negatively?
>
> ➤ when requested to make a presentation?
>
> ➤ when others refer to me as a leader, coach or specialist?

How often are my words a complaint or a negative statement?

What do I say to myself when an unpleasant task requires completion?

What does my self-talk say when I approach a person with whom I am not comfortable? (Client, co-worder, different gender or culture, salesperson or person in authority)

What does my self-talk say when I sense another person's objection by their facial expressions, posture or sighing?

Are there issues that I reflect on and become extremely agitated?

In what situations do I use the words—*wish, hope, would be nice if?*

Do my comments and thoughts express doubt or uncertainty?

How often do I think about negative situations or events?

Do I expect more good or bad outcomes?

Do situations turn out as badly as I feared they would?

How often do I think about enjoyable events in my life?

How often do I imagine positive outcomes?

What is my explanation for not completing my last project?

> What was I saying to myself while I was engaged in the project?

> What did I say to myself to justify quitting?

Do I think about how well I manage my money or do I dwell on financial concerns?

Do I focus on opportunities or limitations?

How do I feel about my future?

What do I say to myself—

> When I'm commuting to work?

> When I'm returning home?

> When a social engagement cannot be avoided?

> When I'm by myself?

> This moment?

Appendix "B"

Listening to My Solar Plexus

(Supplemental Questions to Chapter 15)

When I assert that I am a confident and dynamic person, what do I feel in my solar plexus and what is the first response that I hear in my self-talk?

How do I feel when someone compliments me?

What do I sense is blocking me from achieving a desired goal?

When do I feel stress—at home, job, socially?

Where or with whom can I relax and be comfortable?

What situations or activities make me uncomfortable?

Where or with whom do I feel out of place?

How do I react to new situations?

Are there situations where I sense hostility toward me?

When do I feel confident?

Who intimidates me? Why?

Am I at ease talking to my boss?

How do I feel about people who are different than me?

Where do I give begrudgingly and not with an open heart?

Do I feel pressured or expected to do things?

Why do I feel I cannot say what I want?

What does my solar plexus tell me to do?

Why am I not doing it?

If you are not a manager by title in your career, how do you feel about being the manager in charge of your life?

In answering each question, are my answers reflective of the true feelings in my solar plexus, or are my answers influenced by what others might think or want me to say or do?

Appendix "C"

Simulation and Visualization

(Supplemental Questions to Chapter 16)

In what situations do you hear your self-talk saying, "I just can't see myself doing, being or having...".

When you hear yourself saying, "I just can't see myself doing, saying, being...". in one sentence or phrase, immediately assess what it is that you think, feel or see that is blocking you.

Review each aspect of your life and the goals you identified on pages 39-40. Practice imagining the outcome of what you desire, complete with feelings, as if the situation is true and occurring. Close your eyes and with the power of a quantum leap, visualize yourself doing, being and having what you desire in each aspect of your life:

Relationship – Imagine yourself attracting and sharing your life with a compatible partner.

Education – Imagine yourself emersed in studies you enjoy. (Academic, Technical, Hobbies, General Interest)

Physical Activities – Imagine yourself participating in activities you enjoy.

Health and Exercise – Imagine yourself healthy and in great shape.

Career – Imagine yourself employed in an enjoyable environment.

Finances – Imagine a situation of bounty and surplus.

Spiritual or Peace of Mind – Imagine yourself calm and relaxed.

Overcoming Internal Barriers

Visualizing a clear picture of exactly what you want is critical to utilizing the powers of your mind. To benefit from this powerful ability, challenge yourself to determine what it is that you desire or is holding you back by asking:

Can I see myself achieving my goals?

Yes _____ *No* _____ *If not, why not?*

Can I see myself remaining focused and dedicated to my plan?

Yes _____ *No* _____ *If not, why not?*

Can I see myself managing my activities more effectively?

Yes _____ *No* _____ *If not, what would it take?*

Can I see myself not worrying?

Yes _____ *No* _____ *If not, why not?*

When I set new goals or plans, do I visualize myself successfully achieving and maintaining them?

Yes _____ *No* _____ *If not, why not?*

When I visualize an outcome successfully, do I then doubt that I will achieve it?

If so, why do I doubt the outcome?

Can I see myself preparing a list of challenges that require resolution to achieve my goal?

Yes _____ *No* _____ *If not, why not?*

Appendix "D"

My Master Program

(Supplemental Questions to Chapter 17)

When do I act differently than how I truly see myself?

How do I respond when I receive a compliment?

What do I want but feel that I am not good enough to have or do not deserve?

Why do I feel this way or accept it as true?

What situations or achievements make me feel successful?

What perceived weakness can I turn into a unique advantage?

What do I think about when I am required to attend a function or meet a new person?

What is too good for me? *[This is not a trick question. Carefully consider what you think is too good for you.]*

What size of income is too much for me? *[This is not a trick question.]*

For the income you state, describe how your life would be and how you would responsibly manage that amount of income. Listen carefully for that first subtle response.

Do I feel comfortable expressing new ideas?

Whose lifestyle do I feel manipulated to adopt as my own?

Where does my pride interfere when I need help to achieve a goal?

Do I have a strong desire to watch the activities of others on social media?

Why?

Can I admit to making errors?

Am I comfortable is social environments?

Can I see myself comfortably introducing questions in new situations?

Yes ____ *No*____ *If not, why not?*

Can I see myself making presentations with confidence and ease?

Yes ____ *No*____ *If not, why not?*

Do I believe I can perform effectively in the position that I desire? *Yes* ____ *No*____ *If not, why not?*

When things are going great for me, do I feel they will last?

Yes ____ *No*____ *If not, why do I feel this way?*

How would I rate myself as a—

> Friend?

> Partner/Spouse?

> Employee?

> Parent?

> Manager of my money?

> Communicator—Problem Solver—Negotiator?

What am I discovering about myself?

Am I satisfied with where I live?

When I look at myself, what or who do I feel I am?

> Is it an unpleasant feeling?

> Do I want to continue feeling this way?

> Would I like to change?

> > If so…. *What new program, picture or command do I need to implement to coach and motivate me daily?*

Appendix "E"

The Power of Believing

(Supplemental Questions to Chapter 18)

What do I believe I *can* do?

What do I believe I *can't* do?

What goals do I think are unattainable?

If I set a new goal, is it possible to achieve it without changing my habits?

Am I successful?

Do I believe I *can* be successful in achieving my goal(s)?

Do I believe I *will* be successful in achieving my goal(s)?

Do I demonstrate confidence that my goals are achievable?

When I verbalize an action phrase, do I believe in its power?

At work or in team ventures, do the people I work with believe in the goal or objective of the project?

Do I believe that—

> I am an effective Leader?
>
> I am an effective Communicator?
>
> I am an effective Problem-solver?
>
> I encourage others?

From what I have learned, what is required to suppress the killers that prevent me from believing in myself?

Appendix "F"

My Beliefs and Programs

(Supplemental Questions to Chapter 19)

What image do I have and believe is the real me?

Is that how I want to be?

What are my weak self-image beliefs?

What are my strong self-image beliefs?

What do I believe is preventing me from succeeding or achieving a goal?

What do I have to do to overcome this block or barrier?

Whose support or input do I believe I should seek before making a decision?

Do I believe that my friends have the happy and successful lives that they post on social media?

Do I value the opinions of friends and strangers over the input and suggestions of my partner?

Do family members have expectations that influence my decisions and general happiness?

What traditions, beliefs and customs do I retain that were from my parents or family of origin?

Where has tradition become a hindrance or a burden?

When have I accepted inaccurate information about a person, place or event, only to discover that I prejudged the situation based on the opinions of others?

Am I so fixated on my point of view that it is difficult to consider a different perspective?

What do I believe success would look like for me?

Is my description of success motivated by fashion, family, friends, celebrities, public figures or is it what I deeply desire?

What amount of money is required to be successful?

What social expectations create stress or do not provide me personal satisfaction?

What statements from my parents do I hear in my self-talk that I believe to be true but have never been verified for accuracy?

To whom do I feel that I must be accountable or explain myself?

What beliefs prevent me from participating in independent or solo activities?

What do my siblings, parents, friends and peers think when I make an error?

Does it bother me?

Does it matter what my friends and peers think? Why?

Do I believe spending time on my own is being a loser?

Who do I think has the power to influence or restrict my future success?

Why am I afraid to do something new or different?

What projects, goals or activities have I not started because of what others might think?

What put-downs do I accept or allow?

Are you in a job/career that you chose or did someone else say it is what you should do?

If the latter, what career would I choose?

What do I have to do to prepare to change careers?

Am I prepared to do what is required?

Are the people that I share my ideas with able to assist me or am I merely seeking their approval?

Where do I have difficulties because of a conflict in what I believe?

Appendix "G"

Clarifying My Values

(Supplemental Questions to Chapter 20)

What do I believe provides real meaning in my life?

What would happen if this aspect were removed from my life?

What do I value in a career, financial, social or family life?

What are my standards—Moral—Professional—Personal?

What gives me a sense of security?

What gives me peace of mind?

For the specific goal that I am striving for—

How does this goal provide value in my life?

Am I striving for this goal because of a deep inner desire or is it an idea that others have implied is valuable or that I should attain?

What activities do I enjoy? (i.e., social outings, going to church, work requirements, family events.)

Describe what, where and when the following occurred—

What was the best summer I ever spent?

Winter—

Spring—

Fall—

Weekend—

Time spent alone—

Do I plan for more of these times or activities?

Who do I like and respect?

Why? What did they do? What qualities do they possess?

What values or attitudes do I have that I feel restrict me?

For anything that you value—possessions, beliefs and status, explore—

Who sets the standard?

Why is it valuable?

What does it do for me?

How does it bring me happiness?

Do I place excessive value on specific items or activities?

What do I value that is or will become a financial burden?

Are there expenditures that I refuse to reduce?

How do they affect my overall financial situation, general happiness and stress level?

Are these expenditures worth the overall stress and cost?

To reduce expenditures, have I inquired what others spend and minimized my entertainment costs for TV, internet, phone services, insurance, membership fees, card fees and other items?

What values do I promote in my social group, at work and with my neighbors that may infringe on their beliefs and choices?

Why are my choices and perspective better?

Are my values reflected in my work ethics, management and leadership styles, friendships and partnerships?

In valuing my time, how many hours per week do I spend—

Commuting to work: _____

Working: _____

Maintaining my home or family: _____

Performing tasks/chores/errands for others: _____

Watching TV: _____

Following social media: _____

Exercising: _____

Participating in activities that I *enjoy*: _____

Participating in activities that I *don't* enjoy: _____

Studying: _____

Playing video and computer games: _____

Other: _____

Which activities can I reduce to provide more time to do the things that would enhance my life?

What values and benefits do I gain by following the activities of others on social media?

How do I feel after viewing their activities?

Are the hours I invest following and watching others enhancing my life?

Have I answered the questions above according to my true feelings?

*What you put up with,
you end up with.*

Appendix "H"

Assessing My Attitude

(Supplemental Questions to Chapter 21)

Do I portray a positive attitude?

When do I present a negative attitude?

What do I say about others or about my job that reinforces negative programming?

When I do something wrong, how long do I dwell on it?

In what situations does my attitude influence friendships?

What does my self-talk reveal when I realize that I need to change my behaviors or actions?

What do my self-talk and solar plexus reveal when someone suggests new or different processes or activities?

Am I open to observe and explore or am I quick to criticize?

Do I look for options to improve a situation or do I continue to focus on what might go wrong?

Am I self-motivated or do I have to be pushed, cajoled or convinced into doing something?

Am I aware of how my comments affect others?

Do I notice if those close to me do more things right or wrong?

How do I describe my place of employment?

Are my co-workers winners or losers?

What are their better qualities?

Who do I blame when things go wrong?

After regaining my composure from a crushing blow, do I see hope and believe in a favorable outcome or do I only think of the bad that could still happen?

Appendix "I"

Emotions and Snipers

(Supplemental Questions to Chapter 22)

When evaluating the following questions, the words—Worry, Doubts, Comfort Zones and Fear are synonymous in most situations. A fear is as simple as a minor doubt.

What situations upset me the most?

Do my emotional responses prevent me from being rational?

Do I recognize how my emotional reactions affect others?

Who upsets me?

Why am I not dealing with the person or situation?

What situations do I avoid because they upset me?

What or who do I fear in new situations?

What do I fear when I ask questions, whether it is to qualify clients, make presentations, close sales, coach team members, clarify statements or interact with others?

When is it uncomfortable to provide feedback?

Do I tend to worry?

About what?

Are the reasons for my worries justifiable or are they imagined?

Instead of worrying, what actions can I take?

What do I consider overly risky that prevents me from acting?

Do I avoid taking action because I fear a particular outcome or that the outcome is unknown?

When do emotions, activated by personal attraction or chemistry, interfere with my judgment?

When does fear motivate me or prevent the exploring of new opportunities?

Appendix "J"

Identifying External Killers

(Supplemental Questions to Chapter 23)

How often do I get excited about newly advertised products and services?

Am I driven to acquire these products and services?

Why?

What do they do for me?

How often do friends or family talk me into activities that I don't enjoy?

If I am excited about a new venture, do I let others talk me out of it when they say—No one has ever done that. It can't be done. Why waste your time with that? Well—you can, but I wouldn't?

From whom or where do my ideas originate?

Do I seek approval from others before attempting anything new?

What are the topics of conversation at work? With friends?

Are they positive and encouraging or gossipy and gloomy?

What are the attitudes and values promoted on movies, videos and television programs that I watch or blogs that I follow?

Am I objective and do I keep an open mind?

Do I blindly follow, accepting that is how things are or should be?

When I look at my friends, which ones would I like to trade lives with?

What are they doing that I have chosen not to do?

Would I be better off without certain friends?

What demeaning attitudes do I tolerate from others?

Why?

Appendix J

Do I notice negativity in others?

Does it bother me or does it make me feel supported and in good company?

Are those with whom I socialize supportive or critical of my actions and choices?

What is required for me to rely less on others for direction?

Who do I avoid?

Is it because what they say implies that I should take responsibility for what I am doing or do they put me down?

Could I benefit from their criticism?

Do I accept criticism as:

An opportunity to reflect on my actions and behaviors to improve my performance and presentation?

A put-down or feel grateful that if this person disproves of my activities, it confirms that I am not like them?

How do I feel about complainers? Do I offer positive comments, or do I contribute to their negative topics?

Whom do I view as encouraging and a positive influence?

What is required to become my own best friend to enjoy doing activities on my own?

How does following the activities of friends on social media make me feel?

Why am I not using the time to make my own life exciting, instead of watching what others do on social media?

What negative comments from others are killers that I need to neutralize to restore my confidence and personal power?

What can I say constructively to that person?

What appropriate responses can I develop and practice to respond to future situations and enhance my confidence?

Am I aware when I am being distracted from a task?

What phrase or assertion can I compose that will assist me in staying on track?

Who distracts me the most?

What can I say to this person that will enable me to stay focused on my task?

Will it matter if they get upset if they leave me alone?

What activities do I find distracting?

What activities do I engage in that are controlled by others and make me feel used rather than appreciated for my contributions?

In each aspect of my life, who or what activity distracts or entices me to follow, rather than doing what my true Self desires—

Relationships—

Family—

Career and finances—

Education or continuous learning—

Health and fitness—

Social activities—

How seriously do I want to improve my situation(s)?

If so, what are two actions that I can implement immediately to begin taking control of my life?

1 -_____

2 -_____

Appendix "K"

Repeating Behaviors

(Supplemental Questions to Chapter 24)

Am I aware of my physical cycle, energy level and what I need to perform effectively?

What irritates or annoys me on some days but doesn't bother me at other times?

Are there days when I grasp ideas quickly and other days I require detailed explanations?

What statements of limitation do I repeat in my self-talk?

What situations do I seem to attract or repeat?

Are the situations the same but with different people?

What does the law of attraction repeatedly manifest for me?

Do I see the connection between the words that I say (think) and the events that occur in my life?

When I achieve something, does it continue or does life eventually revert to the way it was?

If it returned to what it was—what words can I recall repeating in my self-talk prior to it returning to the original situation?

Do I tend to give up or quit projects before completion?

How often do I engage in frivolous activities when I should be focusing on a specific task?

Thinking back to a time when I was distracted by what I thought was an important task or issue, was the task actually important?

Do I now see that it was a convenient excuse to avoid an unpleasant task or confrontation?

Did my actions fulfill a program or belief that matches my self-image?

Could that important task or issue have been postponed?

Do I take sick days or not attend family or social events to avoid unpleasant situations?

When was the last time I used *too busy* as an excuse?

Do I look forward to my spare time?

Do I schedule spare time or does my busyness preclude leisure time?

Are my activities supporting the achievement of my goals?

What activities do I perform on a *have to* or *should do* basis rather than doing them freely and willingly?

When am I most creative?

What aspect of my life makes me feel that I am in a rut?

Why do I persist in staying in this rut?

What and/or who do I avoid?

Why?

What are the benefits to addressing these repeating issues?

Why am I not addressing them?

Appendix "L"

Planning and Goal Setting

(Supplemental Questions and Worksheets to Chapter 25)

When was the last time I set a goal and achieved it?

Refer to pages 39-40. Identify one activity or action that you can implement to advance your success in:

Career –

Relationships –

Finances –

Social Life –

Education –

Personal Well-being, Spiritual or Peace of Mind –

List the steps and activities that are required to achieve one of the above goals.

From that list, which ones do I not like doing?

What do I believe is blocking me from completing each step?

Are my beliefs excuses to avoid action?

Would I succeed if I overcame my reluctance and made a habit of doing the things I don't like to do?

When I observe people who are better off than I am, what do they do that appears difficult for me to do or that I don't enjoy doing?

What specifically can I learn to do that will make a difference?

What do I need to do to begin any of the above steps?

Reflecting on a goal that is eluding me, do I really desire to achieve this goal or is it an idle wish?

How would the achievement of that goal affect my life and those around me?

Would the achievement of that goal jeopardize other aspects of my life?

Do I begin activities systematically and in an organized manner?

If not, why not?

Planning

Enter these formats into your computer or electronic device or print one page for each goal and place in a binder. Modify the format to suit your style but avoid spending excessive time planning and not acting. The sooner you begin, the sooner you will succeed.

Clearly define each goal. Apply a quantum leap. Do not describe the steps but clearly describe what the final achievement would look and feel like to you.

Goal:

With regards to this goal, where do I currently see myself?

What identifiable steps are required to complete this goal? In your plan, insert additional steps as required.

What is blocking each step?

Which blocks are beliefs that require addressing as a separate goal?

Am I creating blocks and barriers that don't exist?

Appendix L

What is one activity that I can perform immediately to bring this goal closer to completion?

Am I acting on this?   Yes ___ No ___

If I achieve this goal, what changes will occur in my life?

For better—

_____

_____

For worse—

_____

_____

Repeat this process for each goal.

Reality Check

Is my goal realistic and do I believe it is achievable?

Am I personally suited to perform what is required to achieve that goal? (*Example—You desire a career for its earning potential or status, but dislike or are not capable of performing the duties required*).

If not, what would be a more compatible choice?

How badly do I want to achieve this goal and am I seriously committed to doing what is required to achieve it?

Am I caught in the excitement of a trend or a get-rich-quick scheme, believing minimal or no effort is required to achieve this goal?

Am I willing to give up some of my current activities to allot the time required to achieve this goal?

Am I excited about scheduling activities that will enable me to achieve this goal?

Review your answers on Clarifying My Values—Appendix G.

Goal Clarification

Why do I want to achieve this goal?

How or why will it make me happy?

Goal Compatibility and Lifestyle

The following worksheets will be helpful but may provoke some uncomfortable insights. When we are young, the future seems far away. People often fail to look ahead or assess what their lifestyle will be when their desires become a reality. A goal that we so desperately desired years ago could create a major conflict in our current lifestyle. Planning requires identifying the effects our goal will have on those close to us, the disruption of the status quo by doing things differently and how we will personally grow and change.

Our lives and lifestyle evolve over time. When viewed in a linear and matrix format, future conflicts are predictable. As you complete this exercise, carefully consider—Do my goals and plans reflect how life will evolve for me and the requirements of my (future) family or relationship? What will my life's requirements be in twenty years?

Do my goals include other family members?

Are they in agreement with my goals?

If I achieve my goal, how will it affect my—

Career—

Relationship—

Finances—

Social Life—

Education—

Personal Well-being, Spiritual or Peace of Mind—

If single, what will change if I choose to share my life with someone?

What will I have to compromise?

Do my plans include consideration of a partner's desires?

What do (will) I have to give up for others?

What do I expect others to give up for me?

Is this reasonable?

Appendix L

Assessing the Future

Time does not stand still. How will your life evolve over the next 25 years? (Fill in the ages of each person in your life, or those you plan to attract in the future.)

Age of:	Now	In 5 Years	In 10 Years	In 15 Years	In 20 Years	In 25 Years
Self						
Partner						
Child 1						
Child 2						
Child [n]						
Grandchild						
Parent						
Other-						
Other-						

Modify the following chart to include other goals. You may want to prepare a planning binder or digital file and insert pages as required. Avoid overplanning.

Goal Requirements:	Now	In 5 Years	In 10 Years	In 15 Years	In 20 Years	In 25 Years
Education						
Partner						
Career						
Earnings						
Savings						
Vacations						
Other-						
Other-						
Other-						

Review the completed forms on the previous page and ask—

What activities should I engage in sooner rather than later?

What activities should I defer until it is more suitable?

What requires completion before it will be too late?

When should I/we move into a larger/smaller home?

When will college/university expenses be due?

When am I planning that big holiday for myself or with the family?

Are there certain years it would be advantageous to remain closer to parents or siblings?

Is there a time that I should consider a career change to be more involved with my family?

When would it be better to travel?

In 5, 10 or 15 years, what will be required for—

> vacations?

> schooling?

> assistance for parents?

> my job?

> my health?

Do I have concrete plans or is life going to provide me with *surprises*?

What other activities or surprises am I not planning for?

Critical Points to Ponder:

As you review your responses, reflect on each situation. There are no right or wrong answers. Your choices control the law of attraction to manifest what you describe. Will it be what you want?

Do you set goals to attain them or are they just idle wishes?

Are your goals set sufficiently high to motivate you and provide the pleasure of achieving them, but not so high that they are unrealistic or discouraging?

Do your goals affect others? What are you expecting from them and those close to you?

Are you setting goals with limiting parameters that only one type of job or organization can fulfill? Are you fixating on a limited probability and not noticing the limitless options that are around you?

Avoid focusing on a specific person when attracting a relationship. Focus on compatible values, communication style, interests, and activities. With billions of people in the world, no one person could be the only compatible partner for you.

Recognizing that changes will occur in all aspects of your life, when you achieve your goals, will they be what you want?

If not, what do you really want?

A goal may be determined by a time frame, as in an achievement or an activity. If your goal is a lifelong goal, ensure your plans include a process to maintain your activities so that your success continues?

What other desires have you been setting aside?

_____

_____

Appendix "M"

Locating Hidden Programs

(Supplemental Questions to Chapter 27)

When I ask myself a question regarding my situation, whose voice(s) do I hear and what do they say?

What do I fear will occur if I achieved my goal?

What are the benefits of not achieving my goal?

Am I dismissing that subtle first response because it seems silly or ridiculous?

What response do I receive when I ask, "Why do I repeat or attract...?"

What beliefs interfere with my achieving...?

What prevents me from...?

What is the benefit of not being or having...?

What would happen if...?

Why do I insist on doing...?

What would I have to change if I achieved...?

How would achieving my goal affect or change my life?

Attaining a Desired Weight:

Does attaining a desired weight generate thoughts of undesirable expectations for or from the *new me*?

Will I be expected to participate in activities that I don't enjoy?

Will my partner want to be more intimate?

Will I attract undesirable suitors?

What are other negative scenarios that could occur when I reach a desired weight?

Will I be comfortable or embarrassed when others compliment me on my new look?

What comments echo from my younger years that imply anything about my weight or appearance?

What do I fear will be required to maintain the new me?

What is preventing me from reaching my desired weight?

Regarding my desired weight, what does my self-talk reveal when I ask these questions?

Career and Advancement:

What monologues do I hear in my self-talk that describe or dismiss my successes or failures or why I will not achieve my goal?

What conflicts or requirements could a new job or promotion create?

Regarding my career, what does my self-talk reveal when I explore these questions?

Attracting a Compatible Relationship:

Am I free of other relationships to enter a new one?

What expectations or secrets do I conceal when I meet a prospective new partner?

What do I fear others may notice or discover about me?

Am I open and honest or do I hide my true character?

Am I so desperate that I might accept the first person who shows interest in me?

What words flow through my mind advising me who I should attract? Is the voice mine? Whose voice is it?

Is the advice that I hear in my self-talk compatible with the characteristics of what I desire in a relationship?

What does my self-talk reveal when I ask these questions?

Am I a rescuer or an enabler?

Am I looking for a servant, a benefactor or an equal partner?

Have I prepared a list of qualities and behaviors that I expect in the partner I desire to attract?

Have I identified my values and am I seeking a partner with similar values?

When meeting new prospects, do I explore where conflicts could occur regarding religion, politics, sex and intimacy, family dynamics, money and spending habits, manners, sensitivity and discretion, sports activities, entertainment choices, pets, hygiene, personal organization, vacations, careers, general interests and anything and everything else that people in relationships experience?

Have I prepared a list of relationship deal breakers?

What is required to prepare myself for terminating an association in its early stages when I recognize specific deal breakers?

In my angst, am I pushing the river of life or am I relaxed and open to the flow and the law of attraction?

What does my self-talk reveal when I explore these questions?

Appendix "N"

Communication Saboteurs

(Supplemental Questions to Chapter 28)

With whom do I disagree or argue with most often?

What is the primary issue of the disagreements?

When I think of previous conversations, what may I have said that provoked the conflict?

What do people say that upsets me?

What do I say that upsets others?

What type of responses do I need to prepare in advance?

Do salespeople take advantage of me?

What script can I prepare and practice to defend myself against salespeople who attempt to manipulate me?

If I cannot exit the situation, and silence is not an option, what scripts can I prepare and practice that will enable me to retain my composure when I encounter aggressive people?

What statements or comments do I make at work that initiate conflict, inflame the situation or cause others to be silent?

To prepare myself and improve social interactions or engage in conversation with others, what topics could I inquire about or introduce?

With [Name]   Topic of interest to inquire about or introduce:

_____   _____

_____   _____

_____   _____

_____   _____

_____   _____

Appendix "O"

Suggestions for Self-Coaching

(In Random Order)

Slowly repeat each phrase or statement until your solar plexus and self-talk generate a feeling of success and contentment. Only by understanding the power of words, questions and how they control your behaviors will these self-coaching aids be of benefit.

Focus on what you want and NOT on what you don't want—
I now focus on...[Describe].
What can I say to resolve my issue with [name/situation]?
With the free will and for the good of all concerned, I now attract a positive solution for....

Create quiet time – turn off digital devices or social media—
I enjoy quiet time.
I enjoy time to think.
An Off phone is my zone.
I feel good disconnecting from social media for a few hours.

Begin or complete an unpleasant task—
How will I feel when this is completed?
What is the next step required to continue?
Right now, what is the best use of my time?

Find the energy to push on when a goal seems too far away—
How will I feel when I achieve...?
What is one thing I can I do today that advances my goal?
I will work at...[goal]... until it is finished.
How far have I advanced in the last [week, month, year]?
Is my plan current?

Feeling at a standstill when nothing seems to be advancing—
Why am I not acting?
What is blocking my goal?
What am I overlooking?
What can I do right now?
Will there be negative outcomes if I achieve this goal?

Appendix O

Feeling stressed—
I am calm. I breathe slowly and deeply. I am in control.
This too shall pass. I will continue with my day.
I will attract the right solution.
Every day and in every way I get better and better.

Nurturing the Law of Attraction—
I am open to and recognize new opportunities.
I notice new opportunities everywhere.
I am a lucky person. I attract all that I require.

Relationships—
I now attract a compatible partner.
My partner and I communicate better and better every day.
My relationship with [name] gets better and better.
I am patient, caring and loving.
I carefully evaluate new relationships.
I now attract caring and respectful people into my life.

Education—
I enjoy learning.
I seek new ways to do things.
I am receptive to constructive coaching.
I attract new opportunities that enhance my life.

Physical and Health—
I achieve and maintain a desired weight of [x kg / lbs.]
I enjoy exercising.
I choose foods that help me achieve my goals.
Every day and in every way I get closer to my goal of [Describe].
How do I feel each time I complete my work out?
I am energetic and feel great!

Health—[Note: some situations cannot or may never improve. It is important to focus on doing the best that you can.]
My health is improving.
I now notice more activities that are suitable for me.
I enjoy [name activity].
Every day I feel better and better.
I am relaxed and tomorrow will be better.
Maybe today was tough. Tomorrow will be better.

Career and Finances—

I attract financial abundance and am comfortable.
I manage my finances exceptionally well.
I enjoy my job.
I attract the perfect job for me.
My job is important. I manage each situation effectively.
Every day I get better and better at my job.
I create constructive ways to deal with [name, issues, customers].

Social and Friends—

I attract positive, interesting and supportive friends.
I am strong and stand my ground with arrogant people.
I am confident and remove myself from unpleasant situations.
I attract compatible friends.
Real friends treat me respectfully. Does [name] treat me respectfully?

Improve Time Management—

I am an efficient planner.
I am punctual.
I am organized.

Spiritual and Peace of Mind—

I am a free thinker.
My beliefs are based on reason and respect for myself and others.
I am at peace and find solace in nature.
I am strong and can stand alone.
I am cautious about strangers who are too friendly.
I enjoy being me.
It's a beautiful day.

Cheering Yourself Up—

This too shall pass.
This sucks, but I don't. Every day I get better and better.
What or who makes me smile?
Every day and in every way, I get better and better.
What do I consider enjoyable?
Prepare a list of the activities that you enjoy or cause you to smile.
Each time you recall an event, add it to the list. Review the list when you are feeling down.

Neutralizing old thoughts as they casually surface—

Those are my old thoughts and they are no longer of value. With the free will and for the good of all concerned I now attract... [your desire].

Altering Your Mode Of Communication or Engaging Others—

What is it that you need or require? (listen for a key word)
What do you think or how do you see or feel about...?
Can you look at this and tell me what you see or feel needs to be altered? Improved? Removed?

Dealing with Aggressive People—

Why do you insist your way is better?
Why are you not open to my perspective?
What specifically do you want from me?
Can we talk about this another time?
What is it specifically that is so upsetting?
If you want me to respond, could you calmly restate your request?

When the dynamics are deteriorating—

What can I say to make this better?
What can I say to calm things down?
I am calm. This too shall pass.

Feeling pressured to respond or buy—

Let me think about this and I'll advise you later.
Why do you insist on an immediate answer?
Actually, it's not a "got-to-have." I'll give it some thought.

Question yourself:

Is the requirement for an immediate decision a pressure tactic?
If I miss this opportunity, is it the end of the world?

To Change Your Thinking When You Say Or Feel—

Discouraged—

I am feeling better and better.
I will find a way to make this work.

I don't have time—

This is important. I will make this happen.
I will complete this by... [date or time].

Tempted to abandon your diet and eat junk food—
I achieve and maintain a desired weight of [x kg / lbs.]
I choose healthy foods.
That's like poison. Junk food is poison.
That food in not in my plan.

This isn't going to work—
How can I make this work?
What is the next step required to advance this project/task?
Why is this not working?

I'm going to be late—
I will prepare myself better next time.
I will call and let them know I'll be late.
Take a deep breath. Slow down. I'll be there soon.
It is what it is. I am calm and will get there safely.

I am too tired—
I am energized and feel great.
I feel better and better.
I am focused and energized.
How will I feel when this is completed?

This time won't matter—
That's the killer talking. This time does matter.
Just do it, [Use your name].
How will I feel when this is completed?

Nervous about making a presentation—
I am prepared. I am excited about this presentation.
I will deliver a great presentation.
Every day I become a better presenter.

What you said was inappropriate –
I'm sorry. That didn't come out right. What I meant was...
Oh, that didn't sound right. What I mean is...

You want to become physically active—
List activities you enjoy and evaluate –
    What can I do immediately or schedule to do soon?
    Which activity makes me feel good?
    How will I feel after I go for a [walk, cycle, swim.]

Appendix O

You're bored and there's nothing to do—

List activities that you enjoy and evaluate—
> *What can I enjoy today or plan for soon?*

Am I avoiding a task that requires completing?
What tasks or chores have I been putting off?
Why do I feel like not doing anything?
I'm going to call [name].
What can I set as a goal and achieve?
What have I enjoyed doing in the past?
Why am I not taking action?
Why am I not interested in doing these activities?
(Requires exploring Chapter 14–28)

You need to return an item or deal with a customer service department—

I am calm and present my situation calmly.
I will focus on the malfunction of the product (or delivery issue) and present it calmly.

When they remain silent, ask direct questions—

Why are you not replying?
Can you please reply?
What can you do to correct this?
[Occasionally, you may have to accept the loss and that a bad decision was made or a substandard vendor was selected. Constantly repeating the incident in memory, or to others, will only diminish the enjoyment of your day.]

You need to protect yourself from a person on a negative tirade or complaining—

Those are their thoughts. I am happy and content.
Every day and in every way, I get better and better.
I'm glad I'm me and enjoy my life.

Pressured to follow fashions and fads—

Do I really need that item?
Is this in my budget?
Just say no.
I will pass on that.
You guys carry–on. I'm going to... [your preference].

Your self-talk is putting you down—
Hey, that's not like me. I get better every day.
Whoa! That was the old me. I get better and better every day.
Beat it Killer. I am getting better and better.

You are procrastinating—
What is the best use of my time right now?
How will I feel when this is off my To-Do list? Completed?

Peer Pressure—and need to say "No" to others—
Sorry, I have too many things that require attention.
Sounds like you'll have fun but I'm not interested.
No, I prefer to do [Describe] instead.
No thanks, but you guys go ahead.
Hey, you're a little too pushy. I said no. [The surprise factor of them not expecting this response often has a resounding effect.]

The weather is unpleasant—
I adapt to and enjoy the changes in the weather.
What can I do in this weather that would be fun?
Today is a perfect day to (clean, call, write, explore...).

Pressured to attend a function [family or business] that you do not want to attend—
Do I need to attend this event?
What are the consequences if I don't attend?
Will not attending cause greater complications?
Could this be an opportunity waiting in disguise?
I'll make a showing and quickly exit. This too shall pass.

These are only suggestions. Your situations may be similar but are unique to you. Effective commands require scripting that is compatible with your desired outcome. Prepare, memorize and practice your power phrases until they can be autonomically recited when ambushed by negative thoughts or when you are pondering a situation. *All phrases require silent repetition until the killer words that discourage you are not being recited in your self-talk (conscious mind). By maintaining your focus, a silent energy or force is created that motivates you to act.* This is the essence of mind power. Enjoy.

Acknowledgements

I would like to thank my wife, Lorraine, for her patience, support and assistance over the past few years as I was ever so humbled by the never-ending challenges that writers experience.

I would like to thank Tanja Prokop of bookcoverworld.com for her assistance, guidance and dedication in dealing with all the details of creating the artwork for the book's cover.

The quotations included have been researched to provide credit to the original authors, whenever possible. Several quotations are variations of writings that spanned hundreds or thousands of years. Multiple sources of quotations provide quotes that are adaptations of similar quotes that appear to be credited to multiple individuals. Further complications occur when quotations are translated from different languages. Thankfully, the message or theme of the quotes still conveys the valuable words of wisdom.

I am grateful to live in a time when books, information and knowledge are accessible in the free world. Sharing information for the betterment of all is a daunting but worthwhile challenge. The websites of Gutenberg.org and Wikipedia.com offer easy access. I encourage contributing to their operations to ensure knowledge remains accessible to everyone.

It would be impossible to cite every book read, or seminar, lecture or presentation attended that influenced or inspired my thinking. The *Bibliography* cites those I quoted directly and offers a partial reading list to explore other perspectives.

Most importantly, I would like to thank you, the reader, for taking the time to explore these concepts and processes. Challenge yourself. Question the norm. Initiate those changes you so deeply desire. I also encourage you to contact the publisher and leave a comment or review.

About the Author

A W Anderson, CPHR, is a retired Chartered Professional in Human Resources. He is the author of the *Athena Learning Program©*, a self-development program that explored mind power and behavior. In 1987 the program expanded into the *Professional Skills Training©* program to focus on the personal and social challenges employees, managers and entrepreneurs experience in business.

For over 30 years, *"A W"* has presented the dynamics of mind power and personal discipline for business applications and everyday living. He has trained personnel in the industries of aviation, construction, government, energy, hospitality, insurance, print media, oil and gas, manufacturing, transportation, real estate, retail, service and wholesale distribution.

He is semi-retired and occasionally assists others through online coaching and support. *"A W"* resides with his wife of 24 years in the Canadian Rockies. They share an active lifestyle of kayaking, cycling, golfing, backcountry skiing and a variety of hobbies and interests.

12/14
133/87
wt 193

Made in the USA
Las Vegas, NV
14 January 2023

65613728R00207